October 2018

Important Update: MUST READ

The U.S. Food and Drug Administration updated the FDA Food Code in 2018. The Food Code update has changed information critical to your training and examination. Please refer to this update for the information that will be reflected in the Food Safety Protection Manager exam. These updates are identified in italics.

In Chapter 1: Keeping Food Safe: *Managing Food Safety* and *The Importance of Becoming a Certified Food Protection Manager:* (pg. 1.10 to 1.11)

This new section (in italics) will read:

Managing Food Safety (New Heading)

As you can see, managing food safety in an operation can be challenging. Fortunately, there are things you can do to help keep the food you serve safe.

The Importance of Becoming a Certified Food Protection Manager (New Heading)

The FDA Food Code requires that the person in charge of a foodservice operation become a Certified Food Protection Manager. That person must be onsite at all times during operating hours. A Certified Food Protection Manager must show that he or she has the required knowledge by passing a test from an accredited program. The program must be accredited by an agency approved by a Conference for Food Protection.

Completing the ServSafe Manager Course and passing the ServSafe Food Protection Manager Certification Examination meets this requirement. But, why is it so important to become certified?

A Centers for Disease Control and Prevention study suggests that the presence of a Certified Food Protection Manager reduces the risk of a foodborne illness outbreak for an establishment. The study also suggests that it was a distinguishing factor between restaurants that experienced a foodborne illness outbreak and those that had not.

In addition, the FDA's Retail Food Risk Factor Studies suggest that the presence of a certified manager has a positive correlation with more effective control of certain risk factors, such as poor personal hygiene, in different facility types.

The Food Safety Responsibilities of a Manager (Same heading same content)

Marketing Food Safety (Same heading same content)

In Chapter 1: Keeping Food Safe: *The Food Safety Responsibilities of a Manager* (Pg. 1.11)

Here are the changes to this section (in italics):

- *(New 1st bullet) Food handlers are regularly monitoring food temperatures during hot and cold holding.*

In Chapter 4: The Safe Food Handler: *Infected wounds or boils* (Pg. 4.8)

Here are the changes to this section (in italics):

If the wound or boil is located on the *hand, finger, or wrist*

- Cover it with an impermeable cover *like a finger cot or bandage.* **Impermeable** means that liquid *from the wound* cannot pass through the cover.
- Then place a single-use glove over the cover.

In Chapter 5: The Flow of Food: An Introduction: *Guidelines for Preventing Cross-Contamination between Food* (Pg. 5.3)

Here are the changes to this section (in italics):

Separate raw meat, poultry, and seafood from unwashed and ready-to-eat fruits and vegetables. *Do this during storage, preparation, holding, and display to prevent cross-contamination.*

In Chapter 8: The Flow of Food: Preparation: *Thawing ROP Fish* (Pg. 8.5)

Here are the changes to this section (in italics):

Frozen fish may be supplied in reduced-oxygen packaging (ROP). This fish should usually remain frozen until ready for use. If this is stated on the label, the fish must be removed from the packaging at the following times:

- Before thawing it under refrigeration
- Before or immediately after thawing it under running water

If you are packaging fish using a reduced-oxygen packaging method, the fish must:

- *Be frozen before, during, or after packaging.*
- *Include a label that states the fish must be frozen until used.*

In Chapter 8: The Flow of Food: Preparation: *Prepping Practices That Have Special Requirements* (Pg. 8.9 to 8.10)

Here are the changes to this section (in italics):

A variance is a document issued by your regulatory authority that allows a regulatory requirement to be waived or changed. You will need a variance if your operation plans to prep food in any of the following ways:

- Packaging fresh juice on-site for sale at a later time, unless the juice has a warning label that complies with local regulations.
- Smoking food as a way to preserve it (but not to enhance flavor).
- Using food additives or adding components such as vinegar to preserve or alter the food so that it no longer needs time and temperature control for safety.
- Curing food.
- Custom-processing animals for personal use. For example, a hunter brings a deer to a restaurant for dressing and takes the meat home for later use.
- Packaging food using a reduced-oxygen packaging (ROP) method. This includes MAP, vacuum-packed, and sous vide food, as shown in the photo at left.
- Sprouting seeds or beans.
- Offering live shellfish from a display tank.

When applying for a variance, your regulatory authority may require you to submit a HACCP plan.

- *The HACCP plan must account for any food safety risks related to the way you plan to prep the food item.*
- *You must comply with the HACCP Plan and procedures submitted*
- *You must maintain and provide records requested by the regulatory authority which show that you are regularly:*
  - *Following procedures for monitoring Critical Control Points.*
  - *Monitoring the Critical Control Points.*
  - *Verifying the effectiveness of the operation or process.*
  - *Taking the necessary corrective actions if there is a failure at a critical control point.*

In Chapter 8: The Flow of Food: Preparation: Minimum Internal Cooking Temperatures (Pg. 8.11)

Here are the changes to this section (in italics):

Table 8.2: **Minimum Internal Cooking Temperatures**	
	**165°F (74°C)** ***for <1 second (instantaneous)*** • Poultry—including whole or ground chicken, turkey, or duck • Stuffing made with fish, meat, or poultry • Stuffed meat, seafood, poultry, or pasta • Dishes that include previously cooked TCS ingredients (raw ingredients should be cooked to their required minimum internal temperatures)
	**155°F (68°C)** ***for 17 seconds*** • Ground meat—including beef, pork, and other meat • Injected meat—including brined ham and flavor-injected roasts • Mechanically tenderized meat • *Ground meat from game animals commercially raised and inspected* • Ratites (mostly flightless birds with flat breastbones)—including ostrich and emu • Ground seafood—including chopped or minced seafood • Shell eggs that will be hot held for service

In Chapter 8: The Flow of Food: Preparation: *Minimum Internal Cooking Temperatures* (Pg. 8.12)

Here are the changes to this section (in italics):

Table 8.2: **Minimum Internal Cooking Temperatures** *(continued)*

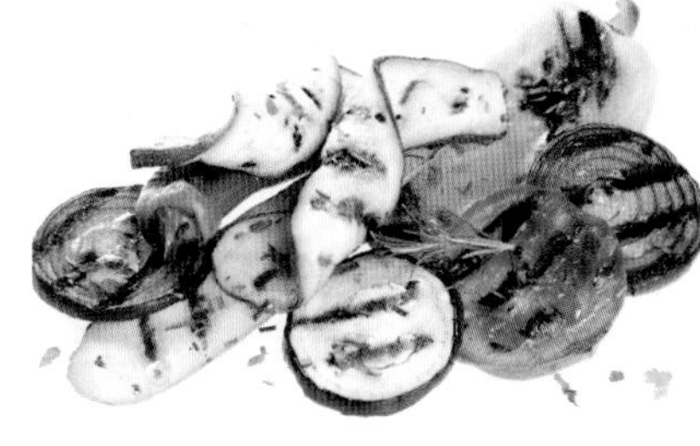

135°F (57°C) (no minimum time)

- *Food from plants,* including fruits, vegetables, grains (e.g., rice, pasta), and legumes (e.g., beans, refried beans) that will be hot held for service

In Chapter 8: The Flow of Food: Preparation: *Study Questions* (Pg. 8.23)

Here are the changes to this section (in italics):

8 What is the minimum internal cooking temperature for ground beef?

A *135°F (57°C)*

B 145°F (63°C) for 15 seconds

C 155°F (68°C) for *17 seconds*

D 165°F (74°C) for *<1 second*

In Chapter 9: The Flow of Food: Service: *Holding Food without Temperature Control* (Pg. 9.3)

Here are the changes to this section (in italics):

If your operation displays or holds TCS food without temperature control, it must do so under certain conditions. *This includes:*

- *preparing written procedures and getting written approval in advance by the regulatory authority*
- *maintaining those procedures in the operation*
- *making sure those procedures are made available to the regulatory authority on request.*

There are other conditions that may apply. Also note that the conditions for holding cold food are different from those for holding hot food. Before using time as a method of control, check with your local regulatory authority for specific requirements.

In Chapter 10: Food Safety Management Systems: *The Seven HACCP Principles* (Pg. 10.7)

Here are the changes to this section (in italics):

Principle 3: Establish Critical Limits. In the example:

With cooking identified as the CCP for Enrico's chicken breasts, a critical limit was needed. Management determined that the critical limit would be cooking the chicken to a minimum internal temperature of 165°F (74°C) *for <1 second.*

Principle 4: Establish Monitoring Procedures. In the example:

...The grill cook must check the temperature of each chicken breast after cooking. Each chicken breast must reach the minimum internal temperature of 165°F (74°C) *for <1 second.*

In Chapter 10: Food Safety Management Systems: *Imminent Health Hazards* (Pg. 10.15)

This new content (in italics) will be added to the end of the section:

The regulatory authority may allow an operation to continue operating in the event of a water or electrical interruption under the following conditions:

- *The operation has a written emergency operating plan approved in advance by the regulatory authority.*
- *An immediate corrective action is taken to prevent, eliminate, or control any food safety risk and imminent health hazard associated with the interruption.*
- *The regulatory authority is informed upon implementing the emergency operating plan.*

In Chapter 10: Food Safety Management Systems: *Something to Think About: Maria's Challenge* (Pg. 10.23)

Here are the changes to this section (in italics):

...Next, she identified critical limits for each CCP. For grilled hamburgers, she determined that cooking them to 150°F (66°C) for 15 seconds would reduce pathogens to a safe level. For grilled chicken, she knew it was necessary to cook it to 165°F (74°C) *for <1 second.*

In Chapter 12: Cleaning and Sanitizing:

Types of Cleaners **(Pg. 12.2)**

Here are the changes to this section (in italics):

Cleaners are chemicals that remove food, dirt, rust, stains, minerals, and other deposits. They must be stable, noncorrosive, and safe to use. *They must also be provided and available to employees during all hours of operation.* Ask your suppliers to help you pick cleaners that meet your needs.

In Chapter 12: Cleaning and Sanitizing:

Chemical Sanitizing **(Pg. 12.4)**

Here are the changes to this section (in italics):

Three common types of chemical sanitizers are chlorine, iodine, and quaternary ammonium compounds, or quats. Chemical sanitizers are regulated by state and federal environmental protection agencies. *They must be provided and available to employees during all hours of operation.*

In Chapter 12: Cleaning and Sanitizing:

Cleaning Up after People Who Get Sick **(Pg. 12.13)**

Here are the changes to this section (in italics):

To be effective, operations must have *written* procedures for cleaning up vomit and diarrhea. These procedures must address specific actions that employees must take to minimize contamination and exposure to food, surfaces, and people. It is critical that employees be trained on these procedures.

In Chapter 15: Staff Food Safety Training:

Training Videos and DVDs **(Pg. 15.7)**

The following portion of this section will be deleted:

~~Trainers generally believe that learners retain information from their training sessions in the following ways:~~

- ~~10 percent of what they read.~~
- ~~20 percent of what they hear.~~
- ~~30 percent of what they see.~~
- ~~50 percent of what they see and here.~~

In the Answer Key: 1.15 Keeping Food Safe: *Something to Think About* (Pg. AK.3)

This new bulleted point (in italics) will be added between the bulleted point that begins "Food handlers are monitored to make sure TCS food is cooked ..." and the one that begins "Food handlers are monitored to make sure TCS food is cooled ...":

- *Food handlers are regularly monitoring food temperatures during hot and cold holding.*

In the Answer Key: 4.18 The Safe Food Handler: *Discussion Questions* (Pg. AK.9)

Here are the changes to this section (in italics):

3 How an infected wound is covered depends on where it is located:

- Cover wounds *or boils* on the hand, *finger*, or wrist with an impermeable cover, *like* a bandage or finger cot. Next, place a single-use glove over the cover.

In the Answer Key: 8.19 The Flow of Food: Preparation: *Discussion Questions* (Pg. AK.21)

Here are the changes to this section (in italics):

1 The minimum internal cooking temperatures are:

- Poultry: 165°F (74°C) *for <1 second (instantaneous)*
- Fish: 145°F (63°C) for 15 seconds
- Pork: 145°F (63°C) for 15 seconds (roasts for four minutes)
- Ground beef: 155°F (68°C) *for 17 seconds*

In the Answer Key: 10.23 Food Safety Management Systems: *Something to Think About: Maria's Challenge* (Pg. AK.31)

Here are the changes to this section (in italics):

2 Here is what Maria should have done differently:

- She should have established the correct critical limit for grilled hamburgers. This would include cooking them to 155°F (68°C) *for 17 seconds.*

Disclaimer

Copyright Permissions
National Restaurant Association Solutions
233 S. Wacker Drive, Suite 3600
Chicago, IL 60606-6383

Email: permissions@restaurant.org

Coursebook, CBX7 (with exam answer sheet) ISBN 978-1-58280-334-0

Coursebook, CBV7 (with online exam voucher) ISBN 978-1-58280-333-3

Coursebook, CB7 (text only) ISBN 978-1-58280-332-6

Printed in the USA
10 9 8 7 6 5 4

Contents

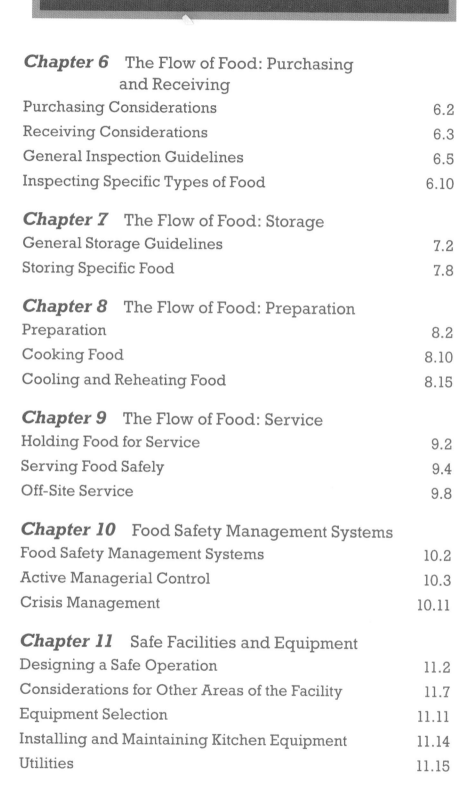

Contents

A Message from the National Restaurant Association

Congratulations! By opening this book, you are joining millions of foodservice professionals in taking the first step in a commitment to food safety. ServSafe® training helps you understand all of the food safety risks faced by your operation. Once you're aware of these risks, you can find ways to reduce them. This will help you keep your operation, your staff, and your customers safe.

Created by Foodservice Industry Leaders You can be confident knowing the ServSafe program was created by leaders in the foodservice industry. The topics you will learn in this book were determined by those who deal with the same food safety issues you face every day. From the basics of handwashing, to more complex topics such as foodborne pathogens, your industry peers have provided you with the building blocks to keep food safe throughout your operation.

Performed and Reinforced by You Food safety doesn't stop once you've completed your training and certification. It is now your responsibility to take the knowledge you learned and share it with your staff. When you return to your operation, start by answering the following questions to assess your food handler training:

- Do you have food safety training programs for both new and current staff?
- Do you have assessment tools to identify staff's food safety knowledge?
- Do you keep records documenting that staff have completed training?

About Your Certification To access your ServSafe Food Protection Manager Certification Exam results, register on ServSafe.com. You will need your class number, which your instructor will provide. Depending on how soon we receive your exam, results will be available approximately 10 business days after you take the exam.
For security purposes, your exam results cannot be provided over the phone or sent through e-mail.

Your ServSafe Food Protection Manager Certification is valid for five years from your exam date. Local laws apply. Check with your local regulatory authority or company for specific recertification requirements.

If you have any questions about your certification or additional food handler training, please call (800) ServSafe (800.737.8723), or e-mail us at servicecenter@restaurant.org.

Staying Connected with the National Restaurant Association

The National Restaurant Association (NRA) has the resources and tools to support you throughout your education and career in the restaurant and foodservice industry. Through scholarships, educational programs, industry certifications, and member benefits, the NRA is your partner now and into the future.

Scholarships The NRA's philanthropic foundation, the National Restaurant Association Educational Foundation (NRAEF), offers scholarships to college students through its NRAEF Scholarship Program. These scholarships can help pave your way to an affordable higher education and may be applied to a culinary, restaurant management, or foodservice-related program at an accredited college or university. We encourage you to investigate the opportunities, which include access to special program scholarships for ProStart students who earn the National Certificate of Achievement, as well as ManageFirst Program® students. You may be awarded one NRAEF scholarship per calendar year—make sure you keep applying every year! The NRAEF partners with state restaurant associations to offer student scholarships. Check with your state to see if they offer additional scholarship opportunities. The NRAEF also offers professional development scholarships for educators. Visit ChooseRestaurants.org/scholarships for information.

College education As you research and apply to colleges and universities to continue your industry education, look for schools offering the NRA's ManageFirst Program. Just like Foundations of Restaurant Management & Culinary Arts, the ManageFirst Program and curriculum materials were developed with input from the restaurant and foodservice industry and academic partners. This management program teaches you practical skills needed to face real-world challenges in the industry, including interpersonal communication, ethics, accounting skills, and more. The program includes the ten topics listed below, plus ServSafe Food Safety and ServSafe Alcohol®:

- Controlling Foodservice Costs
- Hospitality and Restaurant Management
- Hospitality Human Resources Management and Supervision
- Customer Service
- Principles of Food and Beverage Management
- Purchasing
- Hospitality Accounting
- Bar and Beverage Management
- Nutrition
- Hospitality and Restaurant Marketing

You can also earn the ManageFirst Professional® (MFP™) credential by passing five required ManageFirst exams and completing 800 work hours in the industry. Having the MFP on your resume tells employers that you have the management skills needed to succeed in the industry. To learn more about ManageFirst or to locate ManageFirst schools, visit managefirst.restaurant.org.

Certification In the competitive restaurant field, industry certifications can help you stand out among a crowd of applicants.

The NRA's ServSafe Food Protection Manager Certification is nationally recognized. Earning your certification tells the industry that you know food safety and the critical importance of its role—and enables you to share food safety knowledge with every other employee.

Through ServSafe Food Safety, you'll master sanitation, the flow of food through an operation, sanitary facilities, and pest management. ServSafe is the training that is learned, remembered, shared, and used. And that makes it the strongest food safety training choice for you. For more information on ServSafe, visit ServSafe.com.

The challenges surrounding alcohol service in restaurants have increased dramatically. To prepare you to address these challenges, the NRA offers ServSafe Alcohol. As you continue to work in the industry, responsible alcohol service is an issue that will touch your business, your customers, and your community. Armed with your ServSafe Alcohol Certificate, you can make an immediate impact on an establishment. Through the program, you'll learn essential responsible alcohol service information, including alcohol laws and responsibilities, evaluating intoxication levels, dealing with difficult situations, and checking identification. Please visit ServSafe.com/alcohol to learn more about ServSafe Alcohol.

National Restaurant Association membership As you move into the industry, seek out careers in restaurants that are members of the NRA and your state restaurant association. Encourage any operation you are part of to join the national and state organizations. During your student years, the NRA also offers student memberships that give you access to industry research and information that can be an invaluable resource. For more information, or to join as a student member, visit restaurant.org.

Management credentials After you've established yourself in the industry, strive for the industry's highest management certification—the NRA's Foodservice Management Professional® (FMP®). The FMP certification recognizes exceptional managers and supervisors who have achieved the highest level of knowledge, experience, and professionalism that is most valued by our industry. You become eligible to apply and sit for the FMP exam after you've worked as a supervisor in the industry for three years.

Staying Connected with the National Restaurant Association

Passing the FMP exam places you in select company; you will have joined the ranks of leading industry professionals. The FMP certification is also an impressive credential to add to your title and resume. For more information on the Foodservice Management Professional certification, visit managefirst.restaurant.org.

Make the NRA your partner throughout your education and career. Take advantage of the NRA's scholarship, training, certification, and membership benefits that will launch you into your career of choice. Together we will lead this industry into an even brighter future.

Acknowledgments

The development of the *ServSafe CourseBook* would not have been possible without the expertise of our many advisors and manuscript reviewers. Thank you to the following people and organizations for their time, effort, and dedication to creating this seventh edition.

Chirag Bhatt, Bloomin' Brands, Inc.

Debra Boyette, Bojangles' Restaurants, Inc.

Linda Lockett Brown, CINET, Inc.

Kristie Costa, Rhode Island Hospitality Association

Joann DeTraglia, Mohawk Valley Community College

Jean Edsall, Compass Group

Matthew Jenkins, Sodexo

Chandra Johnson, Alpha Education

Kendra Kauppi, University of Minnesota

Mahmood Khan, Virginia Polytechnic Institute & State University

Shawn Kohlhaas, Culinary Cultivations

Jaymin Patel, Aramark

Kyle Reynolds, Le Cordon Bleu College of Culinary Arts

Jacob Rhoten, Cedar Fair Entertainment Co., Kings Dominion

Rachel Robinson, KFC/YUM Brands

Michael Sabella, Food Safety Certified, LLC

Gina Scammon, Suffolk County Department of Health New York

Jennifer Singman, Ecolab

Diane Withrow, Cape Fear Community College

Charles Yet, Washtenaw County Public Health

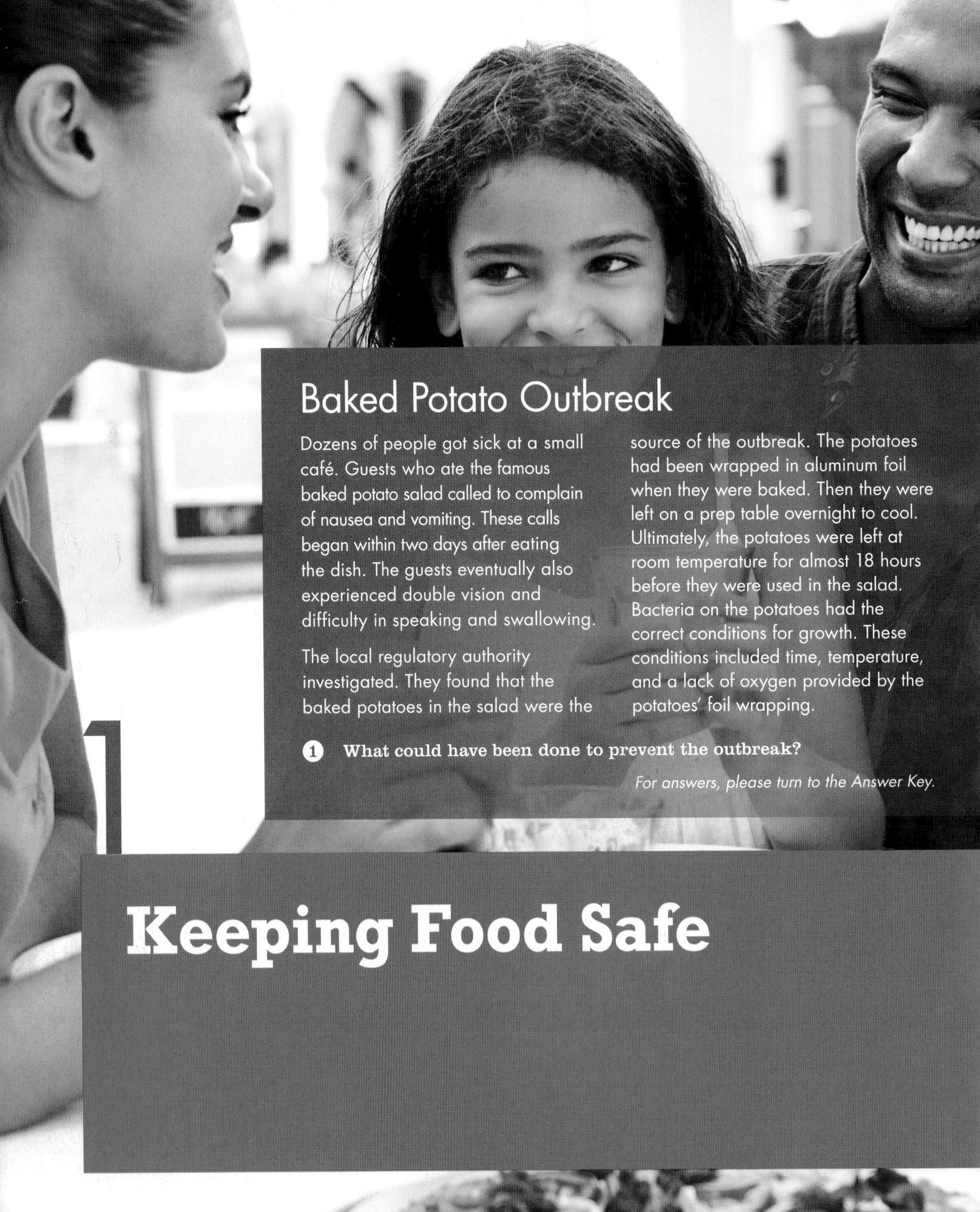

Baked Potato Outbreak

Dozens of people got sick at a small café. Guests who ate the famous baked potato salad called to complain of nausea and vomiting. These calls began within two days after eating the dish. The guests eventually also experienced double vision and difficulty in speaking and swallowing.

The local regulatory authority investigated. They found that the baked potatoes in the salad were the source of the outbreak. The potatoes had been wrapped in aluminum foil when they were baked. Then they were left on a prep table overnight to cool. Ultimately, the potatoes were left at room temperature for almost 18 hours before they were used in the salad. Bacteria on the potatoes had the correct conditions for growth. These conditions included time, temperature, and a lack of oxygen provided by the potatoes' foil wrapping.

1 **What could have been done to prevent the outbreak?**

For answers, please turn to the Answer Key.

1

Keeping Food Safe

Inside This Chapter

- Foodborne Illnesses
- How Foodborne Illnesses Occur
- The Food Safety Responsibilities of a Manager

Objectives

After completing this chapter, you should be able to identify the following:

- What a foodborne illness is and how to determine when one has occurred
- Challenges to food safety
- Costs of a foodborne illness
- Contaminants that can make food unsafe
- How food becomes unsafe
- Food most likely to become unsafe
- Populations at high risk for foodborne illness
- Food safety responsibilities of the person in charge of a foodservice operation

Key Terms

Foodborne illness

Foodborne-illness outbreak

Contamination

Time-temperature abuse

Cross-contamination

TCS food

Ready-to-eat food

High-risk populations

Immune system

Foodborne Illnesses

As a foodservice manager, you are responsible for your operation, your staff, and your guests. The best way to meet your obligations is to keep the food you serve safe. To start, you must know what foodborne illnesses are and whom they most affect. The more you learn about foodborne illnesses, the more you will understand the need for strong food safety practices. The costs of a foodborne-illness outbreak can be devastating.

A **foodborne illness** is a disease transmitted to people by food. An illness is considered a **foodborne-illness outbreak** when two or more people have the same symptoms after eating the same food. However, this requires an investigation by a regulatory authority as well as confirmation by a laboratory. Millions of people contract a foodborne illness each year. Most cases go unreported and do not occur at restaurant or foodservice operations. Those that are reported and investigated help the industry learn about the causes of foodborne illnesses and what can be done to prevent them.

Challenges to Food Safety

You must work hard to maintain high standards of food safety throughout your operation. It is not always easy. Food safety faces many obstacles.

Time Pressure to work quickly can make it hard to take the time to follow food safety practices.

Language and culture Some staff may speak a language different from yours. This can create communication barriers. Cultural differences can influence how staff view food safety as well.

Literacy and education Staff often have varying education levels. This can make teaching food safety to some of them more difficult.

Pathogens Illness-causing pathogens are now found on food that was once considered safe. For example, nontyphoidal *Salmonella* now appears on produce more often than in the past.

Unapproved suppliers Food might be received from suppliers that are not practicing food safety. This can cause a foodborne-illness outbreak.

High-risk populations The number of guests at high risk for getting a foodborne illness is on the rise. One example is the growing elderly population.

Staff turnover Training new staff, as shown at left, leaves less time for food safety training.

The ServSafe program will help you overcome challenges in managing a good food safety program.

The Costs of Foodborne Illnesses

Foodborne illnesses cost the United States billions of dollars each year. National Restaurant Association figures show that a foodborne-illness outbreak can cost an operation thousands of dollars. Some of these costs are shown in Table 1.1.

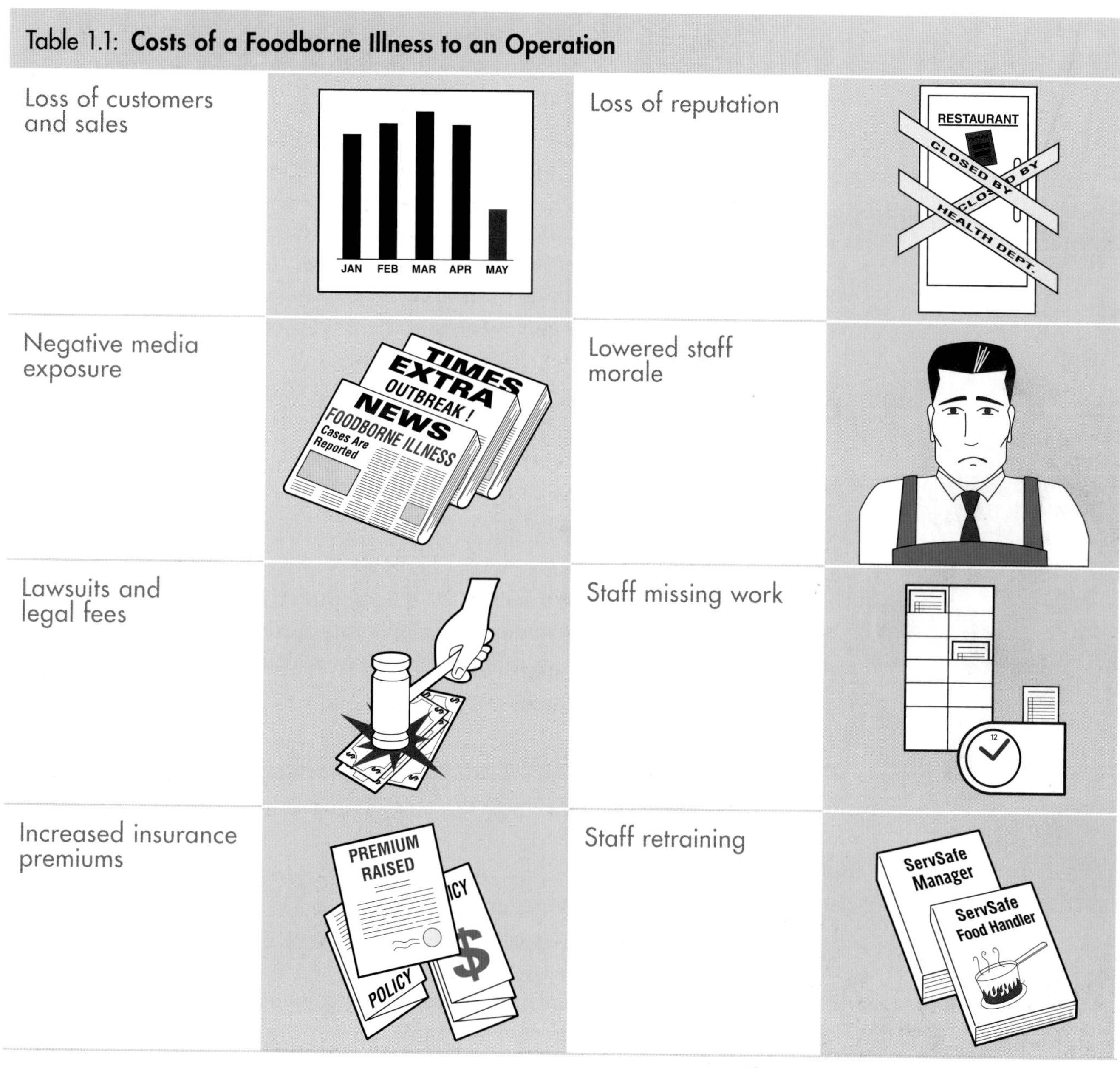

Table 1.1: **Costs of a Foodborne Illness to an Operation**

Loss of customers and sales	Loss of reputation
Negative media exposure	Lowered staff morale
Lawsuits and legal fees	Staff missing work
Increased insurance premiums	Staff retraining

Most important are the human costs. Victims of foodborne illnesses may experience lost work, medical costs and long-term disability, and death.

How Foodborne Illnesses Occur

Unsafe food is usually the result of **contamination**, which is the presence of harmful substances in food. To prevent foodborne illnesses, you must recognize the contaminants that can make food unsafe. These contaminants include pathogens, chemicals, and physical objects. Food contamination can also be caused by certain unsafe practices in your operation.

Contaminants

Contaminants are divided into three categories.

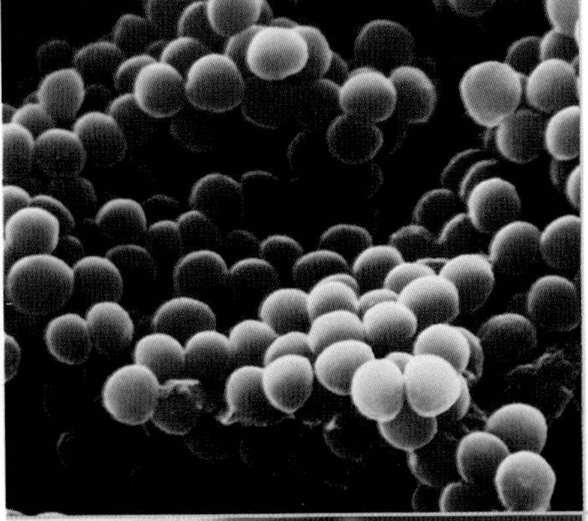

Biological Pathogens are the greatest threat to food safety. They include certain viruses, parasites, fungi, and bacteria, as shown at left. Some plants, mushrooms, and seafood that carry harmful toxins (poisons) are also included in this group.

Chemical Foodservice chemicals can contaminate food if they are used incorrectly. The photo at left shows one example of how chemicals may contaminate food. Chemical contaminants can include cleaners, sanitizers, and polishes.

Physical Foreign objects such as metal shavings, staples, and bandages can get into food. So can glass, dirt, and even bag ties. The photo at left shows this type of physical contaminant. Naturally occurring objects, such as fish bones in fillets, are another example.

Each of these three contaminants is a danger to food safety. But biological contaminants are responsible for most foodborne illnesses.

How Food Becomes Unsafe

If food handlers do not handle food correctly, it can become unsafe. These are the five most common food-handling mistakes, or risk factors, that can cause a foodborne illness:

1 Purchasing food from unsafe sources

2 Failing to cook food correctly

3 Holding food at incorrect temperatures

4 Using contaminated equipment

5 Practicing poor personal hygiene

Purchasing food from unsafe sources can be a big problem. So, purchasing food from approved, reputable suppliers is critical. Keep in mind that food prepared in a private home is also considered to be from an unsafe source and must be avoided, as seen in the photo at right. The other food-handling mistakes listed above are related to four main practices. These include time-temperature abuse, cross-contamination, poor personal hygiene, and poor cleaning and sanitizing. These are identified in Table 1.2.

Table 1.2: **Practices Related to Foodborne Illness**

Time-temperature abuse

Food has suffered **time-temperature abuse** when it has stayed too long at temperatures that are good for the growth of pathogens. A foodborne illness can result if food is time-temperature abused. This can happen in many ways:

- Food is not held or stored at the correct temperature, as shown in the photo at left.
- Food is not cooked or reheated enough to kill pathogens.
- Food is not cooled correctly.

Cross-contamination

Pathogens can be transferred from one surface or food to another. This is called **cross-contamination**. It can cause a foodborne illness in many ways:

- Contaminated ingredients are added to food that receives no further cooking.
- Ready-to-eat food touches contaminated surfaces.
- Contaminated food touches or drips fluids onto cooked or ready-to-eat food, as shown in the photo at left.
- A food handler touches contaminated food and then touches ready-to-eat food.
- Contaminated cleaning cloths touch food-contact surfaces.

Poor personal hygiene

Food handlers can cause a foodborne illness if they do any of the following actions:

- Fail to wash their hands correctly after using the restroom.
- Cough or sneeze on food.
- Touch or scratch wounds and then touch food, as shown in the photo at left.
- Work while sick.

Poor cleaning and sanitizing

Pathogens can be spread to food if equipment has not been cleaned and sanitized correctly between uses. This can happen in the following ways:

- Equipment and utensils are not washed, rinsed, and sanitized between uses.
- Food-contact surfaces are wiped clean rather than being washed, rinsed, and sanitized, as shown in the photo at left.
- Wiping cloths are not stored in a sanitizer solution between uses.
- Sanitizing solutions are not at the required levels to sanitize objects.

Food Most Likely to Become Unsafe: TCS Food

TCS and ready-to-eat food are the most likely food to become unsafe.

TCS Food

Pathogens grow well in the food pictured in Table 1.3. These items need time and temperature control to limit pathogen growth. For this reason, this food is called TCS food—food requiring time and temperature control for safety.

Table 1.3: **TCS Food**

	Milk and dairy products		Shell eggs (except those treated to eliminate nontyphoidal *Salmonella*)
	Meat: beef, pork, and lamb		Poultry
	Fish		Shellfish and crustaceans
	Baked potatoes		Heat-treated plant food, such as cooked rice, beans, and vegetables

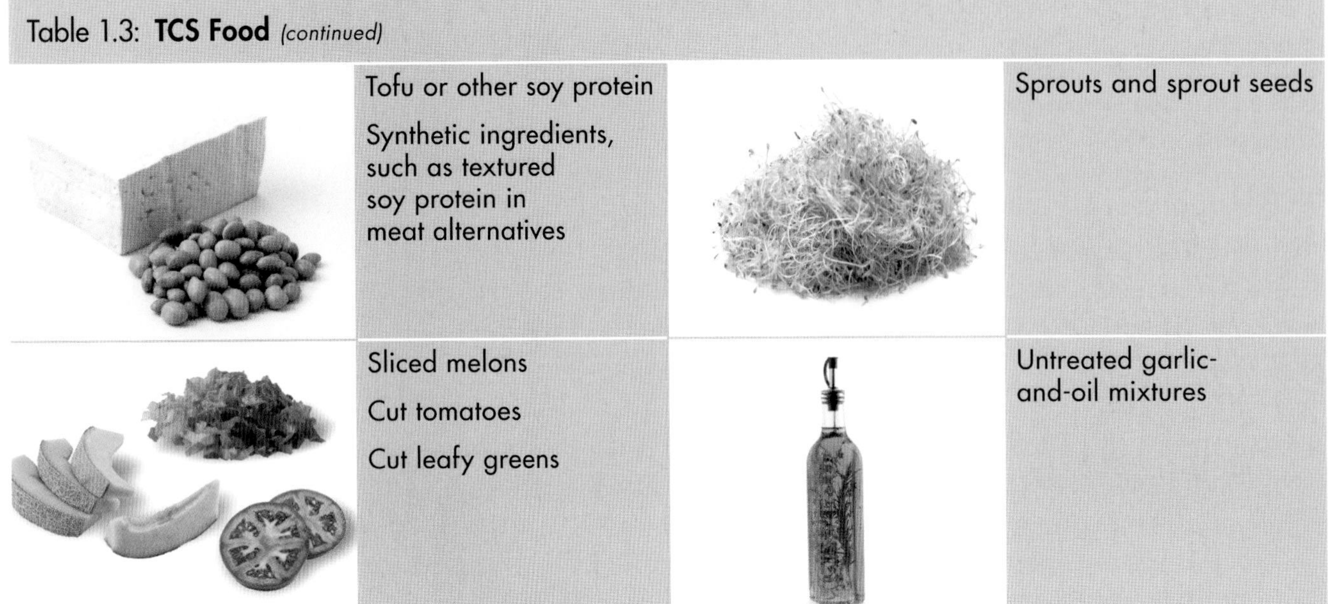

Table 1.3: **TCS Food** *(continued)*

	Tofu or other soy protein Synthetic ingredients, such as textured soy protein in meat alternatives		Sprouts and sprout seeds
	Sliced melons Cut tomatoes Cut leafy greens		Untreated garlic-and-oil mixtures

Ready-to-Eat Food

Like TCS food, ready-to-eat food also needs careful handling to prevent contamination. **Ready-to-eat food** is exactly what it sounds like: food that can be eaten without further preparation, washing, or cooking. Examples include cooked food, washed fruits and vegetables (whole and cut), and deli meat. Bakery items and sugar, spices, and seasonings are other examples of ready-to-eat food.

Populations at High Risk for Foodborne Illness

Some groups of people have a higher risk of getting a foodborne illness than others. These **high-risk populations** include preschool-age children, elderly people, and people with compromised immune systems, as shown in Table 1.4.

Table 1.4: **High-Risk Populations**

Elderly people

As people age, changes occur in their organs. For example, stomach-acid production decreases as people get older. This allows more pathogens to enter the intestines. A change in the stomach and intestinal tract also allows the body to store food for longer periods. This gives toxins more time to form.

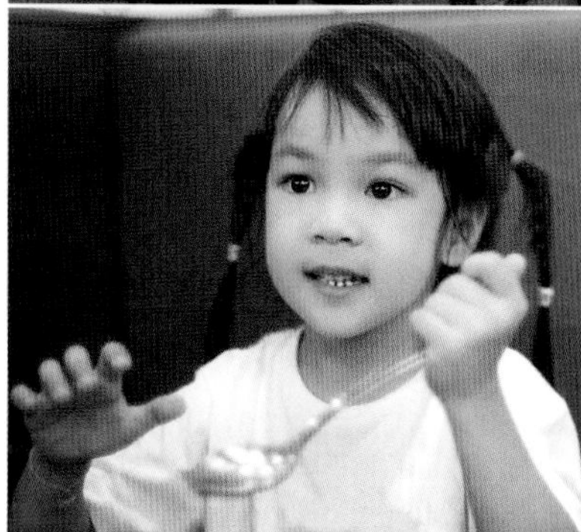

Preschool-age children

Very young children are at a higher risk for getting a foodborne illness because they have not yet built up strong immune systems.

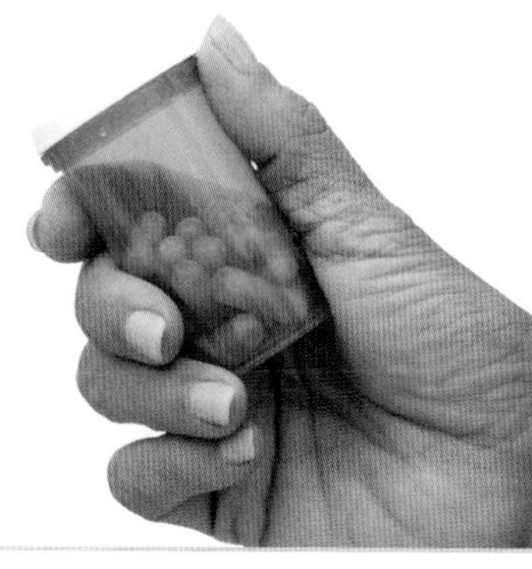

People with compromised immune systems

Certain medical conditions and medications can weaken a person's **immune system**—the body's defense system against illness. These conditions and medications include:

- Cancer or chemotherapy
- HIV/AIDS
- Transplants

People who have had transplants take medication to prevent the body from rejecting the new organ or bone marrow.

Key Practices for Ensuring Food Safety

Now that you know how food can become unsafe, you can focus on the following to keep it safe:

- Purchase food from approved, reputable suppliers.
- Control time and temperature.
- Prevent cross-contamination.
- Practice good personal hygiene.
- Properly clean and sanitize.

Set up standard operating procedures (SOPs) that focus on these areas. The ServSafe program will show you how to design these procedures in later chapters.

The Food Safety Responsibilities of a Manager

The Food and Drug Administration (FDA) recommends that regulatory authorities hold the person in charge of a foodservice operation responsible for ensuring the following standards are met:

- Food is not prepared in a private home or in a room where people are living or sleeping.
- People other than food handlers are restricted from prep, storage, and dishwashing areas. If other people are allowed in these areas, steps are taken to protect food, utensils, and equipment from contamination.
- Maintenance and delivery workers follow food safety practices while in the operation.
- Staff handwashing is monitored in the operation.
- The inspection of deliveries is monitored to ensure that food is received from an approved source, is received at the correct temperature, and has not been contaminated.
- Food delivered after-hours is monitored to make sure it is received from an approved source, stored in the correct location, protected from contamination, and accurately presented.
- Food handlers are monitored to make sure TCS food is cooked to required temperatures. Temperatures are checked using calibrated thermometers, as shown in the photo at left.

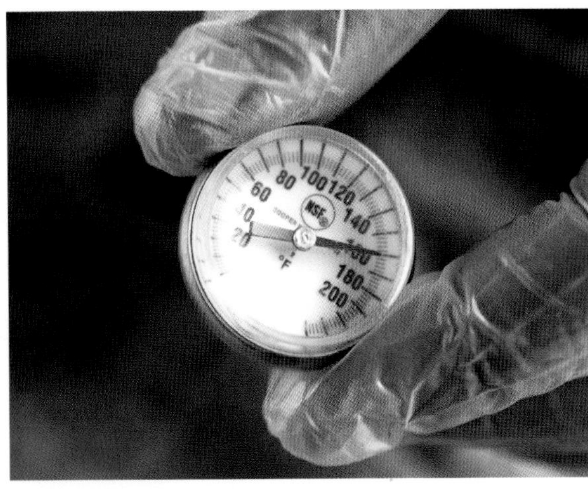

- Food handlers are monitored to make sure TCS food is cooled rapidly.
- Consumer advisories are posted notifying guests of the risk of ordering raw or partially cooked food.
- Cleaning and sanitizing procedures are monitored to make sure that sanitizer solutions are at the correct temperature and concentration and remain in contact with items for the correct amount of time.
- Guests are notified that they must use clean tableware when returning to a self-service area.
- Staff are handling ready-to-eat food with utensils or single-use gloves, as seen in the photo at right.
- Staff are trained in food safety, including allergy awareness.
- Staff, including conditional staff, are reporting illnesses and symptoms of illnesses that can be transmitted through food.
- Food safety procedures are written down, implemented, and maintained where required by the regulatory authority.

Marketing Food Safety

Marketing your food safety efforts will show staff and guests alike that you take food safety seriously. Emphasize your support of food safety training and policies.

You can display your commitment in several other ways as well:

- Offer training courses and evaluate and update them as needed.
- Discuss food safety expectations. Document food-handling procedures and update them as needed.
- Consider awarding certificates for training and small rewards for good food safety records.
- Set an example by following all food safety rules yourself.

You should also show guests that staff know and follow food safety rules. Make sure your staff's hygiene and appearance reflect your food safety focus. Post food safety ideas and information in appropriate locations at your operation. Ensure that staff can answer simple food safety questions when asked.

Chapter Summary

- A foodborne illness is a disease transmitted to people by food. A foodborne illness is considered an outbreak when two or more people have the same symptoms after eating the same food.
- Operations face many challenges to food safety. These include time pressure and potentially unsafe supplies, including food formerly considered safe from pathogens, such as produce. Operations also face an increase in high-risk populations and challenges related to staff.
- A foodborne illness costs both guests and operations. An operation may experience negative publicity, decreased business, lawsuits and legal fees, increased insurance premiums, and personnel issues.
- Three types of contaminants threaten food safety. They are biological, chemical, and physical. Of these, pathogens, which are biological contaminants, pose the greatest danger.
- Food handlers who do not follow correct procedures can also threaten the safety of food. They can do this when they fail to cook food enough and when they hold it at incorrect temperatures. Food handlers can also cause an illness when they use contaminated equipment and when they practice poor personal hygiene.
- Food has been time-temperature abused when it has stayed too long at temperatures that are good for the growth of pathogens. Pathogens can be transferred from one surface or food to another. This is called cross-contamination. Pathogens can be spread to food if equipment has not been cleaned and sanitized correctly between uses.
- Pathogens grow well in TCS food. To prevent this growth, this food needs time and temperature control.
- Some groups are at a higher risk of getting sick from unsafe food. They include preschool-age children, the elderly, people with cancer or on chemotherapy, people with HIV/AIDS, transplant recipients, and people on certain medications.
- Important prevention measures for keeping food safe are controlling time and temperature; preventing cross-contamination; practicing good personal hygiene; purchasing from approved, reputable suppliers; and cleaning and sanitizing items correctly.

Apply Your Knowledge

Use these questions to review the concepts presented in this chapter.

Discussion Questions

1 What are the potential costs associated with foodborne-illness outbreaks?

2 Why are the elderly at a higher risk for getting foodborne illnesses?

3 What are the three major types of contaminants?

For answers, please turn to the Answer Key.

Apply Your Knowledge

Something to Think About

Undercooked Chicken Sends Children to the Hospital

A group of preschool children were on a field trip to the local pumpkin farm for their annual fall outing. Twenty-five children and two chaperones got sick after a stop at a local, family-owned restaurant.

Regulatory authorities determined that chicken used to make chicken sandwiches for the group was not fully cooked. Apparently, the cooks at the operation had a difficult time keeping up after the school bus arrived. As a result, the cooks rushed the cooking process and failed to check the internal temperature of the chicken. Most of the children became severely ill and had to be hospitalized.

The two chaperones recovered quickly.

1 What caused the outbreak?

____

____

____

____

____

____

2 Why did so many children get sick?

____

____

____

____

____

____

For answers, please turn to the Answer Key.

Apply Your Knowledge

Something to Think About

With Power Comes Responsibility

The owner of a popular Italian restaurant needed a new manager. After careful consideration, the owner decided to promote Russell, a young cook who had worked for him for the last three years. Russell showed great promise. He was attending culinary school and had taken and passed the food safety certification program with flying colors. He had a great work record and was rarely late for work.

In his new role as manager, Russell would be directly responsible for food safety in the operation. He knew how important this new role would be, and he took food safety very seriously.

1 What will the regulatory authority hold Russell accountable for in regard to food safety?

For answers, please turn to the Answer Key.

Study Questions

Circle the best answer to each question.

1 **What is a foodborne-illness outbreak?**

A When two or more food handlers contaminate multiple food items

B When an operation serves contaminated food to two or more people

C When two or more people report the same illness from eating the same food

D When the CDC receives information on two or more people with the same illness

2 **What is TCS food?**

A Food requiring thermometer checks for security

B Food requiring trustworthy conditions for service

C Food requiring training commitments for standards

D Food requiring time and temperature control for safety

3 **Why are preschool-age children at a higher risk for foodborne illnesses?**

A Their appetites have increased since birth.

B They have not built up strong immune systems.

C They are more likely to spend time in a hospital.

D They are more likely to suffer allergic reactions.

4 **Which is a TCS food?**

A Bread

B Flour

C Sprouts

D Strawberries

Study Questions

5 **The five common risk factors that can lead to foodborne illness are failing to cook food adequately, holding food at incorrect temperatures, using contaminated equipment, practicing poor personal hygiene, and**

A reheating leftover food.

B serving ready-to-eat food.

C using single-use, disposable gloves.

D purchasing food from unsafe sources.

6 **What is an important measure for preventing foodborne illness?**

A Using new equipment

B Measuring pathogens

C Preventing cross-contamination

D Serving locally grown, organic food

7 **Raw chicken breasts are left out at room temperature on a prep table. What is the main risk that could cause a foodborne illness?**

A Cross-contamination

B Poor personal hygiene

C Time-temperature abuse

D Poor cleaning and sanitizing

8 **A server cleans a dining table with a wiping cloth and then puts the wiping cloth in an apron pocket. What is the risk that could cause a foodborne illness?**

A Cross-contamination

B Poor personal hygiene

C Time-temperature abuse

D Poor cleaning and sanitizing

For answers, please turn to the Answer Key.

Notes

Notes

Shigella Outbreak

Sixteen guests and three catering-hall staff became sick with *Shigella* spp. The guests were part of a large group of National Guard veterans at a reunion. They ate at a popular catering hall located in the southeastern United States. Within one to three days after the catered event, reports began to come into the local regulatory authority. Those who had gotten sick reported very similar symptoms. Each had experienced stomach cramps, fever, and diarrhea. Three people went to the emergency room to seek treatment. The specific food involved was never determined. But the regulatory authority confirmed that the outbreak was likely caused by the catering hall's lead cook, who had prepped the food served at the luncheon. He was not feeling well the morning of the luncheon when he reported to work. He also had failed to wash his hands many times during his morning shift.

1. **What could have been done to prevent the outbreak?**
2. **What should the catering hall's owners and management team do to ensure that an outbreak like this does not occur in the future?**

For answers, please turn to the Answer Key.

2

Understanding the Microworld

Inside This Chapter

- Pathogens
- Bacteria
- Viruses
- Parasites
- Fungi
- Biological Toxins

Objectives

After completing this chapter, you should be able to identify the following:

- Conditions that affect the growth of foodborne bacteria (FAT TOM)
- Major foodborne pathogens and their sources; resulting illnesses and their symptoms
- Ways of preventing viral, bacterial, parasitic, and fungal contamination
- Naturally occurring toxins and ways of preventing illnesses caused by them

Key Terms

Microorganisms

Pathogens

Toxins

Fecal–oral route

Jaundice

Onset time

Bacteria

FAT TOM

pH

Temperature danger zone

Water activity (a_w)

Spore

Virus

Parasite

Fungi

Mold

Yeast

Pathogens

Biological contamination occurs from **microorganisms**. These are small, living organisms that can be seen only through a microscope. Many microorganisms are harmless, but some can cause illness. These are called **pathogens**. Some pathogens make you sick when you eat them. Others produce poisons—or **toxins**—that make you sick. An understanding of pathogens and the toxins that some produce is the first step in preventing foodborne illnesses.

The four types of pathogens that can contaminate food are viruses, bacteria, parasites, and fungi. Many viruses, bacteria, and parasites can cause an illness but cannot be seen, smelled, or tasted. On the other hand, some fungi, such as mold, can change the look, smell, or taste of food but may not make people sick.

How Contamination Occurs

Most pathogens get into food and onto food-contact surfaces because of the way that people handle them. For example, food handlers who do not wash their hands after using the restroom may contaminate food and surfaces with feces from their fingers. Once the food that the food handler touched is eaten, a foodborne illness may result. This is called the **fecal-oral route** of contamination.

Food handlers can also pass on pathogens when they are in contact with a person who is sick. Some pathogens are passed on very easily in any of these ways:

- From person to person
- Through sneezing or vomiting onto food or food-contact surfaces
- From touching dirty food-contact surfaces and equipment and then touching food

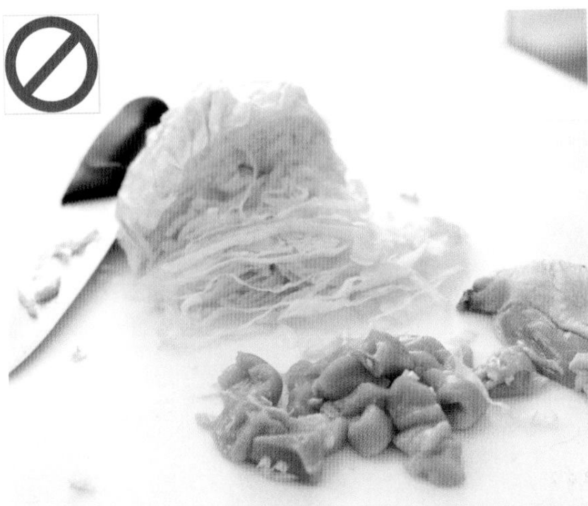

Simple mistakes can result in contamination. For example, allowing ready-to-eat food to touch surfaces that have come in contact with raw meat, seafood, and poultry can lead to contamination. This is shown in the photo at left. Storing food or cleaning products incorrectly can also lead to contamination. So can the failure to spot signs of pests in the operation, because pests are a major source of disease.

Symptoms of a Foodborne Illness

Once pathogens get into food or onto food-contact surfaces, a foodborne illness can result. The symptoms of a foodborne illness vary depending on which illness a person has. But most victims share some common symptoms:

- Diarrhea
- Vomiting
- Fever
- Nausea
- Abdominal cramps
- **Jaundice** (a yellowing of the skin and eyes), as shown at right

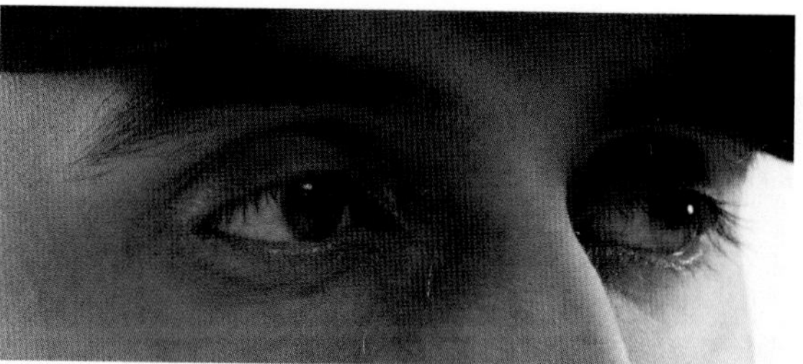

Not every person who is sick with a foodborne illness will have all of these symptoms. Nor are the symptoms of foodborne illness limited to this list. Throughout this chapter, several foodborne illnesses will be presented. Symptoms specific to these illnesses are listed.

How quickly foodborne-illness symptoms appear in a person is known as the **onset time** of the illness. Onset times depend on the type of foodborne illness a person has. They can range from 30 minutes to as long as six weeks. How severe the illness is can also vary from mild diarrhea to death.

The Big Six

According to the Food and Drug Administration (FDA), there are over 40 kinds of bacteria, viruses, parasites, and molds that can occur in food and cause a foodborne illness. Of these, six have been singled out by the FDA, because they are highly contagious and can cause severe illness. These have been dubbed the "Big Six." They include:

- *Shigella* spp.
- *Salmonella* Typhi
- Nontyphoidal *Salmonella* (NTS)
- Shiga toxin-producing *Escherichia coli* (STEC), also known as *E. coli*
- Hepatitis A
- Norovirus

These pathogens are often found in very high numbers in an infected person's feces and can be transferred to food easily. A person does not have to eat much of the pathogen in order to get sick, and that illness is often severe. For this reason, food handlers diagnosed with illnesses from these pathogens cannot work in a foodservice operation while they are sick.

Bacteria

Bacteria are responsible for a large number of foodborne illnesses. Knowing what bacteria are and how they grow can help you control them.

General Information about Bacteria

Bacteria are single-celled, living microorganisms that can spoil food and cause foodborne illness. Bacteria share some basic characteristics.

Location Bacteria can be found almost everywhere. They live in and on our bodies. Some types of bacteria keep us healthy, while others cause illness.

Detection Bacteria cannot be seen, smelled, or tasted.

Growth If conditions are correct, bacteria will grow in rapid numbers.

Toxin production Some bacteria produce toxins in food as they grow and die. People who eat the toxins can get sick. Cooking may not destroy these toxins.

Prevention The most important way to prevent bacteria from causing a foodborne illness is to control time and temperature.

What Bacteria Need to Grow

Bacteria need six conditions to grow. You can remember them by thinking of the words **FAT TOM**, explained in Table 2.1.

Table 2.1: **FAT TOM—Conditions for Bacteria to Grow**

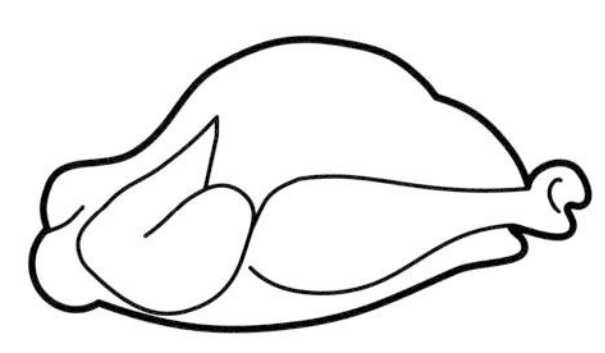

Food

Most bacteria need nutrients such as carbohydrates or proteins to survive. TCS food supports the growth of bacteria better than other types of food. This includes meat, poultry, dairy products, and eggs.

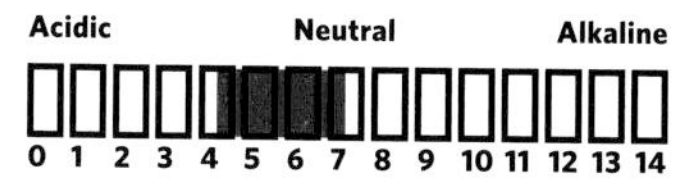

Acidity

Bacteria grow best in food that contains little or no acid. **pH** is the measure of acidity. The pH scale ranges from 0 to 14.0. A value of 0 is highly acidic, while a value of 14.0 is highly alkaline. A pH of 7.0 is neutral. Bacteria grow best in food that is neutral to slightly acidic, a pH of 7.5 to 4.6.

Here are some common types of food and their pH:

- Lemons and limes have a pH of 1.8–2.4.
- Tomatoes have a pH of 3.7–4.0.
- Mayonnaise has a pH of 3.8–4.0.

The following common types of food have a pH that is ideal for bacterial growth:

- Bread has a pH of 5.0–6.0.
- Raw chicken has a pH of 5.5–6.0.
- Cantaloupe has a pH of 6.1–6.5.
- Milk has a pH of 6.4–6.8.
- Cooked corn has a pH of 7.3–7.6.

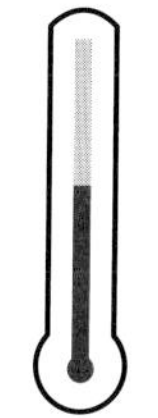

Temperature

Bacteria grow rapidly between 41°F and 135°F (5°C and 57°C). This range is known as the **temperature danger zone**. Bacteria grow even more rapidly from 70°F to 125°F (21°C to 52°C). Bacterial growth is limited when food is held above or below the temperature danger zone.

Time

Bacteria need time to grow. The more time bacteria spend in the temperature danger zone, the more opportunity they have to grow to unsafe levels.

Oxygen

Some bacteria need oxygen to grow. Others grow when oxygen is not there. Bacteria that grow without oxygen can occur in cooked rice, untreated garlic-and-oil mixtures, and temperature-abused baked potatoes.

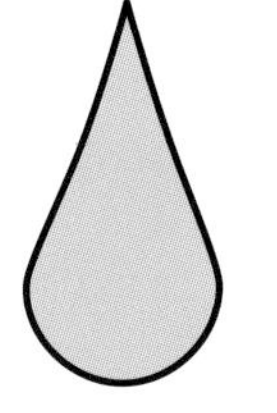

Moisture

Bacteria grow well in food with high levels of moisture. The amount of moisture available in food for this growth is called **water activity (a_w)**. The a_w scale ranges from 0.0 to 1.0. The higher the value, the more available moisture in the food. For example, water has a water activity of 1.0. Food with a water activity of 0.85 or higher is ideal for the growth of bacteria.

Controlling FAT TOM Conditions

You can help keep food safe by controlling FAT TOM. In your operation, however, you will most likely be able to control only time and temperature.

- To control time, limit how long TCS food spends in the temperature danger zone.
- To control temperature, keep TCS food out of the temperature danger zone.

Bacterial Growth

Bacterial growth can be broken into four progressive stages (phases): lag, log, stationary, and death. This growth is shown in the graph below.

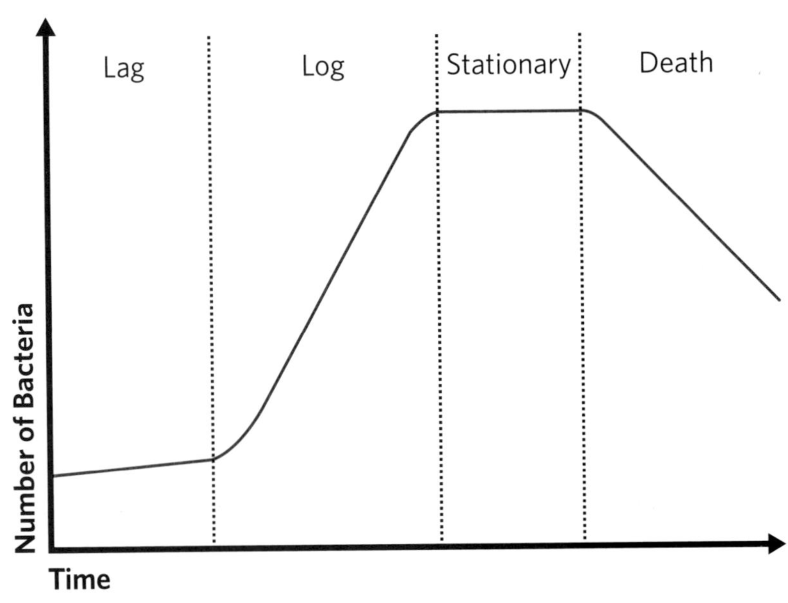

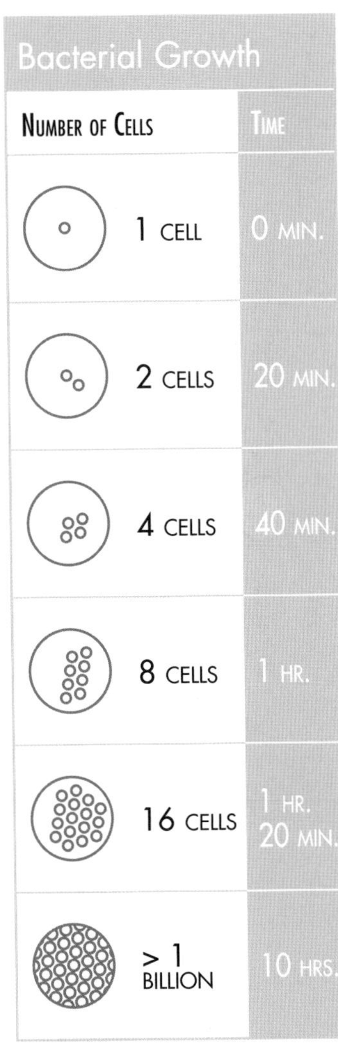

Bacterial Growth

Number of Cells	Time
1 cell	0 min.
2 cells	20 min.
4 cells	40 min.
8 cells	1 hr.
16 cells	1 hr. 20 min.
> 1 billion	10 hrs.

Lag phase Bacteria that are introduced to food go through an adjustment period called the lag phase. Their number is stable as they get ready to grow. To prevent food from becoming unsafe, prolong the lag phase by controlling the conditions for growth: temperature, time, oxygen, moisture, and pH. As mentioned earlier, you have the most control over time and temperature. For example, refrigerating food keeps bacteria in the lag phase.

Log phase Bacteria reproduce by splitting in two. Under the correct conditions, they can double as often as every 20 minutes, as shown in the illustration at left. As a result, food will quickly become unsafe.

Stationary phase **Bacteria can continue to grow until conditions become unfavorable. Eventually, they grow and die at the same rate.**

Death phase **When dying bacteria outnumber growing bacteria, the population declines.**

The time required for bacteria to enter a lag phase and grow in a log phase depends on FAT TOM conditions. The graph below shows how different temperatures affect the growth of *Salmonella* spp. *Salmonella* spp. grows more quickly at warmer temperatures (95°F–99°F [35°C–37°C]) than at colder ones (44°F–50°F [7°C–10°C]). At even colder temperatures (42°F [6°C] and lower), it does not grow at all. But it does not die either, prolonging the lag phase. This is why refrigerating food correctly helps to keep it safe.

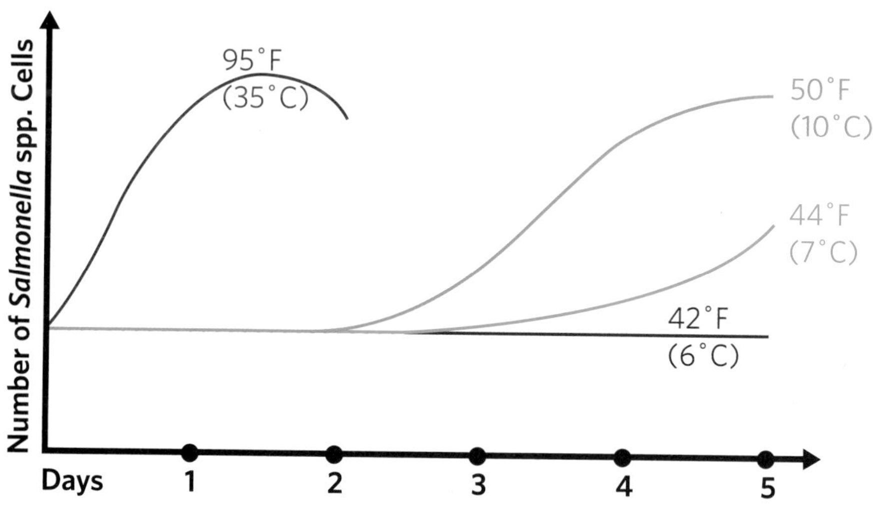

Spores

To keep from dying when they lack nutrients, certain bacteria can change into a form called a spore. Spores are often found in dirt. They can contaminate food grown there, such as potatoes, other vegetables, and rice. They can also contaminate meat, poultry, fish, and other food exposed to dirt or dust.

Spores can resist heat and survive cooking temperatures. They can also change back into a form that grows. You can prevent this by storing food at the correct temperature. You also need to hold and cool food correctly.

Major Foodborne Bacteria

Several different types of bacteria can cause foodborne illness. These are listed on the next several pages. For each type of bacteria, you should understand the common source and food commonly linked with it. You should also be able to identify the most common symptoms associated with the illness caused by the bacteria. Finally, you should be able to determine the most important prevention measures.

Table 2.2 will help you recognize the similarities and differences among the different types of foodborne bacteria. It will help you remember the different types of bacteria as well.

Throughout this chapter, you will see that pathogens have been grouped according to their most important prevention measure. This might include:

- Controlling time and temperature
- Preventing cross-contamination
- Practicing personal hygiene
- Purchasing from approved, reputable suppliers

Controlling Time and Temperature

These bacteria can be prevented through time and temperature control:

- *Bacillus cereus* (page 2.10)
- *Listeria monocytogenes* (page 2.10)
- Shiga toxin-producing *E. coli* (page 2.11)
- *Campylobacter jejuni* (page 2.11)
- *Clostridium perfringens* (page 2.12)
- *Clostridium botulinum* (page 2.12)

Preventing Cross-Contamination

These bacteria can be prevented by preventing cross-contamination:

- Nontyphoidal *Salmonella* (page 2.13)
- *Salmonella* Typhi (page 2.13)

Practicing Personal Hygiene

These bacteria can be prevented by practicing good personal hygiene:

- *Shigella* spp. (page 2.14)
- *Staphylococcus aureus* (page 2.14)

Purchasing from Approved, Reputable Suppliers

These bacteria can be prevented by purchasing products from approved, reputable suppliers:

- *Vibrio vulnificus* and *Vibrio parahaemolyticus* (page 2.15)

Table 2.2: **Major Foodborne Bacteria**

Most Important Prevention Measure		Controlling time and temperature						Preventing cross-contamination		Practicing personal hygiene		Purchasing from approved, reputable suppliers
Bacteria		*Bacillus cereus*	*Listeria monocytogenes*	Shiga toxin-producing *E. coli*	*Clostridium perfringens*	*Clostridium botulinum*	*Campylobacter jejuni*	Nontyphoidal *Salmonella*	*Salmonella* Typhi	*Shigella* spp.	*Staphylococcus aureus*	*Vibrio vulnificus* *Vibrio parahaemolyticus*
Bacteria Characteristics												
Commonly Linked Food	Poultry				•		•	•				
	Eggs							•				
	Meat	•	•	•	•		•					
	Fish											
	Shellfish											•
	Ready-to-eat food		•						•	•	•	
	Produce	•		•		•		•		•		
	Rice/grains	•										
	Milk/dairy products	•	•					•				
	Contaminated water						•		•	•		•
Most Common Illness Symptoms	Diarrhea	•		•	•		•	•		•		•
	Abdominal pain/cramps			•	•		•	•	•	•	•	•
	Nausea	•				•					•	•
	Vomiting	•				•	•	•			•	•
	Fever						•	•	•	•		•
	Headache						•		•			
Prevention Measures	Handwashing								•	•	•	
	Cooking	•	•	•			•	•	•			•
	Holding	•			•	•					•	
	Cooling	•			•	•					•	
	Reheating				•	•					•	
	Approved suppliers			•								•
	Excluding food handlers			•				•	•	•		
	Preventing cross-contamination		•	•			•	•				

Most Important Prevention Measure: Controlling Time and Temperature

Bacteria *Bacillus cereus* *(ba-SIL-us SEER-ee-us)*
Illness *Bacillus cereus* gastroenteritis *(ba-SIL-us SEER-ee-us GAS-tro-EN-ter-I-tiss)*

Bacillus cereus is a spore-forming bacteria found in dirt. It can produce two different toxins when allowed to grow to high levels. The toxins cause different illnesses.

Food Commonly Linked with the Bacteria

Diarrhea illness

- Cooked vegetables
- Meat products
- Milk

Vomiting illness

- Cooked rice dishes, including fried rice and rice pudding

Most Common Symptoms

Diarrhea illness

- Watery diarrhea
- No vomiting

Vomiting illness

- Nausea
- Vomiting

Other Prevention Measures

- Cook food to minimum internal temperatures.
- Hold food at the correct temperatures.
- Cool food correctly.

Bacteria *Listeria monocytogenes* *(liss-TEER-ee-uh MON-o-SI-TAHJ-uh-neez)*
Illness Listeriosis *(liss-TEER-ee-O-sis)*

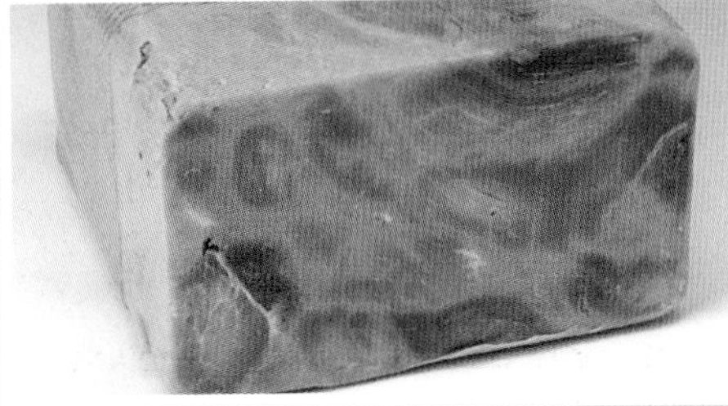

Listeria monocytogenes is found in dirt, water, and plants. Unlike other bacteria, it grows in cool, moist environments. The illness is uncommon in healthy people, but high-risk populations are especially vulnerable—particularly pregnant women.

Food Commonly Linked with the Bacteria

- Raw meat
- Unpasteurized dairy products
- Ready-to-eat food, such as deli meat, hot dogs, and soft cheeses

Most Common Symptoms

Pregnant women

- Miscarriage

Newborns

- Sepsis
- Pneumonia
- Meningitis

Other Prevention Measures

- Throw out any product that has passed its use-by or expiration date.
- Cook raw meat to minimum internal temperatures.
- Prevent cross-contamination between raw or undercooked food and ready-to-eat food.
- Avoid using unpasteurized dairy products.

Bacteria Shiga toxin-producing *Escherichia coli* *(ess-chur-EE-kee-UH KO-LI) (STEC)*, also known as *E. coli*, including O157:H7, O26:H11, O111:H8, and O158:NM

Illness Hemorrhagic colitis *(hem-or-RA-jik ko-LI-tiss)*

Shiga toxin-producing *E. coli* can be found in the intestines of cattle. It is also found in infected people. The bacteria can contaminate meat during slaughtering. Eating only a small amount of the bacteria can make a person sick. Once eaten, it produces toxins in the intestines, which cause the illness. The bacteria are often in a person's feces for weeks after symptoms have ended.

Food Commonly Linked with the Bacteria

- Ground beef (raw and undercooked)
- Contaminated produce

Most Common Symptoms

- Diarrhea (eventually becomes bloody)
- Abdominal cramps
- Kidney failure (in severe cases)

Other Prevention Measures

- Cook food, especially ground beef, to minimum internal temperatures.
- Purchase produce from approved, reputable suppliers.
- Prevent cross-contamination between raw meat and ready-to-eat food.
- Exclude food handlers with diarrhea who have been diagnosed with an illness caused by shiga toxin-producing *E. coli* from the operation.

Bacteria *Campylobacter jejuni* *(Camp-ee-lo-BAK-ter jay-JUNE-ee)*

Illness Campylobacteriosis *(CAMP-ee-lo-BAK-teer-ee-O-sis)*

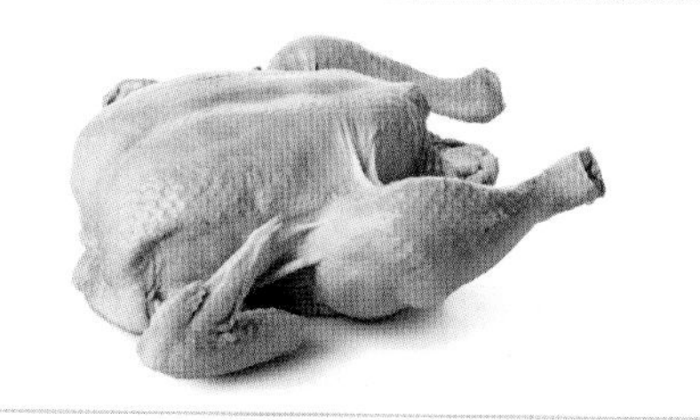

Though *Campylobacter jejuni* is commonly associated with poultry, it has been known to contaminate water. Illness often occurs when poultry is incorrectly cooked and when raw poultry has been allowed to cross-contaminate other food and food-contact surfaces. The pathogen is best controlled through correct cooking and the prevention of cross-contamination.

Food Commonly Linked with the Bacteria

- Poultry
- Water contaminated with the bacteria
- Meat
- Stews/gravies

Most Common Symptoms

- Diarrhea (may be watery or bloody)
- Abdominal cramps
- Fever
- Vomiting
- Headaches

Other Prevention Measures

- Cook food, particularly poultry, to required minimum internal temperatures.
- Prevent cross-contamination between raw poultry and ready-to-eat food.

Bacteria *Clostridium perfringens* *(klos-TRID-ee-um per-FRIN-jins)*
Illness *Clostridium perfringens* gastroenteritis *(klos-TRID-ee-um per-FRIN-jins GAS-tro-EN-ter-I-tiss)*

Clostridium perfringens is found in dirt, where it forms spores that allow it to survive. It is also carried in the intestines of both animals and humans.

Clostridium perfringens does not grow at refrigeration temperatures. It does grow rapidly in food in the temperature danger zone. Commercially prepped food is not often involved in outbreaks. People who get sick usually do not have nausea, fever, or vomiting.

Food Commonly Linked with the Bacteria

- Meat
- Poultry
- Dishes made with meat and poultry, such as stews and gravies

Most Common Symptoms

- Diarrhea
- Severe abdominal pain

Other Prevention Measures

- Cool and reheat food correctly.
- Hold food at the correct temperatures.

Bacteria *Clostridium botulinum* *(klos-TRID-ee-um BOT-chew-LINE-um)*
Illness Botulism *(BOT-chew-liz-um)*

Clostridium botulinum forms spores that are often found in water and dirt. These spores can contaminate almost any food. The bacteria do not grow well in refrigerated or highly acidic food or in food with low moisture. However, *Clostridium botulinum* grows without oxygen and can produce a lethal toxin when food is time-temperature abused. Without medical treatment, death is likely.

Food Commonly Linked with the Bacteria

- Incorrectly canned food
- Reduced-oxygen packaged (ROP) food
- Temperature-abused vegetables, such as baked potatoes
- Untreated garlic-and-oil mixtures

Most Common Symptoms

Initially

- Nausea and vomiting

Later

- Weakness
- Double vision
- Difficulty in speaking and swallowing

Other Prevention Measures

- Hold, cool, and reheat food correctly.
- Inspect canned food for damage.

Most Important Prevention Measure: Preventing Cross-Contamination

Bacteria Nontyphoidal *Salmonella* *(SAL-me-NEL-uh)*
Illness Salmonellosis *(SAL-men-uh-LO-sis)*

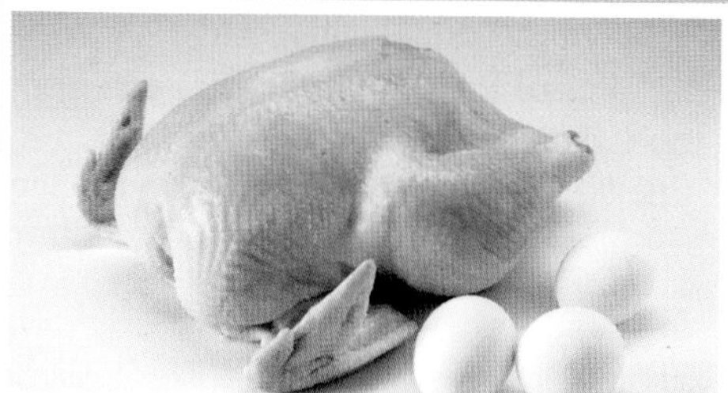

Many farm animals carry nontyphoidal *Salmonella* naturally. Eating only a small amount of these bacteria can make a person sick. How severe symptoms are depends on the health of the person and the amount of bacteria eaten. The bacteria are often in a person's feces for weeks after symptoms have ended.

Food Commonly Linked with the Bacteria

- Poultry and eggs
- Meat
- Milk and dairy products
- Produce, such as tomatoes, peppers, and cantaloupes

Most Common Symptoms

- Diarrhea
- Abdominal cramps
- Vomiting
- Fever

Other Prevention Measures

- Cook poultry and eggs to minimum internal temperatures.
- Prevent cross-contamination between poultry and ready-to-eat food.
- Exclude food handlers who are vomiting or have diarrhea and have been diagnosed with an illness caused by nontyphoidal *Salmonella* from the operation.

Bacteria *Salmonella* Typhi *(SAL-me-NEL-uh Ti-fee)*
Illness Typhoid fever

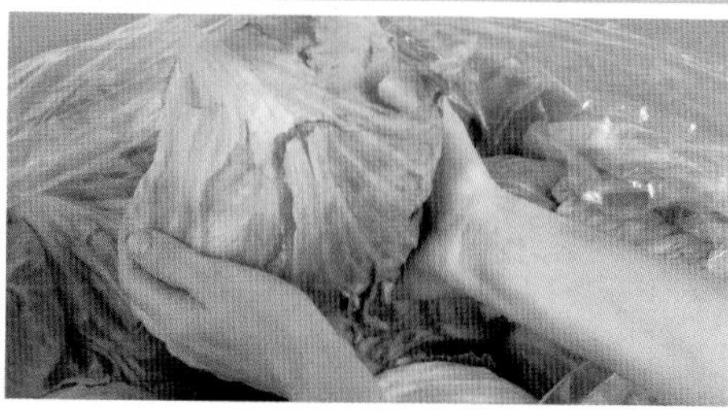

Salmonella Typhi lives only in humans. People with typhoid fever carry the bacteria in their bloodstream and intestinal tract. Eating only a small amount of these bacteria can make a person sick. The severity of symptoms depends on the health of the person and the amount of bacteria eaten. The bacteria are often in a person's feces for weeks after symptoms have ended.

Food Commonly Linked with the Bacteria

- Ready-to-eat food
- Beverages

Most Common Symptoms

- High fever
- Weakness
- Abdominal pain
- Headache
- Loss of appetite
- Rash

Other Prevention Measures

- Exclude food handlers who have been diagnosed with an illness caused by *Salmonella* Typhi from the operation.
- Wash hands.
- Cook food to minimum internal temperatures.

Most Important Prevention Measure: Practicing Good Personal Hygiene

Bacteria *Shigella* spp. *(shi-GEL-uh)*
Illness Shigellosis *(SHIG-uh-LO-sis)*

Shigella spp. is found in the feces of humans with the illness. Most illnesses occur when people eat or drink contaminated food or water. Flies can also transfer the bacteria from feces to food. Eating only a small amount of these bacteria can make a person sick. High levels of the bacteria are often in a person's feces for weeks after symptoms have ended.

Food Commonly Linked with the Bacteria
- Food that is easily contaminated by hands, such as salads containing TCS food (potato, tuna, shrimp, macaroni, and chicken)
- Food that has made contact with contaminated water, such as produce

Most Common Symptoms
- Bloody diarrhea
- Abdominal pain and cramps
- Fever (occasionally)

Other Prevention Measures
- Exclude food handlers who have diarrhea and have been diagnosed with an illness caused by *Shigella* spp. from the operation.
- Wash hands.
- Control flies inside and outside the operation.

Bacteria *Staphylococcus aureus (STAF-uh-lo-KOK-us OR-ee-us)*
Illness Staphylococcal gastroenteritis *(STAF-ul-lo-KOK-al GAS-tro-EN-ter-I-tiss)*

Staphylococcus aureus can be found in humans—particularly in the hair, nose, and throat; and in infected cuts. It is often transferred to food when people carrying it touch these areas on their bodies and then handle food without washing their hands. If allowed to grow to large numbers in food, the bacteria can produce toxins that cause the illness when eaten. Cooking cannot destroy these toxins, so preventing bacterial growth is critical.

Food Commonly Linked with the Bacteria
- Food that requires handling during prepping
- Salads containing TCS food (egg, tuna, chicken, and macaroni)
- Deli meat

Most Common Symptoms
- Nausea
- Vomiting and retching
- Abdominal cramps

Other Prevention Measures
- Wash hands, particularly after touching the hair, face, or body.
- Cover wounds on hands and arms.
- Hold, cool, and reheat food correctly.

Most Important Prevention Measure: Purchasing from Approved, Reputable Suppliers

Bacteria *Vibrio vulnificus* and *Vibrio parahaemolyticus*
(VIB-ree-o vul-NIF-ih-kus and VIB-ree-o PAIR-uh-HEE-mo-lit-ih-kus)

Illness *Vibrio* gastroenteritis *(VIB-ree-o GAS-tro-EN-ter-I-tiss)*
Vibrio vulnificus primary septicemia *(VIB-ree-o vul-NIF-ih-kus SEP-ti-SEE-mee-uh)*

These bacteria are found in the waters where shellfish are harvested. They can grow very rapidly at temperatures in the middle of the temperature danger zone. People with chronic conditions (such as diabetes or cirrhosis) who get sick from these bacteria may get primary septicemia. This severe illness can lead to death.

Food Commonly Linked with the Bacteria
- Oysters from contaminated water

Most Common Symptoms
- Diarrhea
- Abdominal cramps and nausea
- Vomiting
- Low-grade fever and chills

Other Prevention Measures
- Cook oysters to minimum internal temperatures.

Viruses

As a manager, you should know what viruses are and about the illnesses they can cause. Most important, you should understand how to keep viruses from making your guests sick.

General Information about Viruses

The **virus** is the smallest of the microbial food contaminants. Viruses share some basic characteristics.

Location Viruses are carried by human beings and animals. They require a living host to grow. While viruses do not grow in food, they can be transferred through food and still remain infectious in food.

Sources People can get viruses from food, water, or any contaminated surface. Foodborne illnesses from viruses typically occur through the fecal-oral route. Norovirus is one of the leading causes of foodborne illness. It is often transmitted through airborne vomit particles.

Transfer Viruses can be transferred from person to person, from people to food, and from people to food-contact surfaces. When guests get sick from food contaminated with viruses, it is usually because their food was handled by an infected person. That person could be the operation's food handler, a staff member of the food manufacturer, or anyone else who has the virus. People carry viruses in their feces and can transfer them to their hands after using the restroom. For example, ready-to-eat food can become contaminated if hands are not washed correctly.

Prevention measures Viruses are not destroyed by normal cooking temperatures. That is why it is important to practice good personal hygiene when handling food and food-contact surfaces. The quick removal and cleanup of vomit is also important. Here are the best ways to prevent the spread of viruses in your operation:

- Prohibit food handlers who are vomiting or who have diarrhea or jaundice from working.
- Make sure food handlers wash their hands regularly and correctly, as shown in the photo at left.
- Avoid bare-hand contact with ready-to-eat food.

Major Foodborne Viruses

Norovirus and Hepatitis A are two viruses that are highly contagious and can cause severe illness. Food handlers diagnosed with these viruses must not work in a foodservice operation while they are sick. To have a good understanding of these viruses, you should become familiar with the following characteristics of each:

- Common sources
- Foods commonly linked with it
- Most common symptoms
- Most important prevention measures

Table 2.3 will help you recognize the similarities and differences between each virus. You will also see that the viruses are grouped according to their most important prevention measure—practicing good personal hygiene. Other prevention measures for the illnesses are listed in the tables as well.

Practicing Good Personal Hygiene

Illnesses from the following viruses can be prevented by practicing good personal hygiene:

- Hepatitis A (page 2.18)
- Norovirus gastroenteritis (page 2.18)

Table 2.3: **Major Foodborne Viruses**

Most Important Prevention Measure		Controlling time and temperature		Preventing cross-contamination		Practicing personal hygiene		Purchasing from approved, reputable suppliers		
Virus						**Hepatitis A**	**Norovirus**			
Virus Characteristics										
Commonly Linked Food	Poultry									
	Eggs									
	Meat									
	Fish									
	Shellfish					•	•			
	Ready-to-eat food					•	•			
	Produce									
	Rice/grains									
	Milk/dairy products									
	Contaminated water					•	•			
Most Common Illness Symptoms	Diarrhea						•			
	Abdominal pain/cramps					•	•			
	Nausea					•	•			
	Vomiting						•			
	Fever					•				
	Headache									
Prevention Measures	Handwashing					•	•			
	Cooking									
	Holding									
	Cooling									
	Reheating									
	Approved suppliers					•	•			
	Excluding food handlers					•	•			
	Preventing cross-contamination									

Most Important Prevention Measure: Practicing Personal Hygiene

Virus Hepatitis A *(HEP-a-TI-tiss)*
Illness Hepatitis A

Hepatitis A is mainly found in the feces of people infected with it. The virus can contaminate water and many types of food. It is commonly linked with ready-to-eat food. However, it has also been linked with shellfish from contaminated water.

The virus is often transferred to food when infected food handlers touch food or equipment with fingers that have feces on them. Eating only a small amount of the virus can make a person sick. An infected person may not show symptoms for weeks but can be very infectious. Cooking does not destroy hepatitis A.

Food Commonly Linked with the Virus

- Ready-to-eat food
- Shellfish from contaminated water

Most Common Symptoms

- Fever (mild)
- General weakness
- Nausea
- Abdominal pain
- Jaundice (appears later)

Other Prevention Measures

- Exclude food handlers who have been diagnosed with hepatitis A from the operation.
- Exclude food handlers who have had jaundice for seven days or less from the operation.
- Wash hands.
- Avoid bare-hand contact with ready-to-eat food.
- Purchase shellfish from approved, reputable suppliers.

Virus Norovirus *(NOR-o-VI-rus)*
Illness Norovirus gastroenteritis

Like hepatitis A, Norovirus is commonly linked with ready-to-eat food. It has also been linked with contaminated water. Norovirus is often transferred to food when infected food handlers touch food or equipment with fingers that have feces on them.

Eating only a small amount of Norovirus can make a person sick. It is also very contagious. People become contagious within a few hours after eating it. The virus is often in a person's feces for days after symptoms have ended.

Food Commonly Linked with the Virus

- Ready-to-eat food
- Shellfish from contaminated water

Most Common Symptoms

- Vomiting
- Diarrhea
- Nausea
- Abdominal cramps

Other Prevention Measures

- Exclude food handlers who are vomiting or have diarrhea and have been diagnosed with Norovirus from the operation.
- Wash hands.
- Avoid bare-hand contact with ready-to-eat food.
- Purchase shellfish from approved, reputable suppliers.

Parasites

An illness from a **parasite** is not as common as one caused by a virus or bacteria. However, it is still important to understand these pathogens to prevent the foodborne illnesses they cause.

Characteristics of Parasites

Parasites share some basic characteristics.

Location Parasites cannot grow in food. They require a host to live and reproduce.

Sources Parasites are commonly associated with seafood, wild game, and food processed with contaminated water, such as produce.

Prevention measures The most important way to prevent foodborne illnesses from parasites is to purchase food from approved, reputable suppliers. Cooking food to required minimum internal temperatures is also important. Also, make sure that fish that will be served raw or undercooked has been correctly frozen by the manufacturer.

Major Foodborne Illnesses Caused by Parasites

For each major foodborne illness caused by parasites, you should understand the following characteristics:

- Common sources
- Food commonly linked with it
- Most common symptoms
- Most important prevention measures

Table 2.4 will help you recognize the similarities and differences among foodborne illnesses caused by parasites. It will help you remember each parasite as well.

Purchasing from Approved, Reputable Suppliers

These parasites can be prevented by purchasing products from approved, reputable suppliers:

- *Anisakis simplex* (page 2.21)
- *Cryptosporidium parvum* (page 2.21)
- *Giardia duodenalis* (page 2.22)
- *Cyclospora cayetanensis* (page 2.22)

Table 2.4: **Major Foodborne Parasites**											
Most Important Prevention Measure		Controlling time and temperature		Preventing cross-contamination		Practicing personal hygiene		Purchasing from approved, reputable suppliers			
Parasite								*Anisakis simplex*	*Cryptosporidium parvum*	*Giardia duodenalis*	*Cyclospora cayetanensis*
Parasite Characteristics											
Commonly Linked Food	Poultry										
	Eggs										
	Meat										
	Fish							•			
	Shellfish										
	Ready-to-eat food										
	Produce								•	•	•
	Rice/grains										
	Milk/dairy products										
	Contaminated water								•	•	•
Most Common Symptoms	Diarrhea								•	•	•
	Abdominal pain/cramps								•	•	•
	Nausea								•	•	•
	Vomiting										
	Fever									•	•
	Headache										
Prevention Measures	Handwashing								•	•	•
	Cooking							•			
	Holding										
	Cooling										
	Reheating										
	Approved suppliers							•	•	•	•
	Excluding food handlers								•	•	•
	Preventing cross-contamination										

Most Important Prevention Measure: Purchasing from Approved, Reputable Suppliers

Parasite *Anisakis simplex* *(ANN-ih-SAHK-iss SIM-plex)*
Illness Anisakiasis *(ANN-ih-SAH-KYE-ah-sis)*

People can get sick when they eat raw or undercooked fish containing this parasite.

Food Commonly Linked with the Parasite

Raw and undercooked fish:

- Herring
- Cod
- Halibut
- Mackerel
- Pacific salmon

Most Common Symptoms

- Tingling in throat
- Coughing up worms

Other Prevention Measures

- Cook fish to minimum internal temperatures.
- If serving raw or undercooked fish, purchase sushi-grade fish that has been frozen to the correct time-temperature requirements.

Parasite *Cryptosporidium parvum* *(KRIP-TOH-spor-ID-ee-um PAR-vum)*
Illness Cryptosporidiosis *(KRIP-TOH-spor-id-ee-O-sis)*

Photo courtesy of Boskovich Farms, Inc.

Cryptosporidium parvum can be found in the feces of infected people. Food handlers can transfer it to food when they touch food with fingers that have feces on them. Day-care and medical communities have been frequent locations of person-to-person spread of this parasite. Symptoms will be more severe in people with weakened immune systems.

Food Commonly Linked with the Parasite

- Contaminated water
- Produce

Most Common Symptoms

- Watery diarrhea
- Abdominal cramps
- Nausea
- Weight loss

Other Prevention Measures

- Use correctly treated water.
- Keep food handlers with diarrhea out of the operation.
- Wash hands.

Parasite *Giardia duodenalis (jee-ARE-dee-uh do-WAH-den-AL-is)*, also known as *G. lamblia* or *G. intestinalis*

Illness Giardiasis *(JEE-are-DYE-uh-sis)*

Photo courtesy of Boskovich Farms, Inc.

Giardia duodenalis can be found in the feces of infected people. Food handlers can transfer the parasite to food when they touch food with fingers that have feces on them.

Food Commonly Linked with the Parasite

- Incorrectly treated water
- Produce

Most Common Symptoms

Initially

- Fever

Later

- Diarrhea
- Abdominal cramps
- Nausea

Other Prevention Measures

- Use correctly treated water.
- Keep food handlers with diarrhea out of the operation.
- Wash hands.

Parasite *Cyclospora cayetanensis (SI-klo-spor-uh KI-uh-te-NEN-sis)*

Illness Cyclosporiasis *(SI-klo-spor-I-uh-sis)*

Cyclospora cayetanensis is a parasite that has been found in contaminated water and has been associated with produce irrigated or washed with contaminated water. It can also be found in the feces of infected people. Food handlers can transfer the parasite to food when they touch it with fingers containing feces. For this reason, food handlers with diarrhea must be excluded from the operation. It is also critical to purchase produce from approved, reputable suppliers.

Food Commonly Linked with the Parasite

- Incorrectly treated water
- Produce such as berries, lettuce, or basil

Most Common Symptoms

- Nausea
- Abdominal cramps
- Mild fever
- Diarrhea alternating with constipation
- Loss of weight
- Loss of appetite

Other Prevention Measures

- Purchase produce from approved, reputable suppliers.
- Keep food handlers with diarrhea out of the operation.
- Wash hands.

Fungi

So far, you have learned about pathogens that cause foodborne illnesses. **Fungi** are pathogens that only sometimes make people sick. Mostly, they spoil food. They are found in air, dirt, plants, water, and some food. **Mold** and **yeast** are examples.

Mold

Molds share some basic characteristics.

Effects **Molds spoil food and sometimes cause illness.**

Toxins **Some molds produce toxins, such as aflatoxins.**

Growth **Molds grow under almost any condition. They grow particularly well in acidic food with low water activity, such as jams, jellies, and cured, salty meat (e.g., ham, bacon, and salami).**

Temperature **Cooler or freezer temperatures may slow the growth of molds, but they do not kill them.**

Prevention measures **Some molds produce toxins that can cause allergic reactions, nervous system disorders, and kidney and liver damage. For example, aflatoxin, produced by the molds *Aspergillus flavus* and *Aspergillus parasiticus*, can cause liver disease. Food such as corn and corn products, peanuts and peanut products, cottonseed, milk, and tree nuts (such as Brazil nuts, pecans, pistachio nuts, and walnuts) have been associated with aflatoxins.**

Throw out all moldy food, unless the mold is a natural part of the product (e.g., cheese such as Brie, Camembert, and Gorgonzola). The FDA recommends cutting away moldy areas in hard cheese—at least one inch (2.5 centimeters) around them. You can also use this procedure on food such as salami and firm fruits and vegetables.

Yeast

Yeasts share some basic characteristics.

Signs of spoilage **Yeasts can spoil food quickly. Signs of spoilage can include a smell or taste of alcohol. The yeast itself may look like a white or pink discoloration or slime, as show in the photo at right. It also may bubble.**

Growth **Like molds, yeasts grow well in acidic food with little moisture, such as jellies, jams, syrup, honey, and fruit or fruit juice.**

Prevention measure **Throw out any food that has been spoiled by yeast.**

Biological Toxins

You learned earlier that most foodborne illnesses are caused by pathogens, a form of biological contamination. But you also must be aware of biological toxins or poisons that can make people sick.

Seafood, plant, and mushroom toxins can all cause illness. You should know what these toxins are and which illnesses they can cause. Most important, you should understand how to prevent them.

Seafood Toxins

Seafood toxins cannot be smelled or tasted. They also cannot be destroyed by freezing or cooking once they form in food. There are two groups of seafood toxins.

Fish toxins Some fish toxins are a natural part of the fish. These are called systemic toxins. Puffer fish, moray eels, and freshwater minnows all produce them. Because of the extreme risk it poses, puffer fish should not be served unless the chef has been licensed to prepare it.

Other toxins are made by pathogens on the fish. Some fish can also become contaminated when they eat smaller fish that have eaten a toxin.

Shellfish toxins Shellfish, such as oysters, can be contaminated when they eat marine algae that have a toxin.

Major Seafood Toxins

For each major seafood toxin, you should understand the following characteristics:

- Common sources
- Food commonly linked with it
- Most common symptoms
- Most important prevention measures

Table 2.5 will help you recognize the similarities and differences among seafood toxins. It will help you remember each seafood toxin as well.

Purchasing from Approved, Reputable Suppliers

These toxins can be prevented by purchasing products from approved, reputable suppliers:

- **Histamine** (page 2.26)
- **Ciguatoxin** (page 2.26)
- **Saxitoxin** (page 2.27)
- **Brevetoxin** (page 2.27)
- **Domoic acid** (page 2.28)

Table 2.5 **Major Seafood Toxins**

Most Important Prevention Measure		Controlling time and temperature	Preventing cross-contamination	Practicing personal hygiene	Purchasing from approved, reputable suppliers				
Seafood Toxin					Histamine	Ciguatoxin	Saxitoxin	Brevetoxin	Domoic acid
Seafood Toxin Characteristics									
Commonly Linked Food	Fish				•	•			
	Shellfish						•	•	•
Most Common Symptoms	Diarrhea				•		•	•	•
	Abdominal pain/cramps								•
	Nausea					•	•		
	Vomiting				•	•	•	•	•
	Fever								
	Headache				•				
	Neurological symptoms				•	•	•	•	•
Prevention Measures	Handwashing								
	Cooking								
	Holding				•				
	Cooling								
	Reheating								
	Approved suppliers				•	•	•	•	•
	Excluding food handlers								
	Preventing cross-contamination								

Most Important Prevention Measure: Purchasing from Approved, Reputable Suppliers

Toxin Histamine *(HISS-ta-meen)*
Illness Scombroid poisoning *(SKOM-broyd)*

Histamine poisoning can occur when high levels of histamine in scombroid and other species of fish are eaten. When the fish are time-temperature abused, bacteria on the fish make the toxin. It cannot be destroyed by freezing, cooking, smoking, or curing.

Food Commonly Linked with the Toxin

- Tuna
- Bonito
- Mackerel
- Mahimahi

Most Common Symptoms

Initially

- Reddening of the face and neck
- Sweating
- Headache
- Burning or tingling sensation in the mouth or throat

Possibly later

- Diarrhea
- Vomiting

Other Prevention Measures

- Prevent time-temperature abuse during storage and prepping.

Toxin Ciguatoxin *(SIG-wa-TOX-in)*
Illness Ciguatera fish poisoning *(SIG-wa-TAIR-uh)*

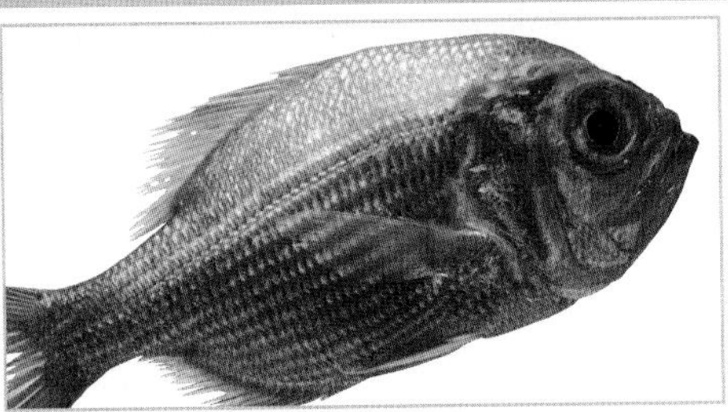

Ciguatoxin is found in some marine algae. The toxin builds up in certain fish when they eat smaller fish that have eaten the toxic algae. Ciguatoxin cannot be detected by smell or taste. It is not eliminated by cooking or freezing the fish. Symptoms may last months or years depending on how severe the illness is.

Food Commonly Linked with the Toxin

Predatory tropical reef fish from the Pacific Ocean, the western part of the Indian Ocean, and the Caribbean Sea:

- Barracuda
- Grouper
- Jacks
- Snapper

Most Common Symptoms

- Reversal of hot and cold sensations
- Nausea
- Vomiting
- Tingling in fingers, lips, or toes
- Joint and muscle pain

Other Prevention Measures

- Purchase predatory tropical reef fish from approved, reputable suppliers.

Toxin	Saxitoxin *(SAX-ih-TOX-in)*
Illness	Paralytic shellfish poisoning (PSP) *(PAIR-ah-LIT-ik)*

Some types of shellfish can become contaminated as they filter toxic algae from the water. People can get sick with paralytic shellfish poisoning (PSP) when they eat these shellfish. Saxitoxin cannot be smelled or tasted. It is not destroyed by cooking or freezing. Death from paralysis may result if high levels of the toxin are eaten.

Food Commonly Linked with the Toxin

Shellfish found in colder waters, such as those of the Pacific and New England coasts:

- Clams
- Mussels
- Oysters
- Scallops

Most Common Symptoms

- Numbness
- Tingling of the mouth, face, arms, and legs
- Dizziness
- Nausea
- Vomiting
- Diarrhea

Other Prevention Measures

- Purchase shellfish from approved, reputable suppliers.

Toxin	Brevetoxin *(BREV-ih-TOX-in)*
Illness	Neurotoxic shellfish poisoning (NSP) *(NUR-o-TOX-ik)*

Some types of shellfish can become contaminated as they filter toxic algae from the water. People can get sick with neurotoxic shellfish poisoning (NSP) when they eat these shellfish. Brevetoxin cannot be smelled or tasted. It is not destroyed by cooking or freezing.

Food Commonly Linked with the Toxin

Shellfish found in the warmer waters of the west coast of Florida, the Gulf of Mexico, and the Caribbean Sea:

- Clams
- Mussels
- Oysters

Most Common Symptoms

- Tingling and numbness of the lips, tongue, and throat
- Dizziness
- Reversal of hot and cold sensations
- Vomiting
- Diarrhea

Other Prevention Measures

- Purchase shellfish from approved, reputable suppliers.

Toxin	Domoic acid *(duh-MO-ik)*
Illness	Amnesic shellfish poisoning (ASP) *(am-NEE-zik)*

Some types of shellfish can become contaminated as they filter toxic algae from the water. People can get sick with amnesic shellfish poisoning (ASP) when they eat these shellfish. The severity of symptoms depends on the amount of toxin eaten and the health of the person. Domoic acid cannot be smelled or tasted. It is not destroyed by cooking or freezing.

Food Commonly Linked with the Toxin

Shellfish found in the coastal waters of the Pacific Northwest and the east coast of Canada:

- Clams
- Mussels
- Oysters
- Scallops

Most Common Symptoms

Initially

- Vomiting
- Diarrhea
- Abdominal pain

Possibly later

- Confusion
- Memory loss
- Disorientation
- Seizure
- Coma

Other Prevention Measures

- Purchase shellfish from approved, reputable suppliers.

Mushroom Toxins

Foodborne illnesses linked with mushrooms are almost always caused by toxic wild mushrooms collected by amateur hunters. Most cases happen because toxic mushrooms are mistaken for edible ones. The symptoms of illness depend on the type of toxic mushrooms eaten.

Mushroom toxins are not destroyed by cooking or freezing. Use only mushrooms and mushroom products purchased from approved, reputable suppliers, as shown in the photo at left.

Plant Toxins

Plant toxins are another form of biological contamination. Illnesses from plant toxins usually happen because an operation has purchased plants from an unapproved source. Some illnesses, however, are caused by plants that have not been cooked correctly. The following are examples of items that have made people sick:

- Toxic plants, such as fool's parsley or wild turnips, mistaken for the edible version
- Honey from bees allowed to harvest nectar from toxic plants
- Undercooked kidney beans

Purchase plants and items made with plants only from approved, reputable suppliers. Then cook and hold dishes made from these items correctly.

Chapter Summary

- Bacteria need certain conditions to grow. They include food, acidity, temperature, time, oxygen, and moisture (FAT TOM). Food items with the correct FAT TOM conditions favor greater bacterial growth. They are also often involved in foodborne-illness outbreaks.
- Bacteria can usually be controlled by keeping food out of the temperature danger zone (41°F–135°F [5°C–57°C]). Some bacteria can change into spores to preserve themselves when lacking nutrients. Others can produce toxins in food that can make people sick.
- Viruses are the leading cause of foodborne illness. They cannot grow in food, but they can survive refrigeration and freezer temperatures. Good personal hygiene helps prevent the spread of viruses.
- Parasites need to be in another animal to survive. They can contaminate both food and water—particularly water used to irrigate produce. Purchasing products from approved, reputable suppliers helps prevent foodborne illnesses caused by parasites.
- Fungi, such as molds and yeasts, mostly spoil food. However, some molds can produce harmful toxins. Food containing mold should always be discarded unless the mold is a natural part of the product. Yeasts can spoil food quickly. Food spoiled by yeast should also be thrown out.
- Fish toxins can be a natural part of the fish. Other toxins are made by pathogens on the fish. Some also occur when fish eat smaller fish containing the toxin. Shellfish, such as oysters, can likewise become contaminated when they eat marine algae that have a toxin. Purchasing products from approved, reputable suppliers is the most important prevention measure for seafood toxins.
- Foodborne illnesses linked with mushrooms are almost always caused by eating toxic wild mushrooms collected by amateur hunters. Foodborne illnesses can also be caused by other naturally occurring plant toxins. Purchasing products from approved, reputable suppliers helps prevent these types of foodborne illnesses.

Apply Your Knowledge

Use these questions to review the concepts presented in this chapter.

Discussion Questions

1 What are the six conditions that support the growth of bacteria?

2 What two FAT TOM conditions are easiest for an operation to control?

3 How can an outbreak of Norovirus be prevented?

4 What measures should be taken to prevent a seafood-specific foodborne illness?

5 What six pathogens have been dubbed the "Big Six"? Why have they been singled out by the FDA?

For answers, please turn to the Answer Key.

Apply Your Knowledge

Something to Think About

Rice Makes Children Sick

A day-care center decided to prepare stir-fried rice to serve for lunch the next day. The rice was cooked to the correct temperature at 1:00 p.m. It was then covered and placed on a countertop, where it was allowed to cool at room temperature. At 6:00 p.m., the cook placed the rice in the cooler. At 9:00 a.m. the following day, the rice was combined with the other ingredients for stir-fried rice and cooked to 165°F (74°C) for at least 15 seconds. The cook covered the rice and left it on the stove until noon, when she reheated it. Within an hour of eating the rice, several of the children complained that they were nauseous and began to vomit.

1 What pathogen caused the illness and why?

For answers, please turn to the Answer Key.

Study Questions

Circle the best answer to each question.

1 **What are the most common symptoms of a foodborne illness?**

A Diarrhea, vomiting, fever, nausea, abdominal cramps, and dizziness

B Diarrhea, vomiting, fever, nausea, abdominal cramps, and headache

C Diarrhea, vomiting, fever, nausea, abdominal cramps, and jaundice

D Diarrhea, vomiting, fever, nausea, abdominal cramps, and tiredness

2 **What is the most important way to prevent a foodborne illness caused by bacteria?**

A Control time and temperature.

B Prevent cross-contamination.

C Practice good personal hygiene.

D Practice correct cleaning and sanitizing.

3 **Shiga toxin-producing *E. coli* is commonly linked with what type of food?**

A Potato salad

B Thick stews

C Dairy products

D Raw ground beef

4 **What is the most important way to prevent foodborne illnesses caused by viruses?**

A Control time and temperature.

B Prevent cross-contamination.

C Practice good personal hygiene.

D Practice correct cleaning and sanitizing.

5 **A guest called an operation and told the manager about getting sick after eating there. The guest complained of vomiting and diarrhea a few hours after eating the raw oysters. What pathogen probably caused the illness?**

A Norovirus

B *Shigella* spp.

C *Salmonella* Typhi

D Shiga toxin-producing *E. coli*

Study Questions

6 Parasites are commonly linked with what type of food?

A Rice
B Poultry
C Seafood
D Canned food

7 A guest had a reversal of hot and cold sensations after eating seafood. What most likely caused the illness?

A Toxin
B Virus
C Bacteria
D Parasite

8 Which pathogens are found in high numbers in an infected person's feces, are highly infectious, and can cause severe illness?

A Histamine, aflatoxin, brevetoxin, ciguatoxin, saxitoxin, and domoic acid
B Hepatitis A, Norovirus, *Salmonella* Typhi, nontyphoidal *Salmonella*, *Shigella* spp., and Shiga toxin-producing *E. coli*
C *Anisakis simplex, Cryptosporidium parvum, Giardia duodenalis, Vibrio vulnificus,* and *Clostridium botulinum*
D *Bacillus cereus, Listeria monocytogenes, Staphylococcus aureus, Clostridium perfringens, Campylobacter jejuni,* and *Vibrio parahaemolyticus*

9 Aside from temperature, which other FAT TOM condition will a foodservice operation be most able to control?

A Acidity
B Time
C Oxygen
D Moisture

10 Which pathogen can be controlled by washing hands and controlling flies inside and outside the operation?

A Hepatitis A
B *Shigella* spp.
C *Clostridium botulinum*
D *Vibrio parahaemolyticus*

For answers, please turn to the Answer Key.

Notes

Notes

Man Hospitalized after Allergic Reaction

A man was hospitalized after dining at a local, family-owned restaurant in a small southeastern town. The man, who was allergic to shellfish, was hospitalized after eating a steak at the operation.

The man told the server about his allergy and was assured that his steak would not touch any shellfish while it was being prepared. Authorities determined that the grill used to prepare the steak was also used to grill shrimp and other shellfish.

1. **How could this allergic reaction have been prevented?**

For answers, please turn to the Answer Key.

3 Contamination, Food Allergens, and Foodborne Illness

Inside This Chapter

- Physical and Chemical Contaminants
- The Deliberate Contamination of Food
- Food Allergens

Objectives

After completing this chapter, you should be able to identify the following:

- Physical and chemical contaminants and methods of prevention
- Points in the operation where food is at risk from deliberate contamination
- The most common food allergens and their associated symptoms
- Methods of preventing allergic reactions

Key Terms

Food defense program

A.L.E.R.T.

Food allergen

Anaphylaxis

Cross-contact

Physical and Chemical Contaminants

Although biological contaminants are the leading cause of foodborne illness, physical and chemical contaminants also pose a risk to food safety.

Physical Contaminants

Food can become contaminated when objects get into it. It can also happen when natural objects are left in food, such as bones in a fish fillet.

Sources Some common objects that can get into food include:

- Metal shavings from cans, as shown in the photo at left
- Wood
- Fingernails
- Staples
- Bandages
- Glass
- Jewelry
- Dirt

Naturally occurring objects, such as fruit pits and bones, can also be contaminants.

Symptoms Bleeding and pain may be the most outward symptoms. Mild to fatal injuries are possible. This could include:

- Cuts
- Dental damage
- Choking

Prevention Purchase food from approved, reputable suppliers to prevent physical contamination. Closely inspect the food you receive. Take steps to make sure no physical contaminants can get into it. This includes making sure that food handlers practice good personal hygiene.

Chemical Contaminants

Many people have gotten sick after consuming food and beverages contaminated with foodservice chemicals. To keep food safe, follow these guidelines.

Sources Chemicals can contaminate food if they are used or stored the wrong way. The following chemicals can be risks:

- Cleaners
- Sanitizers
- Polishes
- Machine lubricants
- Pesticides
- Deodorizers
- First-aid products
- Health and beauty products, such as hand lotions and hair sprays

Certain types of kitchenware and equipment can also be risks for chemical contamination. These include items made from pewter, copper (as seen in the photo at right), zinc, and some types of painted pottery. These materials are not always safe for food and can cause contamination. This is especially true when acidic food, such as tomato sauce, is held in them.

Symptoms Symptoms vary depending on the chemical consumed. Most illnesses occur within minutes. Vomiting and diarrhea are typical. If an illness is suspected, call the emergency number in your area and the Poison Control number.

Prevention The chemicals you use must be approved for use in a foodservice operation. They must also be necessary for the maintenance of the facility. Here are some ways to protect food and food-contact surfaces from contamination by chemicals:

- Purchase chemicals from approved, reputable suppliers.
- Store chemicals away from prep areas, food-storage areas, and service areas. Chemicals must be separated from food and food-contact surfaces by spacing and partitioning, as seen in the photo at right. Chemicals must **NEVER** be stored above food or food-contact surfaces.

- Use chemicals for their intended use and follow the manufacturers' directions.
- Only handle food with equipment and utensils approved for foodservice use.
- Make sure the manufacturers' labels on original chemical containers are readable.
- Follow the manufacturers' directions and local regulatory requirements when throwing out chemicals.

The Deliberate Contamination of Food

Certain people could try to tamper with your food. This includes terrorists or activists, disgruntled current or former staff, vendors, or competitors. They may use biological, chemical, or physical contaminants. They may even use radioactive materials. Attacks might occur anywhere in the food supply chain. But they are usually focused on a specific food item, process, or business.

The best way to protect food is to make it very difficult to tamper with. A **food defense program** should address the points in your operation where food is at risk. The Food and Drug Administration (FDA) has created a tool that can be used to develop a food defense program. It is based on the acronym **A.L.E.R.T.** It can be used to help you identify the points in your operation where food is at risk. A.L.E.R.T. stands for the following.

Assure Make sure that products you receive are from safe sources:

- Supervise product deliveries.
- Use approved suppliers who practice food defense.
- Request that delivery vehicles are locked or sealed.

Look Monitor the security of products in the facility:

- Limit access to prep and storage areas. Locking storage areas, as shown at left, is one way to do this.
- Create a system for handling damaged products.
- Store chemicals in a secure location.
- Train staff to spot food defense threats.

Employees Know who is in your facility:

- Limit access to prep and storage areas.
- Identify all visitors and verify credentials.
- Conduct background checks on staff.

Reports Keep information related to food defense accessible:

- Keep receiving logs.
- Maintain office files and documents.
- Create staff files.
- Conduct random food defense self-inspections.

Threat Identify what you will do and who you will contact if there is suspicious activity or a threat at your operation:

- Hold any product you suspect to be contaminated.
- Contact your regulatory authority immediately.
- Maintain an emergency contact list.

Food Allergens

A **food allergen** is a protein in a food or ingredient that some people are sensitive to. These proteins occur naturally. When enough of an allergen is eaten, an allergic reaction can occur. This is when the immune system mistakenly considers the allergen to be harmful and attacks the food protein. There are specific signs that a guest is having an allergic reaction. To protect your guests, you should be able to recognize these signs and know what to do. You also should know the types of food that most often cause allergic reactions to help prevent them from happening.

Allergy Symptoms

Depending on the person, an allergic reaction can happen just after the food is eaten or several hours later. This reaction could include some or all of these symptoms:

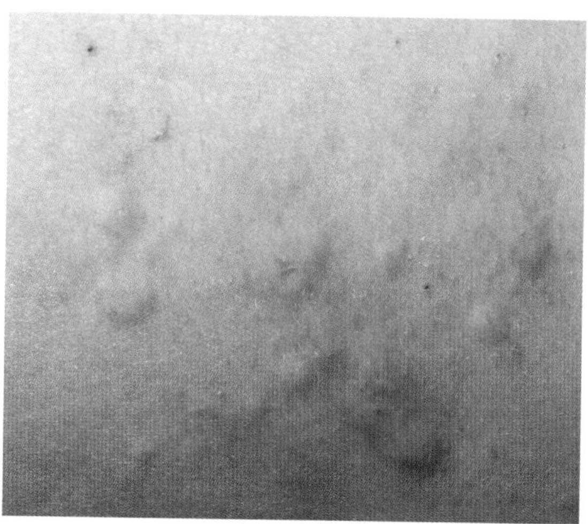

- Nausea
- Wheezing or shortness of breath
- Hives or itchy rashes, as shown in the photo at right
- Swelling of various parts of the body, including the face, eyes, hands, or feet
- Vomiting and/or diarrhea
- Abdominal pain
- Itchy throat

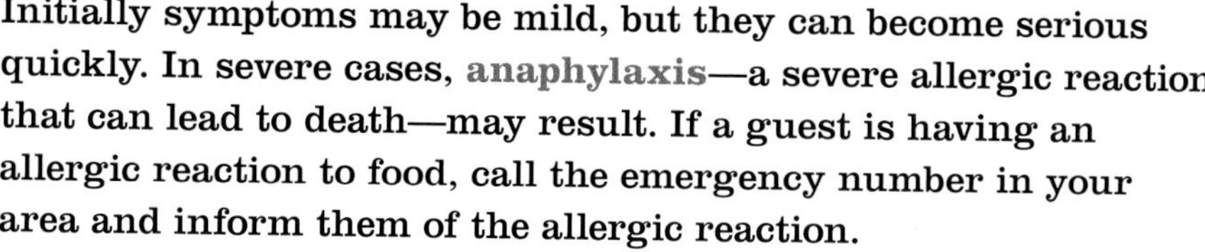

Initially symptoms may be mild, but they can become serious quickly. In severe cases, **anaphylaxis**—a severe allergic reaction that can lead to death—may result. If a guest is having an allergic reaction to food, call the emergency number in your area and inform them of the allergic reaction.

Common Food Allergens

You and your staff must be aware of the most common food allergens and the menu items that contain them.

While more than 160 food items can cause allergic reactions, just eight of these account for 90 percent of all reactions in the United States. These eight food items are known as the Big Eight and are shown in Table 3.1 on the following page.

Table 3.1: **The Big Eight Allergens**

Milk		Soy	
Eggs		Wheat	
Fish, such as bass, flounder, and cod		Crustacean shellfish, such as crab, lobster, and shrimp	
Peanuts	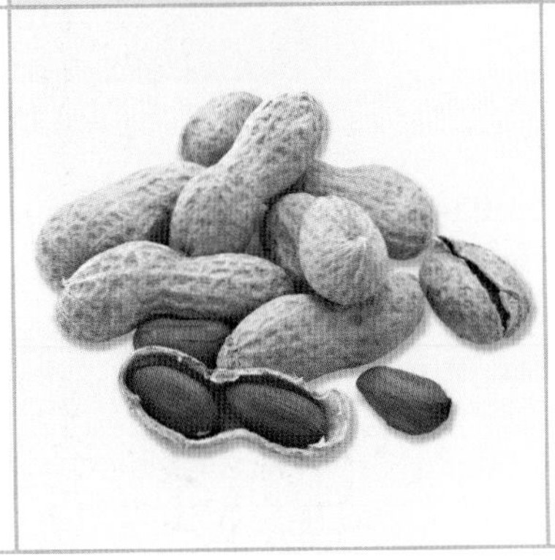	Tree nuts, such as walnuts and pecans	

Preventing Allergic Reactions

Fifteen million Americans have a food allergy, and allergic reactions result in 200,000 emergency room visits every year. Both service staff and kitchen staff need to do their part to avoid serving food containing allergens to people with food allergies. These precautions also apply to any food sensitivities that a guest might mention, such as a gluten intolerance.

Service Staff

Your staff should be able to tell guests about menu items that contain potential allergens. At minimum, have one person available per shift to answer guests' questions about menu items. When guests say they have a food allergy, your staff should take it seriously. When working with a guest to place an allergen special order, your staff must be able to do the following.

Describe dishes Tell guests how the item is prepared. Sauces, marinades, and garnishes often contain allergens. For example, peanut butter is sometimes used as a thickener in sauces or marinades. This information is critical to a guest with a peanut allergy.

Identify ingredients Tell guests if the food they are allergic to is in the menu item. Identify any "secret" ingredients. For example, your operation may have a house specialty that includes an allergen.

Suggest items Suggest menu items that do not contain the food that the guest is allergic to.

Identify the allergen special order Clearly mark or otherwise indicate the order for the guest with the identified food allergy. This is done to inform the kitchen staff of the guest's food allergy.

Deliver food Confirm the allergen special order with the kitchen staff when picking up the food. Make sure no garnishes or other items containing the allergen touch the plate. Food should be hand-delivered to guests with allergies. Delivering food separately from the other food delivered to a table, as shown in the photo at right, will help prevent contact with food allergens.

Kitchen Staff

Staff must make sure that allergens are not transferred from food or food-contact surfaces containing an allergen to the food served to the guest. This transfer of allergens is called **cross-contact**. Here are examples of how it can happen:

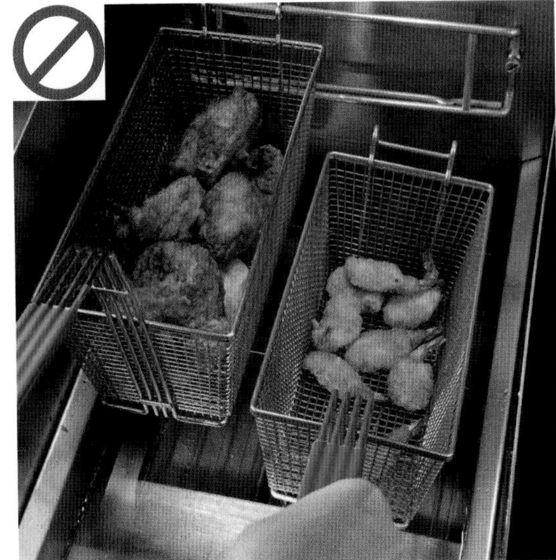

- Cooking different types of food in the same fryer oil. In the photo at left, shrimp allergens could be transferred to the chicken being fried in the same oil.
- Letting food touch surfaces, equipment, or utensils that have touched allergens. For example, putting chocolate chip cookies on the same parchment paper that was used for peanut butter cookies can transfer some of the peanut allergen.

Food Labels

Food labels are an important tool used to identify allergens in the products that you purchase. Federal law requires manufactured products containing one or more of the Big Eight allergens to clearly identify them on the ingredient label. The allergen may be included in the common name of the food, such as "buttermilk," or it may be shown in parentheses after the ingredient. Often, allergens will be shown in a "contains" statement, such as in the photo below.

Calories per gram:
Fat 9 • Carbohydrate 4 • Protein 4
INGREDIENTS: CHICKEN BROTH, CONTAINS LESS THAN 1% OF THE FOLLOWING: SALT, DEXTROSE, CHICKEN FAT, MONOSODIUM GLUTAMATE, HYDROLYZED WHEAT GLUTEN, NATURAL FLAVORS, AUTOLYZED YEAST EXTRACT, CARROT JUICE CONCENTRATE, MONO AND DIGLYCERIDES, XANTHAN GUM, ONION JUICE CONCENTRATE.
CONTAINS: WHEAT.

How to Avoid Cross-Contact

Staff can avoid cross-contact by following these procedures:

- Check recipes and ingredient labels to confirm that the allergen is not present.
- Wash, rinse, and sanitize cookware, utensils, and equipment before prepping food. This includes food-prep surfaces. Some operations use a separate set of cooking utensils just for allergen special orders, as shown in the photo at right.

- Make sure the allergen does not touch anything for guests with food allergies, including food, beverages, utensils, equipment, and gloves.
- Wash your hands and change gloves before prepping food.
- Use separate fryers and cooking oils when frying food for guests with food allergies.
- Label food packaged on-site for retail sale. Name all major allergens on the label and follow any additional labeling requirements.

Chapter Summary

- Physical contamination can occur when foreign objects get into food. It can also take place when natural objects are left in food, such as the bones in a fish fillet.
- To prevent contamination, closely inspect the food you receive. Take steps to make sure food will not become physically contaminated during its flow through your operation.
- Chemical contaminants can come from many common substances within an operation. To prevent contamination, use only utensils and equipment that are made for handling food. Also store chemicals away from food, utensils, and equipment used for food. Follow the chemical manufacturers' directions for use as well.
- Take steps to prevent the deliberate contamination of food. The key is to make food very difficult to tamper with at your operation. A food defense program should address where food can be at risk.
- Managers and staff should be aware of the most common food allergens, which include milk, eggs, fish, crustacean shellfish, wheat, soy, peanuts, and tree nuts.
- Service staff should be able to tell guests about menu items that contain potential allergens. Kitchen staff need to make sure that allergens are not transferred from food containing an allergen to food being served to a guest.

Apply Your Knowledge

Use these questions to review the concepts presented in this chapter.

Discussion Questions

1 What are some ways to keep food safe from physical contaminants?

2 What are some ways to keep chemicals from contaminating food?

3 What are some ways to prevent the deliberate contamination of food?

Apply Your Knowledge

4 What measures can be taken to help ensure the safety of guests with food allergies?

For answers, please turn to the Answer Key.

Apply Your Knowledge

Something to Think About

The 1984 Rajneeshee Bioterror Attack

In the fall of 1984, the single largest bioterrorist attack in the United States occurred in Oregon. It was carried out by members of a cult who had hoped to influence the turnout of a local election. They sprinkled *Salmonella* Typhimurium on salad bars at 10 local restaurants. As a result, over 750 people got sick, with 45 being hospitalized. The victims suffered from symptoms including fever, chills, diarrhea, nausea, and vomiting. Most had abdominal pain, diarrhea, and bloody stools. Fortunately, there were no fatalities. Those responsible for the attacks spread a liquid containing the pathogen over the food on the salad bars. They also poured the liquid into the salad dressing.

1 What could have been done to prevent what happened?

For answers, please turn to the Answer Key.

Study Questions

Circle the best answer to each question.

1 **A prep cook stores a bottle of sanitizer on a shelf above a prep table. To prevent chemical contamination, what should be done differently?**

A Store the sanitizer bottle away from the prep area.
B Store the sanitizer bottle on the floor between uses.
C Store the sanitizer bottle on the work surface of the prep table.
D Store the sanitizer bottle with food supplies below the prep table.

2 **Which food contains a common allergen?**

A Potatoes sautéed in duck fat
B Smoked salmon wrapped in a lettuce leaf
C Melon slices wrapped with prosciutto (ham)
D Green beans dressed with olive oil and garlic

3 **Which food contains a common allergen?**

A Squash sautéed in corn oil
B Brown rice mixed with herbs
C Mixed green salad with apples and raisins
D Mushrooms seasoned with soy sauce and brown sugar

4 **Wheezing and shortness of breath are symptoms of what?**

A Hepatitis A
B *Bacillus cereus*
C An allergic reaction
D Hemorrhagic colitis

5 **What should food handlers do to prevent food allergens from being transferred to food?**

A Use cleaned and sanitized utensils when prepping the order.
B Cook food to the appropriate minimum internal temperature.
C Store cold food at 41°F (5°C) or lower.
D Label chemical containers correctly.

6 **To prevent the deliberate contamination of food, a manager should know who is in the facility, monitor the security of products, keep information related to food security on file, and know**

A when to register with the EPA.
B how to fill out an incident report.
C where to find the chemicals in the operation.
D whom to contact about suspicious activity.

For answers, please turn to the Answer Key.

Notes

Hepatitis A Scare

Hepatitis A vaccinations were offered to thousands of guests who had visited a local casual-dining operation in the Gulf Coast region of the United States. The vaccinations were made available by the local regulatory authority after a food handler at the operation tested positive for Hepatitis A, exposing the guests to the virus. The identified food handler was responsible for preparing and setting up items on the salad bar.

The food handler was excluded from work until approved to return by a physician and the regulatory authority. The local regulatory authority also worked with the operation's owners and management team to ensure they had all of the correct processes in place to protect guests and staff.

1. **What could have been done to prevent the outbreak?**

For answers, please turn to the Answer Key.

4 The Safe Food Handler

Inside This Chapter

- Personal Hygiene and Contamination
- A Good Personal Hygiene Program

Objectives

After completing this chapter, you should be able to identify the following:

- How food handlers can contaminate food
- The correct handwashing procedure
- When and where hands should be washed
- Hand antiseptics and when to use them
- Hand-maintenance requirements
- The correct way to cover infected wounds
- The importance of avoiding bare-hand contact with ready-to-eat food
- How to use single-use gloves and when to change them
- Requirements for staff work attire
- Jewelry that poses a hazard to food safety
- Policies regarding eating, drinking, and smoking as they relate to food safety
- Criteria for excluding staff from the operation or restricting them from working with exposed food, utensils, and equipment
- Illnesses that need to be reported to the regulatory authority

Key Terms

Carriers

Hand antiseptics

Impermeable

Hair restraint

Personal Hygiene and Contamination

Food handlers can contaminate food and cause guests to get sick at every step in the flow of food through the operation. Good personal hygiene is a critical protective measure against foodborne illness.

How Food Handlers Can Contaminate Food

You have learned that staff can make people sick by transferring pathogens to food they touch. These pathogens often come from the food handlers themselves. Food handlers can contaminate food in any of the following situations:

- When they have a foodborne illness.
- When they have wounds or boils that contain a pathogen.

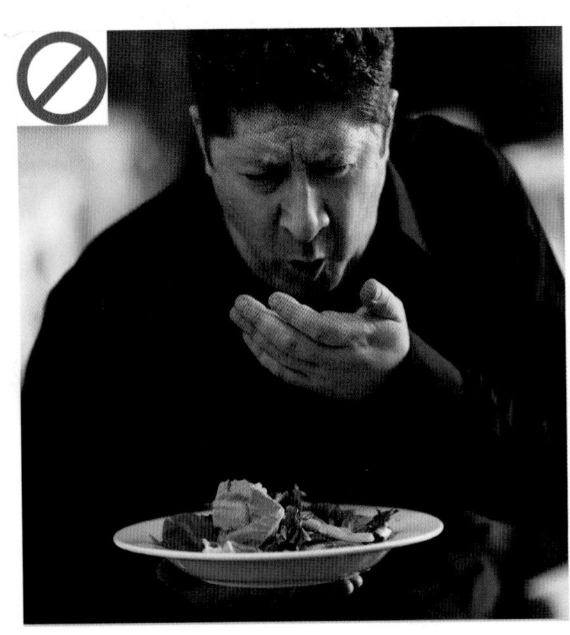

- When sneezing or coughing, as the food handler is doing in the photo at left.
- When they have contact with a person who is ill.
- When they use the restroom and do not wash their hands. These food handlers may contaminate food and surfaces with feces from their fingers. Once someone eats food contaminated this way, a foodborne illness may result. This is called the fecal–oral route of contamination.
- When they have symptoms such as diarrhea, vomiting, or jaundice—a yellowing of the eyes or skin.

With some illnesses, a person may infect others before showing symptoms. For example, a person could spread Hepatitis A for weeks before having any symptoms. With other illnesses, such as Norovirus, a person may infect others for days after symptoms are gone.

Some people also carry pathogens and infect others without getting sick themselves. These people are called **carriers**. The bacteria *Staphylococcus aureus* is carried in the nose of 30 to 50 percent of healthy adults. About 20 to 35 percent of healthy adults carry it on their skin as well. Food handlers transfer this bacteria to food when they touch the infected areas of their bodies and then touch food.

These scenarios show how easily food can be contaminated:

- A deli food handler diagnosed with salmonellosis failed to inform his manager that he was sick. He was later determined to be the cause of an outbreak involving more than 200 guests through 12 different items.
- A food handler with diarrhea did not wash his hands after using the restroom. He made close to 5,000 people sick when he mixed a vat of buttercream frosting with his bare hands and arms.

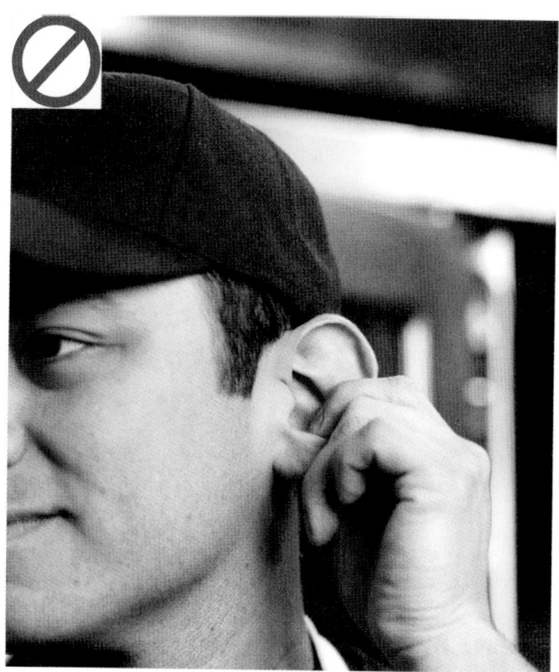

Simple acts, such as running fingers through the hair, wiping or touching the nose, rubbing an ear (shown at right), scratching the scalp, coughing or sneezing into the hand, spitting in the operation, or touching a pimple or an infected wound/boil can also contaminate food. For this reason, food handlers need to monitor what they do with their hands.

Diseases Not Transmitted through Food

The public has expressed growing concern over communicable diseases spread through intimate contact or by direct exchange of bodily fluids. Diseases such as AIDS (acquired immunodeficiency syndrome), Hepatitis B and C, and tuberculosis are spread in this fashion but are not spread through food.

As a manager, you should be aware of the following laws concerning staff who have tested positive for the human immunodeficiency virus (HIV), which can lead to the disease AIDS if left untreated, or who have tuberculosis or Hepatitis B or C:

- The Americans with Disabilities Act (ADA) provides civil-rights protection to those who are HIV positive or who have Hepatitis B. This prohibits employers from firing people or transferring them out of food-handling duties simply because they have these diseases.
- Employers should maintain the confidentiality of any staff who have an illness that is not foodborne.

A Good Personal Hygiene Program

Food handlers must not only have the correct knowledge, skills, and attitudes toward personal hygiene, but also know how they can contaminate food if they are not careful. To keep food handlers from contaminating food, your operation needs a good personal hygiene program. A good personal hygiene program also helps everyone feel confident in the cleanliness of the business. As a manager, you must make sure this program succeeds.

Do not underestimate your role in a personal hygiene program. You have a responsibility to create the program and make sure it works. Some things to support a personal hygiene program include:

- Creating personal hygiene policies.
- Training food handlers on those policies and retraining them regularly.

- Modeling the correct behavior at all times.
  The manager in the photo at left is modeling good personal hygiene practices. He is wearing clean clothes and a hair restraint. He is also using gloves.
- Supervising food safety practices at all times.
- Revising personal hygiene policies when laws or science change.

Handwashing

Every day our hands touch surfaces covered with pathogens that we cannot see. Remember, even healthy people can spread pathogens. For this reason, handwashing is the most important part of personal hygiene. It may seem basic and routine; however, many food handlers fail to wash their hands correctly and as often as needed. You must train your food handlers to wash their hands, and then you must monitor them.

Where to Wash Hands

Hands must be washed in a sink designated for handwashing. Monitor food handlers to make sure they do this. They should **NEVER** wash their hands in sinks designated for food prep or dishwashing or sinks used for discarding waste water. The food handler in the photo at left is using a designated handwashing sink.

How to Wash Hands

To wash hands or prosthetic devices correctly, use the steps that follow. The whole process should take at least 20 seconds.

1 **Wet hands and arms.** Use running warm water.

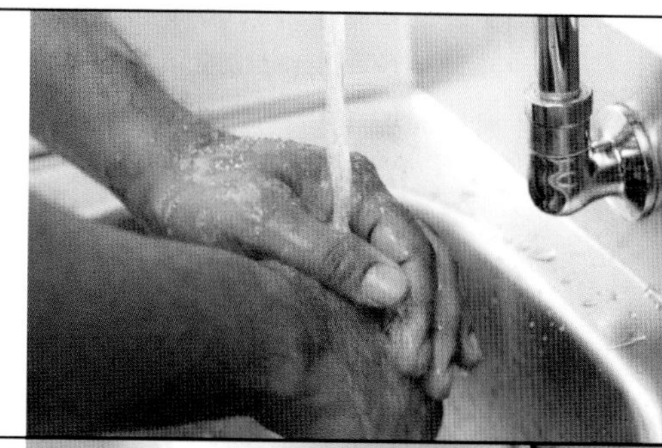

2 **Apply soap.** Make sure there is enough soap to build up a good lather. Follow the manufacturer's recommendations.

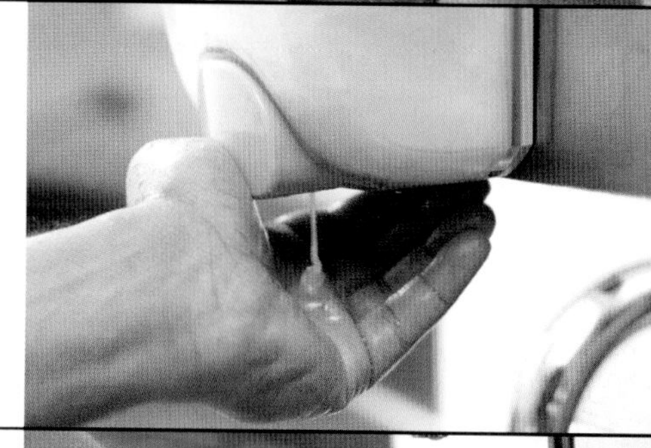

3 **Scrub hands and arms vigorously for 10 to 15 seconds.** Clean the fingertips, under fingernails, and between fingers.

4 **Rinse hands and arms thoroughly.** Use running warm water.

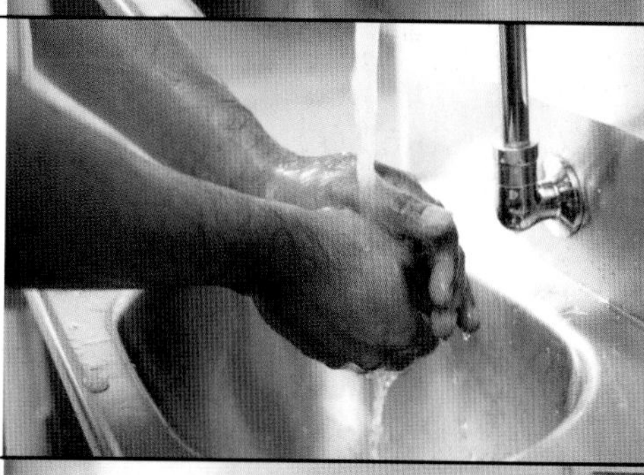

5 **Dry hands and arms.** Use a single-use paper towel or a hand dryer.

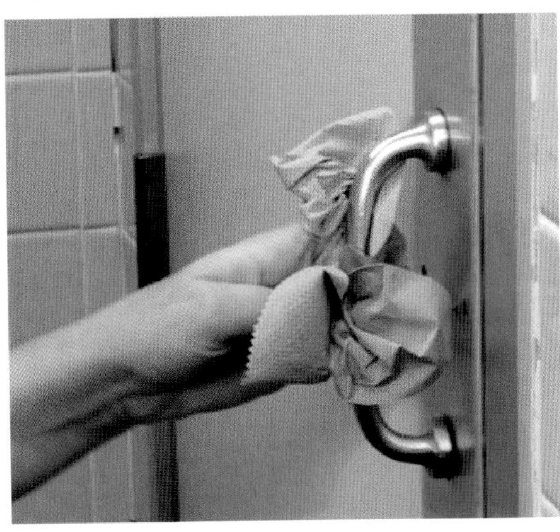

If you are not careful, you can contaminate your hands after washing them. Consider using a paper towel to turn off the faucet and to open the door when leaving the restroom. The food handler in the photo at left is using a paper towel to open the restroom door in order to avoid contamination.

When to Wash Hands

Food handlers must wash their hands before preparing food or working with clean equipment and utensils. They must also wash their hands before putting on single-use gloves. The buser pictured below washed his hands before unloading the clean glasses.

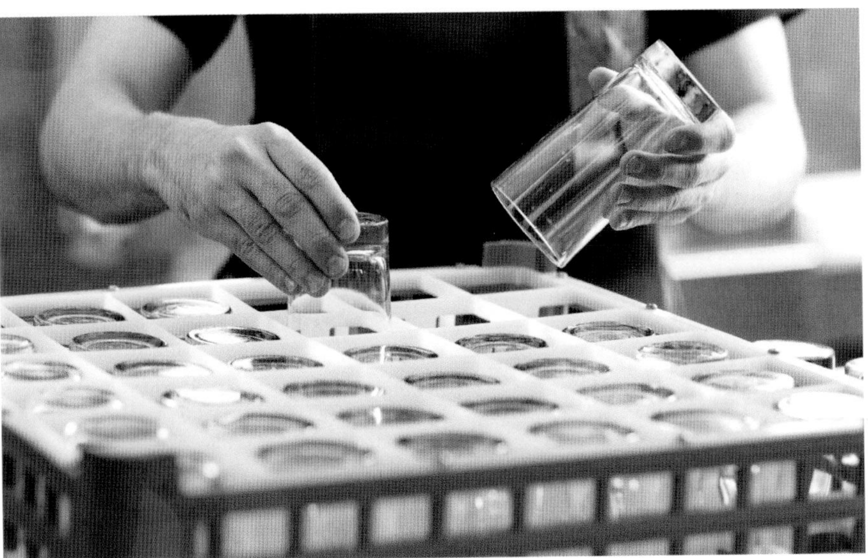

Food handlers must wash their hands after the following activities:

- Using the restroom.
- Touching the body or clothing.
- Coughing, sneezing, blowing their nose, or using a handkerchief or tissue.
- Eating, drinking, smoking, or chewing gum or tobacco.
- Handling soiled items.
- Handling raw meat, poultry, and seafood.

- Taking out garbage.
- Handling service animals or aquatic animals.
- Handling chemicals that might affect food safety.
- Changing tasks (before beginning a new task).
- Leaving and returning to the kitchen/prep area.
- Handling money.
- Using electronic devices. The food handler in the photo at right must wash his hands before working with food or clean equipment and utensils.
- Touching anything else that may contaminate hands, such as dirty equipment, work surfaces, or cloths.

Corrective Action

If you see food handlers who are not following proper handwashing procedures, correct the situation immediately. If they have touched food or food-contact surfaces with unclean hands:

- Dispose of the contaminated food.
- Clean potentially contaminated equipment and utensils.
- Retrain or coach food handlers who are not following proper handwashing procedures if necessary.

Hand Antiseptics

Hand antiseptics, also called hand sanitizers, are liquids or gels that help lower the number of pathogens on skin. If used, they must comply with the Code of Federal Regulations (CFR) and Food and Drug Administration (FDA) standards.

Only use hand antiseptics after handwashing. **NEVER** use them in place of it. Wait for a hand antiseptic to dry before you touch food or equipment.

Hand Care

In addition to washing, hands need other care to prevent the spread of pathogens. Make sure food handlers follow the guidelines in Table 4.1, on the next page.

Table 4.1: **Hand-Care Guidelines**

Topic	Guidelines
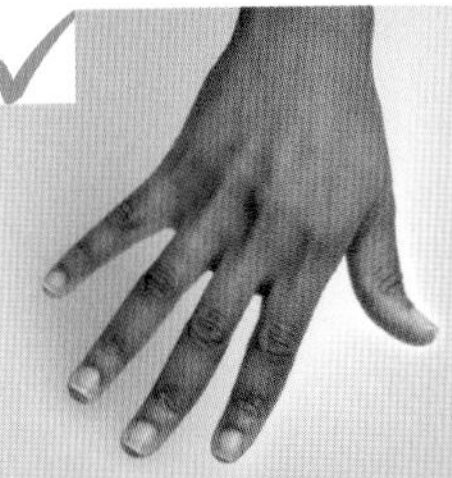	**Fingernail length** Keep fingernails short and clean. Long fingernails may be hard to keep clean and can rip gloves. They can also chip and become physical contaminants. Fingernails should be kept trimmed and filed. This will allow nails to be cleaned easily. Ragged nails can be hard to keep clean. They may also hold pathogens and break off—becoming physical contaminants.
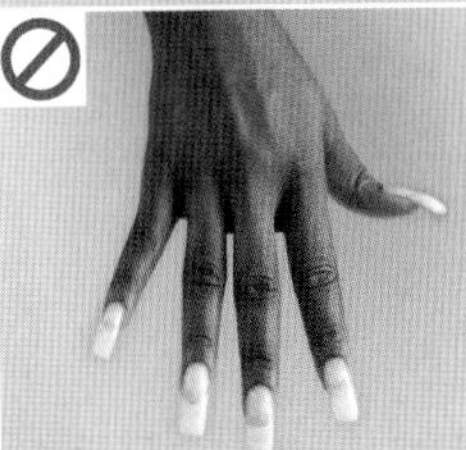	**False fingernails** Do **NOT** wear false fingernails. They can be hard to keep clean. False fingernails also can break off into food. However, false fingernails can be worn if the food handler wears single-use gloves.
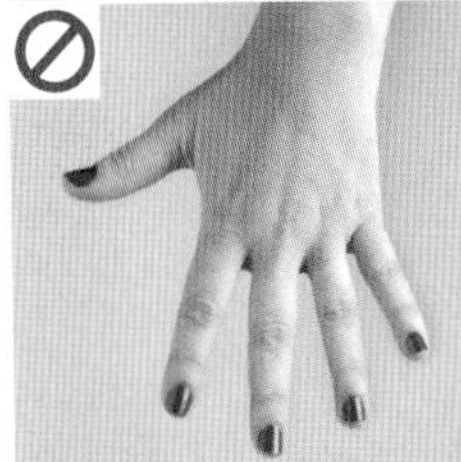	**Nail polish** Do **NOT** wear nail polish. It can disguise dirt under nails and may flake off into food. However, nail polish can be worn if the food handler wears single-use gloves.

Infected wounds or boils

Infected wounds, cuts, and boils contain pus. They must be covered if they are open or draining to prevent pathogens from contaminating food and food-contact surfaces. How an infected wound or boil is covered depends on where it is located.

	If the wound or boil is located on the hand or wrist	Then cover it with an impermeable cover like a finger cot. **Impermeable** means that liquid cannot pass through the cover. Examples include bandages and finger cots. Place a single-use glove over the cover.
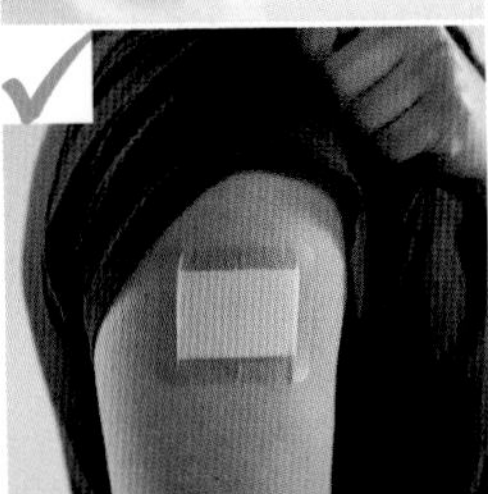	If the wound or boil is located on the arm	Then cover it with an impermeable cover, such as a bandage. The wound must be completely covered.
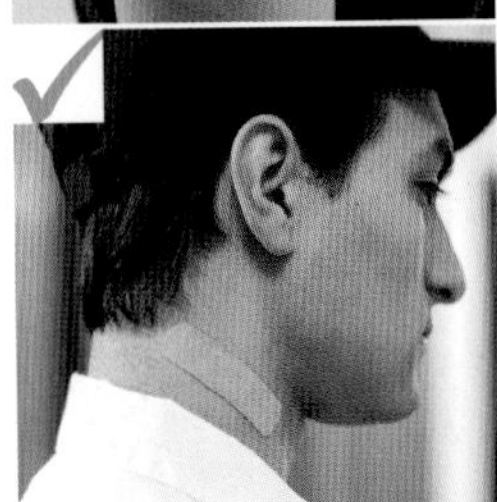	If the wound or boil is located on another part of the body	Then cover it with a dry, durable, tight-fitting bandage.

Bare-Hand Contact with Ready-to-Eat Food

Food can become contaminated when it has been handled with bare hands. This is especially true when hands have not been washed correctly or have infected cuts or wounds. For this reason, do **NOT** handle ready-to-eat food with bare hands. And, if you primarily serve a high-risk population, **NEVER** handle ready-to-eat food with bare hands.

However, there may be exceptions. It may be acceptable to handle ready-to-eat food with bare hands in these situations:

- The food will be added as an ingredient to a dish that does not contain raw meat, seafood, or poultry, but will be cooked to at least 145°F (63°C). For example, adding cheese to pizza dough.
- The food will be added as an ingredient to a dish containing raw meat, seafood, or poultry, and the dish will be cooked to the required minimum internal temperature of the raw items. For example, adding seasonings to raw meat, as shown in the photo at right.

Some regulatory authorities allow bare-hand contact with ready-to-eat food. If your jurisdiction allows this, you should have specific policies in place about staff health. You must also train staff in handwashing and personal hygiene practices. Check your local regulatory requirements.

Single-Use Gloves

Many operations use single-use gloves when handling food. As the name implies, single-use gloves are designed for one task, after which they must be discarded. Used properly, they can help keep food safe by creating a barrier between hands and food. However, single-use gloves should **NEVER** be used in place of handwashing.

Single-use gloves should always be worn when handling ready-to-eat food, as shown in the photo at right. Gloves do not need to be worn when washing produce. They also do not need to be worn when handling ready-to-eat ingredients for a dish that will be cooked to the correct internal temperature.

Buying Gloves

Follow these guidelines when purchasing single-use gloves.

Approved gloves **Purchase only gloves approved for foodservice.**

Disposable gloves **Buy only single-use gloves for handling food. NEVER wash and reuse gloves.**

Different types **Supply different gloves for different tasks. Long gloves, for example, should be used for hand-mixing salads. Colored gloves can also be used to help prevent cross-contamination.**

Multiple sizes **Provide gloves of varying sizes.**

Latex alternatives **Some food handlers and guests may be sensitive to latex. Consider providing gloves made from other materials.**

How to Use Gloves

When using single-use gloves, follow these guidelines to prevent contamination:

- **Wash your hands before putting on gloves when starting a new task. You do not need to rewash your hands each time you change gloves as long as you are performing the same task and your hands have not become contaminated.**

- **Choose the correct glove size. Gloves that are too big will not stay on. Those that are too small will tear or rip easily. The photo at left shows a correct fit.**
- **Hold gloves by the edge when putting them on. Avoid touching the glove as much as possible.**
- **Once you have put them on, check the gloves for rips or tears.**
- **NEVER blow into gloves.**
- **NEVER roll gloves to make them easier to put on.**
- **NEVER wash and reuse gloves.**

When to Change Gloves

Food handlers must change single-use gloves at these times:

- As soon as the gloves become dirty or torn
- Before beginning a different task
- After an interruption, such as taking a phone call
- After handling raw meat, seafood, or poultry and before handling ready-to-eat food
- After four hours of continuous use

Gloves can give food handlers a false sense of security, especially if they are not changed as often as they should be. Reinforce correct glove use with all food handlers.

Other Good Personal Hygiene Practices

Personal hygiene can be a touchy subject for some. But because it is so important to food safety, managers should address the subject with every food handler.

Personal Cleanliness

Pathogens can be found on hair and skin. They have a greater risk of being transferred to food and food equipment if food handlers do not shower or bathe before work. Make sure all staff members do this.

Correct Work Attire

Food handlers in dirty clothes may give a bad impression of your operation. More important, dirty clothing may carry pathogens that can cause foodborne illnesses. These pathogens can be transferred from the clothing to the hands and to the food being prepped. Set up a dress code, and make sure staff follow it. The code should include the guidelines listed in Table 4.2, on the next page.

Table 4.2: **Work Attire Guidelines**

Attire | **Guidelines**

Hair restraints

- Wear a clean hat or other **hair restraint** when in a food-prep area. This can keep hair from falling into food and onto food-contact surfaces.
- Do **NOT** wear hair accessories that could become physical contaminants. Hair accessories should be limited to items that keep hands out of hair and hair out of food.
- Do **NOT** wear false eyelashes. They can become physical contaminants.
- Food handlers with facial hair should also wear a beard restraint.

Clean clothing

- Wear clean clothing daily.
- Change soiled uniforms, including aprons, as needed to prevent contamination.
- If possible, change into work clothes at work.
- Store street clothing and personal belongings in designated areas. This includes items such as backpacks, jackets, electronic devices, keys, and personal medications. Make sure these items are stored in a way that does not contaminate food, food-contact surfaces, and linens.
- Keep dirty clothing that is stored in the operation away from food and prep areas. You can do this by placing dirty clothes in nonabsorbent containers or washable laundry bags. This includes dirty aprons, chef coats, and other uniforms.

Aprons

- Remove aprons when leaving prep areas. For example, aprons should be removed and stored before taking out garbage or using the restroom.
- **NEVER** wipe your hands on your apron.

Jewelry

- Remove jewelry from hands and arms before prepping food or when working around prep areas. Food handlers cannot wear any of the following:
  - Rings, except for a plain band
  - Bracelets, including medical bracelets
  - Watches
- Your company may also require you to remove other types of jewelry. This may include earrings, necklaces, and facial jewelry. These items can fall off and become a physical contaminant. Ornate jewelry can be difficult to clean and can hold pathogens. Servers may wear jewelry if allowed by company policy.

These requirements should be included in written policies that are both monitored and enforced. Newly hired staff who have not started working yet should also be made aware of these policies.

Eating, Drinking, Smoking, and Chewing Gum or Tobacco

Small droplets of saliva can contain thousands of pathogens. Eating, drinking, smoking, or chewing gum or tobacco can transfer saliva to hands or directly to food being handled.

To prevent this, employees should only eat, drink, smoke, or chew gum or tobacco in designated areas. Never do these things when:

- Prepping or serving food
- Working in prep areas
- Working in areas used to clean utensils and equipment

Employees can drink from a covered container if they handle the container carefully to prevent contamination of their hands, the container, and exposed food, utensils, and equipment. A properly covered container will include a lid with a straw or a sip-lid top. The chef in the photo at right is using a proper container and lid.

If food must be tasted during prepping, use an approved utensil, and only use that utensil once. The food handler in the photo at right is tasting food correctly.

Reporting Health Issues

Require staff to let you know when they are sick. This includes newly hired staff who have not started working yet. Your regulatory authority may ask for proof that you have done this. You can provide it in the following ways:

- Presenting signed statements in which staff have agreed to report illness
- Providing documentation showing staff have completed training, which includes information on the importance of reporting illness
- Posting signs or providing pocket cards that remind staff to notify managers when they are sick

Reporting Illness

Staff must report illnesses before they come to work. They should also let you know immediately if they get sick while working, as the food handler in the photo at left is doing.

When food handlers are ill, you may need to restrict them from working with exposed food, utensils, and equipment. Sometimes, you may even need to exclude sick employees from coming into the operation. This is especially important if they have certain symptoms:

- Vomiting
- Diarrhea
- Jaundice (a yellowing of the skin or eyes)
- Sore throat with fever
- Infected wound or boil that is open or draining (unless properly covered)

Staff must also tell you when they have been diagnosed with an illness from one of these pathogens:

- Norovirus
- Hepatitis A
- *Shigella* spp.
- Shiga-toxin producing *E. coli* (STEC)
- *Salmonella* Typhi
- Nontyphoidal *Salmonella*

They must also tell you if they live with someone who has been diagnosed with any of these illnesses, except nontyphoidal *Salmonella*.

If a food handler is diagnosed with an illness from any of these pathogens, you must report the illness to your regulatory authority. See Table 4.3 for more information.

Watching for Staff Illnesses

As a manager, you should watch food handlers for signs of illness. That could include watching for things like:

- Vomiting
- Excessive trips to the bathroom
- Yellowing of the skin, eyes, and fingernails
- Cold sweats or chills (indicating a fever)
- Persistent nasal discharge and sneezing

Restricting or Excluding Staff for Medical Conditions

Use the following chart to help you decide how to handle staff illnesses and other medical conditions that can affect food safety. Note that for most illnesses, however, you should work with your local regulatory authority to determine how to respond.

Table 4.3: **How to Handle Medical Conditions**

If	Then
The food handler has an infected wound or boil that is not properly covered.	**Restrict** the food handler from working with exposed food, utensils, and equipment.
The food handler has a sore throat with a fever.	**Restrict** the food handler from working with exposed food, utensils, and equipment. **Exclude** the food handler from the operation if you primarily serve a high-risk population. The food handler can return to the operation and/or work with or around food when he or she has a written release from a medical practitioner.
The food handler has persistent sneezing, coughing, or a runny nose that causes discharges from the eyes, nose, or mouth.	**Restrict** the food handler from working with exposed food, utensils, and equipment.
The food handler has at least one of these symptoms from an infectious condition: • Vomiting • Diarrhea • Jaundice (yellow skin or eyes)	**Exclude** the food handler from the operation. **Vomiting and diarrhea** Food handlers must meet one of these requirements before they can return to work: • Have had no symptoms for at least 24 hours. • Have a written release from a medical practitioner. **Jaundice** Food handlers with jaundice must be reported to the regulatory authority. Food handlers who have had jaundice for seven days or less must be excluded from the operation. Food handlers must have a written release from a medical practitioner and approval from the regulatory authority before returning to work.

(continued on next page)

Table 4.3: **How to Handle Medical Conditions** ***(continued)***

If	Then
The food handler is vomiting or has diarrhea and has been diagnosed with an illness caused by one of these pathogens: • Norovirus • *Shigella* spp. • Nontyphoidal *Salmonella* • Shiga toxin-producing *E. coli* (STEC) The food handler has been diagnosed with an illness caused by one of these pathogens: • Hepatitis A • *Salmonella* Typhi	**Exclude** the food handler from the operation. **Report** the situation to the regulatory authority. Some food handlers diagnosed with an illness may not experience symptoms, or their symptoms may have ended. Work with the medical practitioner and the local regulatory authority to determine whether the food handlers must be excluded from the operation or restricted from working with exposed food, utensils, and equipment. The medical practitioner and regulatory authority will also determine when the employees can safely return to the operation and/or carry out their regular food handling duties.

This chart is only a guide. Work with your local regulatory authority to determine the best course of action.

Chapter Summary

- Food handlers pose a greater risk for contaminating food when they have a foodborne illness; wounds or boils that contain a pathogen; contact with someone who is ill; or symptoms such as sneezing, coughing, diarrhea, vomiting, or jaundice. The risk is also greater when food handlers use the restroom and do not wash their hands. Other common ways that food handlers can contaminate food include touching their scalp, hair, nose, or ears; touching a pimple or wound; wearing and touching a dirty uniform; coughing or sneezing into their hands; and spitting in the operation.
- Hands must be cared for and washed correctly. They must be washed at a sink designated for handwashing. They also must be washed at the correct times. This includes before preparing food, working with clean equipment and utensils, putting on single-use gloves, and starting a new task. Food handlers must also wash their hands after using the restroom and after many other activities that can contaminate their hands. Hand antiseptics should never be used in place of handwashing.
- Single-use gloves must be worn when handling ready-to-eat food. Wash hands before putting on gloves. Wear gloves that are the correct size. Avoid touching the gloves when you put them on. Change your gloves when they are dirty or torn; before starting a new task; after an interruption in your task; after handling raw meat, seafood, or poultry and before handling ready-to-eat food; and after four hours of continuous use. Never handle ready-to-eat food with bare hands if you primarily serve a high-risk population.
- Food handlers should shower or bathe before going to work. Food handlers also must put on clean clothing and a hair restraint before handling food or working in prep areas. They must remove jewelry from hands and arms. Aprons should always be removed and stored when staff members leave prep areas. If they have a wound or boil, it must be covered correctly.
- Food handlers should never eat, smoke, or chew gum or tobacco in food-prep or service areas, or in areas designated for cleaning.
- Require staff to report health problems to management. Managers should also watch for staff illnesses. Managers must exclude or restrict food handlers who have certain symptoms or medical conditions. Check with your regulatory authority for requirements that apply to your operation.

Apply Your Knowledge

Use these questions to review the concepts presented in this chapter.

Discussion Questions

1 What are some basic work-attire requirements for staff?

2 What personal behaviors can contaminate food?

3 What is the correct procedure for covering infected wounds on hands or arms?

4 What procedures must food handlers follow when using gloves?

Apply Your Knowledge

5 What staff health problems pose a possible threat to food safety? What are the appropriate actions that should be taken?

For answers, please turn to the Answer Key.

Apply Your Knowledge

Something to Think About

Robert's Day

Robert is a food handler at a deli. It is 7:47 a.m., and he has just woken up. He is scheduled to be at work and ready to go by 8:00 a.m. When he gets out of bed, his stomach feels queasy. He blames that on the beer he had the night before. Fortunately, Robert lives only five minutes from work. Despite this, he does not have enough time to take a shower. He grabs the same uniform he wore the day before when prepping chicken. He also puts on his watch and several rings.

Robert does not have luck on his side today. On the way to the deli, his oil light comes on. He is forced to pull off the road and add oil to his car. When he gets to work, he realizes that he has left his hat at home. Robert is greeted by an angry manager. The manager puts Robert to work right away, loading the rotisserie with raw chicken. Robert then moves to serving a guest who orders a freshly made salad. Robert is known for his salads and makes the salad to the guest's approval.

The manager asks Robert to take out the garbage and then make potato salad for the lunch-hour rush. On the way back from the garbage run, Robert tells the manager that his stomach is bothering him. The manager, thinking of his staff shortage, asks Robert to stick it out as long as he can. Robert agrees and gets out the ingredients for the potato salad. Then he heads to the restroom in hope of relieving his symptoms. After quickly rinsing his hands in the restroom, he finds that the paper towels have run out. Short of time, he wipes his hands on his apron.

The manager tells Robert to clean the few tables in the deli that are available for guests. When finished, Robert grabs a piece of chicken from the rotisserie for a snack. He takes the chicken with him to the prep area, so he can get back to making the potato salad.

1 **What did Robert and his manager do wrong?**

____

____

____

____

____

____

____

For answers, please turn to the Answer Key.

Apply Your Knowledge

Something to Think About

Kurt's Dilemma

Kurt had been awake off and on throughout the night with diarrhea and vomiting. When he woke up the next morning, he did not feel that much better, even though the vomiting and diarrhea had stopped. He decided that it might be a good idea to take the day off from the café where he worked. The café was a very popular place to eat among college students in a large university town.

Kurt's boss, Jackie, answered the phone when he called in. At first she could not believe what she was hearing. Kurt was calling in sick when he knew it was going to be an incredibly busy shift. The café was already running short of staff. Jackie questioned Kurt about his symptoms. Then she asked if he could come in long enough to get them through the rush. Jackie was not worried because Kurt was no longer vomiting and did not have diarrhea. Because he needed the money, Kurt decided to go to work, with the promise that he could go home as soon as the lunch rush was over.

1 **What did Jackie do wrong?**

____

____

____

____

____

____

2 **What should she have done differently?**

____

____

____

____

____

____

For answers, please turn to the Answer Key.

Study Questions

Circle the best answer to each question.

1 **After which activity must food handlers wash their hands?**

A Putting on gloves
B Serving guests
C Clearing tables
D Applying hand antiseptic

2 **What should food handlers do after prepping food and before using the restroom?**

A Wash their hands
B Take off their hats
C Change their gloves
D Take off their aprons

3 **Which piece of jewelry can be worn on a food handler's hand or arm?**

A Watch
B Diamond ring
C Plain band ring
D Medical bracelet

4 **When should hand antiseptics be used?**

A After washing hands
B Before washing hands
C When soap is unavailable
D When gloves are not being used

5 **Who is most at risk of contaminating food?**

A A food handler whose spouse works primarily with high-risk populations
B A food handler whose young daughter has diarrhea
C A food handler who gets a lot of aches and pains
D A food handler who eats a lot of rare meat

Study Questions

6 **A cook wore single-use gloves while forming raw ground beef into patties. The cook continued to wear them while slicing hamburger buns. What mistake was made?**

A The cook did not clean and sanitize the gloves before handling the hamburger buns.

B The cook did not wash hands and put on new gloves before slicing the hamburger buns.

C The cook did not wash hands before putting on the same gloves to slice the hamburger buns.

D The cook did not wear reusable gloves while handling the raw ground beef and hamburger buns.

7 **When washing hands, what is the minimum time you should scrub with soap?**

A 5 seconds

B 10 seconds

C 20 seconds

D 40 seconds

8 **A food handler prepares and delivers meals to elderly people. What symptoms require this food handler to stay home from work?**

A Thirst with itching

B Soreness with fatigue

C Sore throat with fever

D Headache with soreness

9 **When is it acceptable to eat in an operation?**

A When prepping food

B When washing dishes

C When handling utensils

D When sitting in a break area

10 **What should a manager of a hospital cafeteria do if a cook calls in with a headache, nausea, and diarrhea?**

A Tell the cook to stay away from work and see a doctor.

B Tell the cook to come in for a couple of hours and then go home.

C Tell the cook to rest for a couple of hours and then come to work.

D Tell the cook to go to the doctor and then immediately come to work.

For answers, please turn to the Answer Key.

Notes

Notes

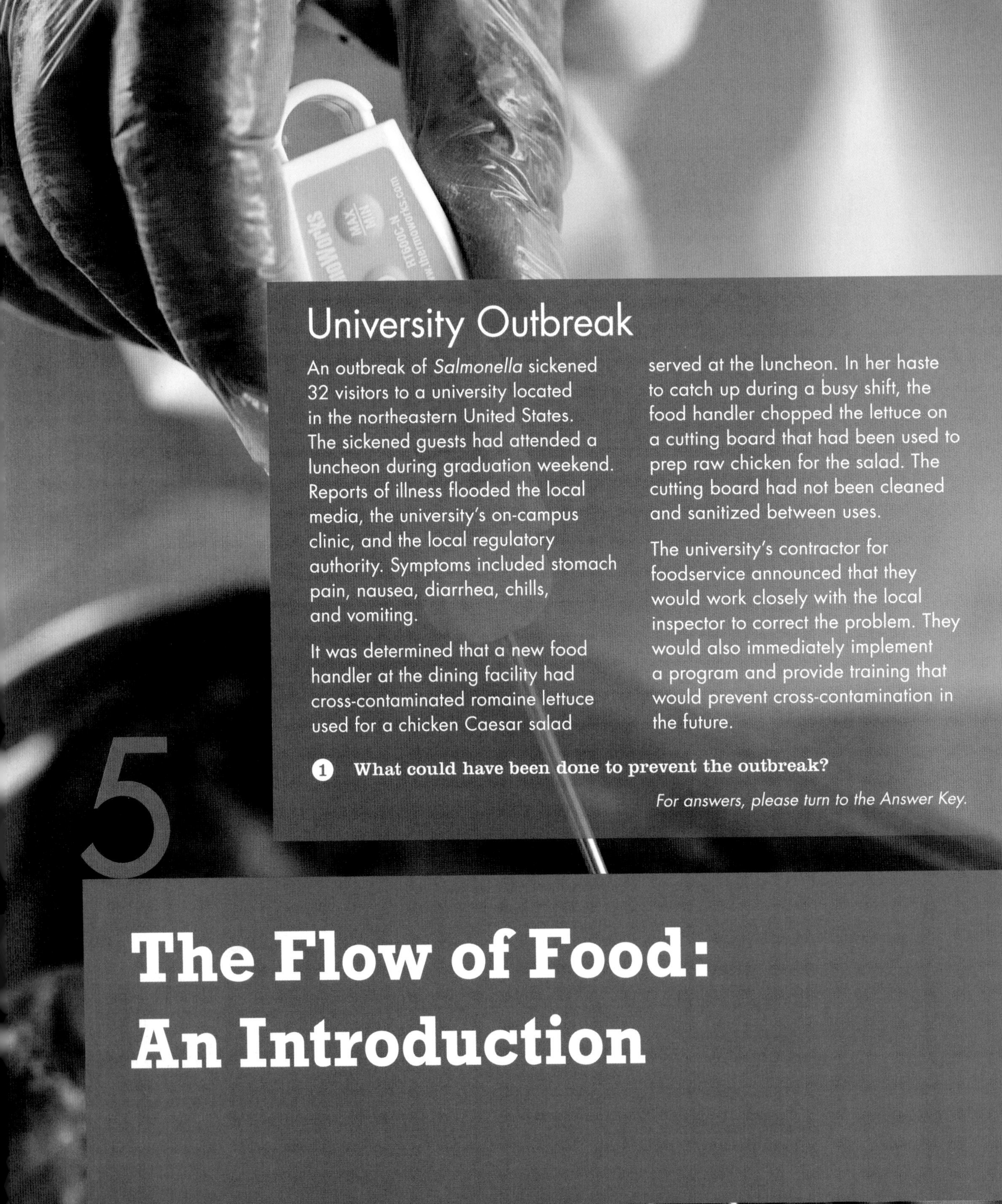

University Outbreak

An outbreak of *Salmonella* sickened 32 visitors to a university located in the northeastern United States. The sickened guests had attended a luncheon during graduation weekend. Reports of illness flooded the local media, the university's on-campus clinic, and the local regulatory authority. Symptoms included stomach pain, nausea, diarrhea, chills, and vomiting.

It was determined that a new food handler at the dining facility had cross-contaminated romaine lettuce used for a chicken Caesar salad served at the luncheon. In her haste to catch up during a busy shift, the food handler chopped the lettuce on a cutting board that had been used to prep raw chicken for the salad. The cutting board had not been cleaned and sanitized between uses.

The university's contractor for foodservice announced that they would work closely with the local inspector to correct the problem. They would also immediately implement a program and provide training that would prevent cross-contamination in the future.

1. **What could have been done to prevent the outbreak?**

For answers, please turn to the Answer Key.

5 The Flow of Food: An Introduction

Inside This Chapter

- Hazards in the Flow of Food
- Monitoring Time and Temperature

Objectives

After completing this chapter, you should be able to identify the following:

- Ways of preventing cross-contamination
- Ways of preventing time-temperature abuse
- Different types of temperature-measuring devices and their uses
- How to calibrate thermometers
- General guidelines for thermometer use

Key Terms

Flow of food

Bimetallic stemmed thermometer

Thermocouples

Thermistors

Time-temperature indicator (TTI)

Calibration

Ice-point method

Boiling-point method

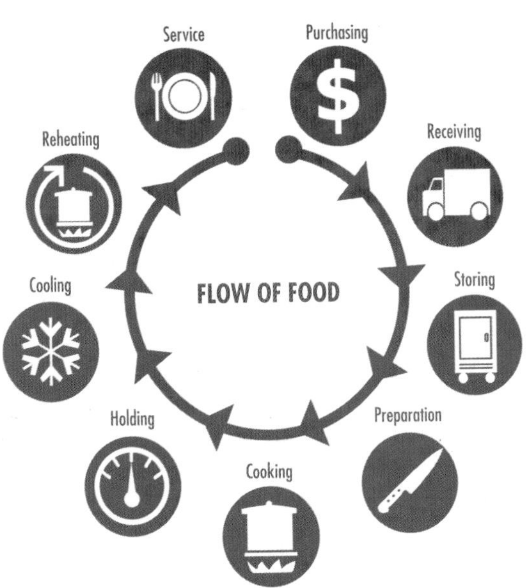

Hazards in the Flow of Food

Many things can happen to food as it moves from purchasing and receiving through storing, prepping, cooking, holding, cooling, reheating, and serving. This path, shown at left, is known as the **flow of food**.

You are responsible for the safety of the food at every point in this flow—and many things can happen to it. For example, a frozen food might be safe when it leaves the processor's plant. However, on the way to the supplier's warehouse, the food might thaw. Once in your operation, the food might not be stored correctly, or it might not be cooked to the correct internal temperature. These mistakes can add up and cause a foodborne illness. That is why it is important to understand how to prevent time-temperature abuse and cross-contamination.

Cross-Contamination

Cross-contamination is a major hazard in the flow of food. Pathogens can be spread from food or unwashed hands to prep tables, utensils, equipment, or other food. Cross-contamination can occur at almost any point within the flow of food. When you know how and where it can happen, it is fairly easy to prevent. The most basic way is to keep raw and ready-to-eat food away from each other. Table 5.1 shows some guidelines for doing this.

Time-Temperature Control

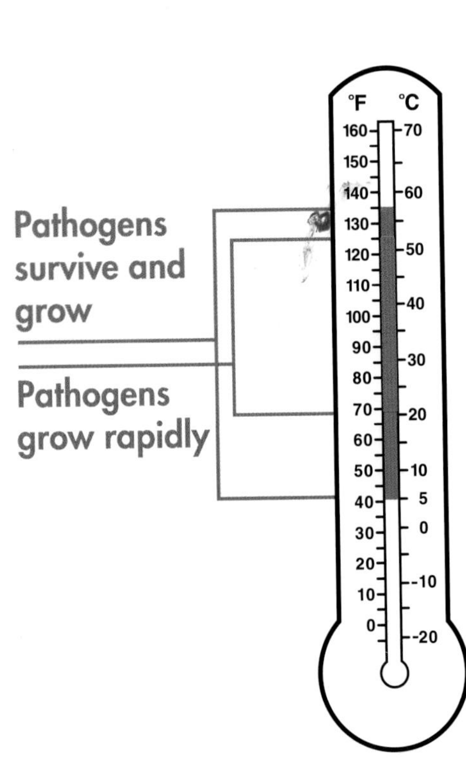

Time-temperature abuse is another major hazard in the flow of food. Remember, TCS food has been time-temperature abused any time it remains between 41°F and 135°F (5°C and 57°C). This is called the temperature danger zone, because pathogens grow in this range. They grow especially fast between 70°F and 125°F (21°C and 52°C). These ranges are shown in the illustration at left.

Food is being time-temperature abused whenever it is handled in the following ways:

- It is cooked to the wrong minimum internal temperature.
- It is held at the wrong temperature.
- It is cooled or reheated incorrectly.

Time also plays a critical role. The longer food stays in the temperature danger zone, the more time pathogens have to grow. To keep food safe, you must reduce the time food spends in this temperature range. TCS food must be thrown out if it stays in the temperature danger zone for four hours or more.

Table 5.1: **Guidelines for Preventing Cross-Contamination between Food**

	**Use separate equipment for raw and ready-to-eat food** Each type of food should have separate equipment. For example, use one set of cutting boards, utensils, and containers for raw poultry. Use another set for raw meat. Use a third set for produce. Colored cutting boards and utensil handles can help keep equipment separate. The color tells food handlers which equipment to use with each food item. You might use yellow for raw chicken, red for raw meat, and green for produce.
	**Clean and sanitize before and after tasks** Clean and sanitize all work surfaces, equipment, and utensils after each task. When you cut up raw chicken, for example, you cannot get by with just rinsing the equipment. Pathogens such as nontyphoidal *Salmonella* can contaminate food through cross-contamination. To prevent this, you must wash, rinse, and sanitize equipment. See chapter 12 for more information on cleaning and sanitizing.
	**Prep raw and ready-to-eat food at different times** If you need to use the same prep table for different types of food, prep raw meat, fish, and poultry at a different time than ready-to-eat food. You must clean and sanitize work surfaces and utensils between each type of food. Also, if you prep ready-to-eat food before raw food, you can reduce the chance for cross-contamination.
	**Buy prepared food** Buy food that does not require much prepping or handling. For example, you could buy precooked chicken breasts or chopped lettuce.

Food handlers should avoid time-temperature abuse by following good policies and procedures. These should address the areas in Table 5.2.

Table 5.2: **Avoiding Time-Temperature Abuse**

Monitoring
Learn which food items should be checked, how often, and by whom. Make sure food handlers understand what to do, how to do it, and why it is important.

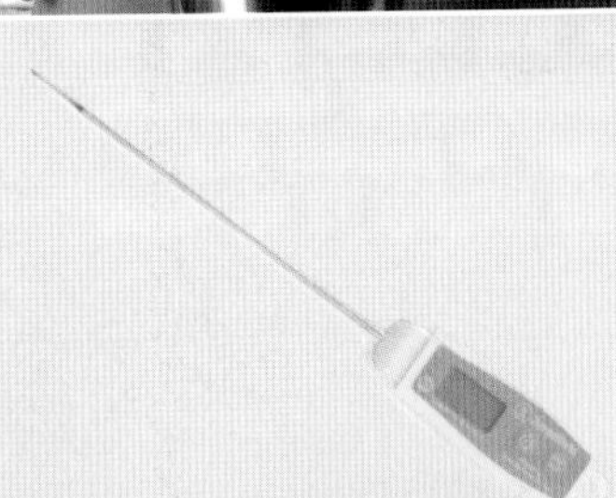

Tools
Make sure the correct kinds of thermometers are available. Give food handlers their own thermometers. Have them use timers in prep areas to check how long food is in the temperature danger zone.

Recording
Have food handlers record temperatures regularly. Make sure they write down when the temperatures were taken. Print simple forms for recording this information. Post them on clipboards outside of coolers and freezers, near prep areas, and next to cooking and holding equipment.

Time and temperature control
Have procedures to limit the time TCS food spends in the temperature danger zone. This might include limiting the amount of food that can be removed from a cooler when prepping the food.

Corrective actions
Make sure food handlers know what to do when time and temperature standards are not met. For example, if you hold soup on a steam table and its temperature falls below 135°F (57°C) after two hours, you might reheat it to the correct temperature or throw it out.

Monitoring Time and Temperature

To keep food safe, you must control the amount of time it spends in the temperature danger zone. This requires monitoring food temperatures. The most important tool you have is the thermometer. There are many types of thermometers. Three types are commonly used in foodservice operations:

- Bimetallic stemmed thermometers
- Thermocouples
- Thermistors

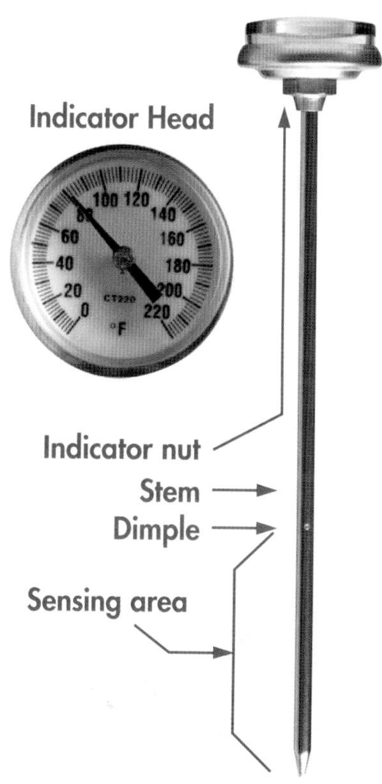

Bimetallic Stemmed Thermometers

A **bimetallic stemmed thermometer**, shown in the photo at right, checks temperatures from 0°F to 220°F (–18°C to 104°C). This makes it useful for checking temperatures during the flow of food. For example, you can use it to check food temperatures both during receiving and in a hot- or cold-holding unit.

A bimetallic stemmed thermometer measures temperatures through a metal stem. When checking temperatures, insert the stem into the food up to the dimple. You must do this because the sensing area goes from the tip of the stem to the dimple. This trait makes the thermometer useful for checking the temperature of large or thick food. It is usually not practical for thin food, such as hamburger patties.

If you purchase bimetallic stemmed thermometers for your operation, make sure they have the following features.

Calibration nut You can make the thermometer accurate by adjusting its calibration nut.

Easy-to-read markings Clear markings reduce the chance that someone will misread the thermometer. The thermometer must be scaled in at least two-degree increments.

Dimple The dimple is the mark on the stem that shows the end of the temperature-sensing area.

Thermocouples and Thermistors

Thermocouples, such as the one in the photo at right, and **thermistors** are also common types of thermometers in foodservice operations. These tools are similar. The difference between them is the technology inside.

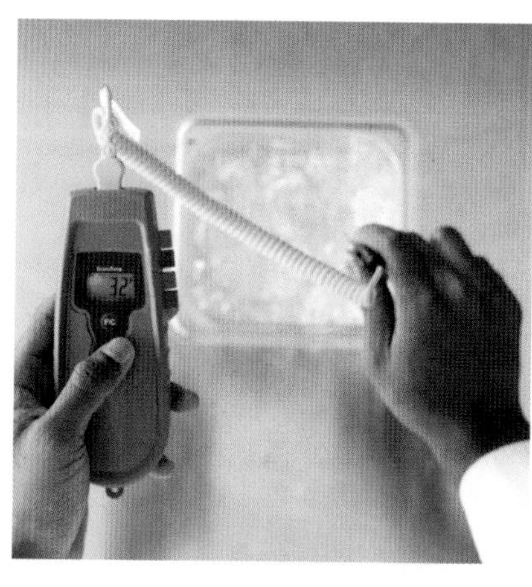

Thermocouples and thermistors measure temperatures through a metal probe. Temperatures are displayed digitally. The sensing area on thermocouples and thermistors is on the tip of their probe. This means you do not have to insert them into the food as far as bimetallic stemmed thermometers to get a correct reading. Thermocouples and thermistors are good for checking the temperature of both thick and thin food.

Thermocouples and thermistors are available in multiple sizes and styles. Many come with different types of probes, shown in Table 5.3.

Table 5.3: **Types of Probes**

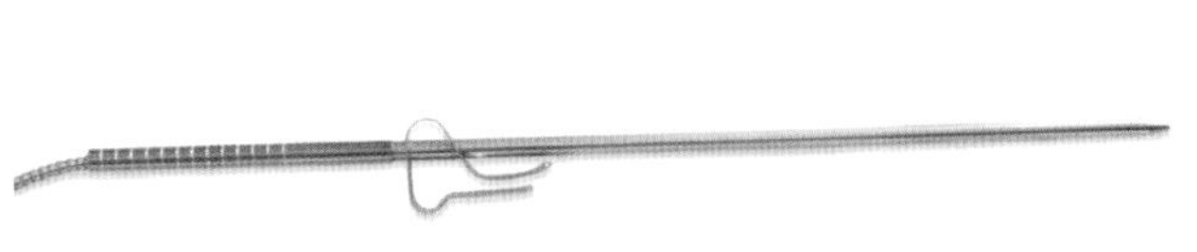	**Immersion probes** Use these to check the temperature of liquids. This could include soups, sauces, and frying oil.
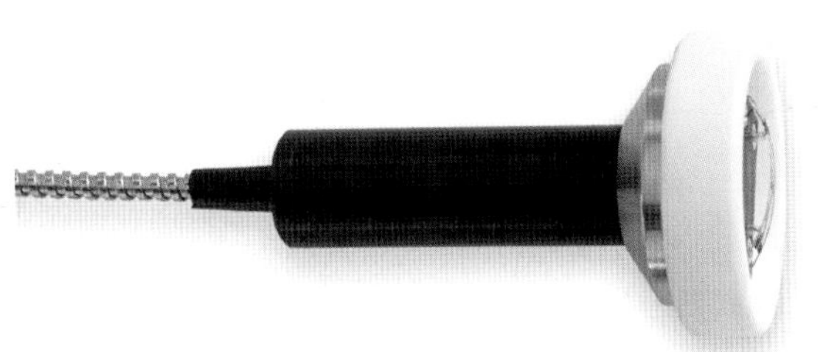	**Surface probes** Use these to check the temperature of flat cooking equipment, such as griddles.
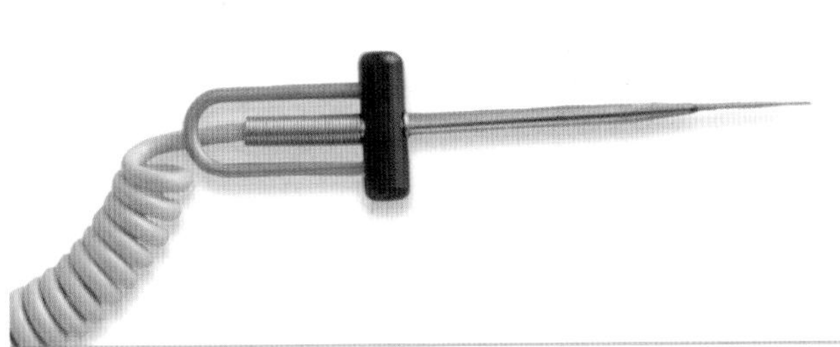	**Penetration probes** Use these to check the internal temperature of food. They are especially useful for checking the temperature of thin food, such as hamburger patties or fish fillets.
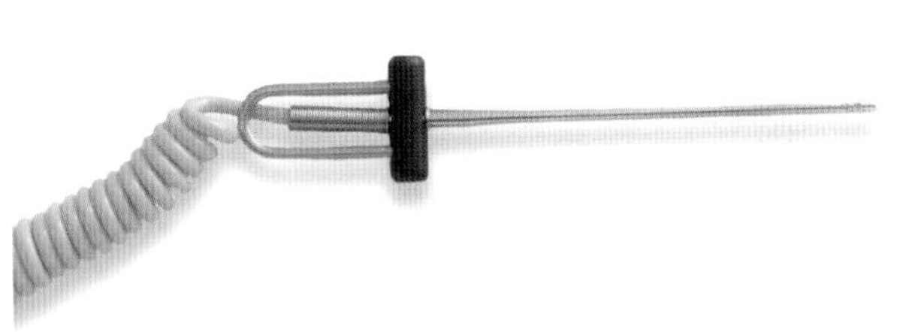	**Air probes** Use these to check the temperature inside coolers and ovens.

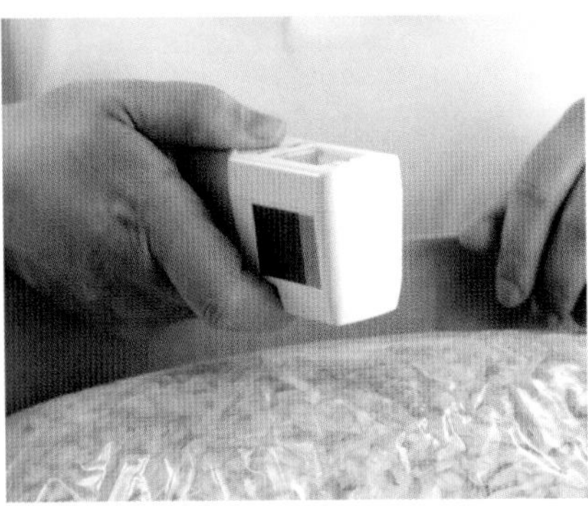

Infrared (Laser) Thermometers

Infrared thermometers, as shown in the photo at left, measure the temperature of food and equipment surfaces. These thermometers are quick and easy to use.

Infrared thermometers do not need to touch a surface to check its temperature. This means there is less chance for cross-contamination and damage to food. However, these thermometers cannot measure air temperature or the internal temperature of food.

Follow these guidelines for using infrared thermometers.

Distance Hold the thermometer as close to the food or equipment as you can without touching it.

Barriers Remove anything between the thermometer and the food, food package, or equipment. Avoid taking readings through metal, such as stainless steel or aluminum, or through glass.

Manufacturer's directions Always follow the manufacturer's guidelines. This should give you the most accurate readings.

Other Temperature-Recording Devices

Other tools are available that can help you monitor temperature. A maximum registering thermometer is one type. This thermometer indicates the highest temperature reached during use. It is used where temperature readings cannot be continuously observed. It works well for checking the final rinse temperature of dishwashing machines.

Some devices monitor both time and temperature. The **time-temperature indicator (TTI)**, shown in the photo at right, is an example. These tags are attached to packaging by the supplier. A color change appears in the TTI window if the food has been time-temperature abused during shipment or storage. This color change is not reversible, so you know if the item has been abused.

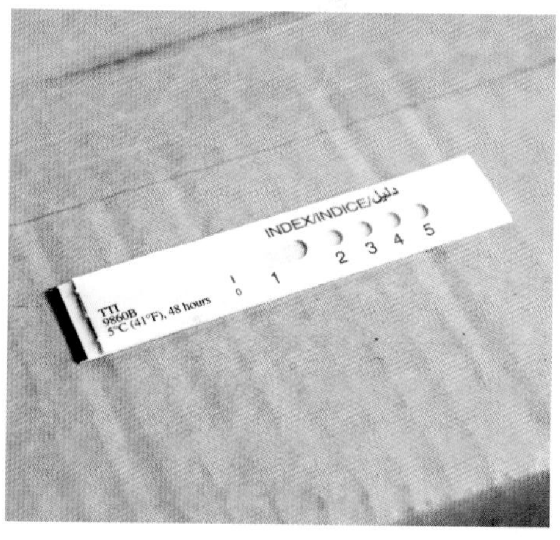

Some suppliers place temperature-recording devices inside their delivery trucks. These devices constantly monitor and record temperatures. You can check the device during receiving to make sure food remained at safe temperatures while it was being shipped.

How to Calibrate Thermometers

Thermometers can lose their accuracy when they are bumped or dropped. It can also happen when they go through a severe temperature change. When this happens, the thermometer needs **calibration**, or an adjustment, to give a correct reading. Thermometers that cannot be calibrated should be replaced. Others might need to be sent back to the manufacturer for calibration. Always follow the manufacturer's directions.

There are two ways to calibrate a thermometer:

- The **ice-point method** involves adjusting the thermometer to the temperature at which water freezes (32°F [0°C]).
- The **boiling-point method** involves adjusting the thermometer to the temperature at which water boils (212°F [100°C], depending on your elevation).

Boiling-Point Method

To calibrate a thermometer using the boiling-point method, follow these steps:

1 **Bring clean tap water to a boil in a deep pan.**

2 **Put the thermometer stem or probe into the boiling water. Make sure the sensing area is submerged. Wait 30 seconds or until the indicator stops moving.**

Note: *Do not let the stem or probe touch the container.*

3 **Adjust the thermometer so it reads 212°F (100°C).**

Notes:

- *This temperature will vary depending on the boiling point for your elevation. Water's boiling point is about 1°F (about 0.5°C) lower for every 550 feet (168 meters) above sea level.*
- *If you are using a bimetallic stemmed thermometer, adjust it by holding the calibration nut with a wrench or other tool.*
- *If you are using a thermocouple or thermistor, some devices will let you press a reset button. Always follow the manufacturer's directions.*

Ice-Point Method

The ice-point method of calibration is easier and safer than the boiling-point method. Follow the steps below to use this method.

1 **Fill a large container with ice. Use crushed ice if you have it. Add tap water until the container is full.**

Note: *Stir the mixture well.*

2 **Put the thermometer stem or probe into the ice water. Make sure the sensing area is submerged.**

Wait 30 seconds or until the indicator stops moving.

Note: *Do not let the stem or probe touch the container.*

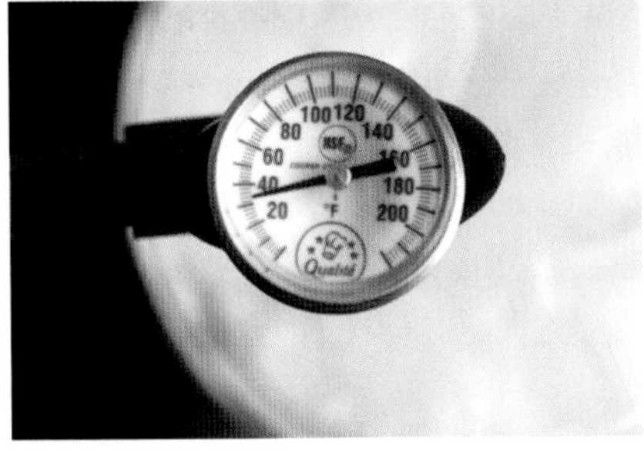

3 **Adjust the thermometer so it reads 32°F (0°C).**

Notes:

- *To calibrate a bimetallic stemmed thermometer, adjust it by holding the calibration nut with a wrench or other tool.*
- *To calibrate a thermocouple or thermistor, follow the manufacturer's directions.*

General Thermometer Guidelines

You should know how to use and care for each type of thermometer in your operation. You can follow the general guidelines below. However, you should always follow manufacturers' directions.

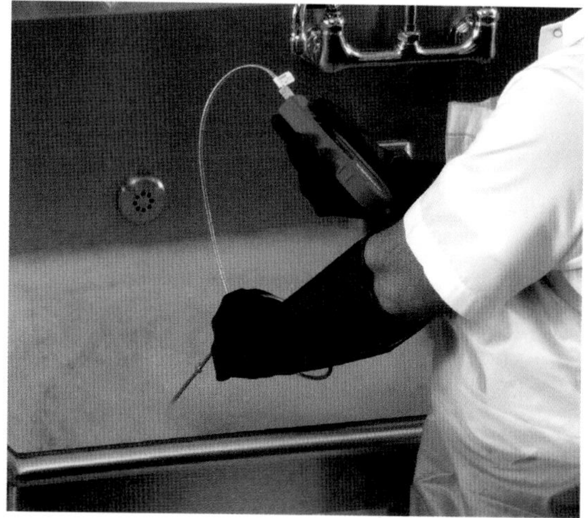

Cleaning and sanitizing Thermometers must be washed, rinsed, sanitized (as shown in the photo at right), and air-dried. Keep storage cases clean as well. Do these things before and after using thermometers to prevent cross-contamination. Be sure the sanitizing solution you are using is for food-contact surfaces. Always have plenty of clean and sanitized thermometers on hand.

Calibration Thermometers can lose their accuracy. Make sure your thermometers are accurate by calibrating them regularly. Calibrate thermometers at these times:

- After they have been bumped or dropped
- After they have been exposed to extreme temperature changes
- Before deliveries arrive
- Before each shift

Keep in mind that some thermometers cannot be calibrated and must be replaced or sent back to the manufacturer for calibration. Always follow the manufacturer's guidelines for calibration.

Accuracy Thermometers used to measure the temperature of food need to be accurate to within ±2°F or ±1°C. Thermometers used to measure air temperature in food storage equipment need to be accurate to within ±3°F or ±1.5°C.

Glass thermometers Glass thermometers, such as candy thermometers, can be a physical contaminant if they break. They can only be used when enclosed in a shatterproof casing.

Checking temperatures When checking the temperature of food:

- Insert the thermometer stem or probe into the thickest part of the food, as shown in the photo at right. This is usually in the center.
- Take another reading in a different spot. The temperature may vary in different areas.

Before recording a temperature, wait for the thermometer reading to steady. While digital thermometers can display the temperature instantly, bimetallic stemmed thermometers need at least 15 seconds after you insert the thermometer stem into the food.

Chapter Summary

- The flow of food is the path food takes in your operation from purchasing to service. Many things can happen to food in its flow through the operation. Two major concerns are cross-contamination and time-temperature abuse.
- To prevent cross-contamination, keep ready-to-eat and raw food separated. When possible, use separate equipment for each type of food. Clean and sanitize all work surfaces, equipment, and utensils before and after each task. When separate equipment cannot be used, prep ready-to-eat food and raw meat, poultry, and fish at different times. Prepping ready-to-eat food first minimizes the chance for contamination. Similarly, you can buy food items that do not require much preparation or handling.
- Time-temperature abuse happens any time food remains between 41°F and 135°F (5°C and 57°C). This range is called the temperature danger zone. You must try to keep food out of this range.
- Have policies and procedures to avoid time-temperature abuse. They should include monitoring food and recording temperatures and times. Also make sure the correct types of thermometers are available. Use timers to check how long food is in the temperature danger zone. Make sure food handlers know what to do if time and temperature standards are not met.
- A thermometer is the most important tool you can use to prevent time-temperature abuse. Different types of thermometers are suited to different tasks. Use the correct type for the food or equipment being checked. Clean and sanitize thermometers before and after each use.
- When checking food temperatures, put the thermometer stem or probe into the thickest part of the food. Then take another reading in a different spot. Before you record the temperature, wait for the thermometer reading to steady. If using a bimetallic stemmed thermometer, put it into the food from the tip to the end of the sensing area. Never use glass thermometers with food items unless they are enclosed in a shatterproof casing.
- Thermometers should be calibrated regularly to keep them accurate. Two methods for calibrating are the ice-point method and the boiling-point method. Follow the manufacturer's directions for calibration.

Apply Your Knowledge

Use these questions to review the concepts presented in this chapter.

Discussion Questions

1 What are some ways food can be time-temperature abused?

2 How can cross-contamination be prevented in the operation?

3 How is a thermometer calibrated using the ice-point method?

For answers, please turn to the Answer Key.

Apply Your Knowledge

Something to Think About

Cross-Contamination Stops Truck in Its Tracks

A popular food truck servicing the boardwalk area of a large beach resort community was cited for cross-contamination by the local regulatory authority.

The operator received violations for prepping raw chicken breasts and then fresh herbs on the same cutting board. The authorities also determined that he was using the same knife to trim raw meat and chop lettuce.

1 What should the operator of the food truck have done differently?

For answers, please turn to the Answer Key.

Apply Your Knowledge

Something to Think About

Tour Canceled by Outbreak

A group of seniors from a local community decided to organize a tour of several nearby wineries. The seniors contracted with a coach bus service and worked out accommodations for the trip. They also ordered box lunches from a local catering company.

The lunches arrived just before 7:00 a.m. on a warm summer morning on the day of the tour. They were immediately placed in the luggage compartment of the bus. The boxes contained chicken salad, sliced ham sandwiches, a small cup of fresh fruit, a bag of baked chips, and a brownie.

The bus pulled over at a picnic area around noon, and the box lunches were passed out to the seniors. Within the hour, 16 seniors got sick with nausea and vomiting. The remainder of the trip was canceled, and the bus returned to the senior center.

1 What caused the illnesses?

2 What could have been done to prevent the illnesses?

For answers, please turn to the Answer Key.

Study Questions

Circle the best answer to each question.

1 **A food handler has finished trimming raw chicken on a cutting board and needs the cutting board to prep vegetables. What must be done to the cutting board?**

- A It must be dried with a paper towel.
- B It must be turned over to the other side.
- C It must be washed, rinsed, and sanitized.
- D It must be rinsed in hot water and air-dried.

2 **How far must a bimetallic stemmed thermometer be inserted into food to give an accurate reading?**

- A Just past the tip of the thermometer stem
- B Halfway between the tip of the thermometer stem and the dimple
- C Up to the dimple in the thermometer stem
- D Past the dimple of the thermometer stem

3 **What probe should be used to check the temperature of a chicken breast?**

- A Air probe
- B Surface probe
- C Immersion probe
- D Penetration probe

4 **What device can be used to record time-temperature abuse during the delivery of food?**

- A Thermocouple
- B Thermistor
- C Time-temperature indicator
- D Bimetallic stemmed thermometer

Study Questions

5 **At what temperatures do most foodborne pathogens grow most quickly?**

A Between 0°F and 41°F (-18°C and 5°C)

B Between 45°F and 65°F (7°C and 18°C)

C Between 70°F and 125°F (21°C and 52°C)

D Between 130°F and 165°F (54°C and 74°C)

6 **Which thermometer is limited to measuring surface temperatures?**

A Thermistor

B Thermocouple

C Infrared thermometer

D Bimetallic stemmed thermometer

7 **A thermometer used to measure the temperature of food must be accurate to what temperature?**

A ±2°F or ±1°C

B ±4°F or ±3°C

C ±6°F or ±5°C

D ±8°F or ±7°C

8 **While getting ready to check the temperature of a roast chicken, a chef dropped a bimetallic stemmed thermometer onto a prep table. What should the chef do next?**

A Check the dimple

B Calibrate the thermometer

C Clean and sanitize the thermometer

D Take the temperature of the roast chicken

For answers, please turn to the Answer Key.

Notes

Notes

6 The Flow of Food: Purchasing and Receiving

More Than They Bargained For

The chef at a newly opened seafood restaurant on the coast of California wanted to outdo her competition by providing the freshest seafood available. She could often be found down on the docks purchasing fresh seafood from the local fishers. On a recent trip to the docks, she purchased some barracuda for the nightly special. That night, the chef told the servers to really push the item. The barracuda sold out quickly.

Several customers called the operation the next morning complaining of nausea and vomiting. Later, the same customers experienced joint and muscle pain and tingling in their fingers. All of them suffered from the reversal of hot and cold sensations. It was later discovered that the customers had contracted ciguatera fish poisoning.

1. **What did the chef do wrong?**
2. **What should she have done differently?**

For answers, please turn to the Answer Key.

Inside This Chapter

- Purchasing Considerations
- Receiving Considerations
- General Inspection Guidelines
- Inspecting Specific Types of Food

Objectives

After completing this chapter, you should be able to identify the following:

- Characteristics of an approved supplier
- Guidelines for receiving and inspecting deliveries
- Requirements for key drop deliveries
- Procedure for handling food recalls
- Procedures for checking the temperatures of various food items
- Temperature requirements when receiving food
- Packaging requirements when receiving food
- Documentation required when receiving food
- Government inspection stamps required when receiving food
- Quality requirements when receiving food
- Receiving criteria for specific food items

Key Terms

Approved suppliers

Key drop delivery

Use-by date

Expiration date

Sell-by date

Best-by date

Shellstock identification tags

Inspection stamp

Purchasing Considerations

The final responsibility for the safety of food entering your operation resides with you. You can avoid many potential food safety hazards by using approved, reputable suppliers. Consider the following when making your selection.

Approved, reputable suppliers **Food must be purchased from approved suppliers. These suppliers have been inspected and can show you an inspection report. Approved suppliers also meet applicable local, state, and federal laws. These standards apply to all suppliers in the food chain, which can include growers, shippers, packers, manufacturers, distributors (trucking fleets and warehouses), and local markets. Develop relationships with all of your suppliers, and verify that they have good food safety practices. In the photo shown at left, an owner is meeting with a supplier and touring the facility.**

Many operations establish supplier lists based on their company specifications, standards, and procedures. However, only approved, reputable suppliers should be included on these lists.

Inspection reports Consider reviewing suppliers' most recent inspection reports. These can be from the U.S. Department of Agriculture (USDA), the Food and Drug Administration (FDA), or a third-party inspector. They should be based on Good Manufacturing Practices (GMP) or Good Agricultural Practices (GAP).

GMPs are the FDA's minimum sanitation and processing requirements for producing safe food. They describe the methods, equipment, facilities, and controls used to process food. Both suppliers and their sources are subject to GMP inspections.

Make sure an inspection report reviews the following areas:

- Receiving and storage
- Processing
- Shipping
- Cleaning and sanitizing
- Personal hygiene
- Staff training
- Recall program
- HACCP program or other food safety system

Receiving Considerations

Receiving Guidelines

Having procedures in place for inspecting food can reduce hazards before they enter your operation. Here are some guidelines that can help you improve the way you receive deliveries.

Scheduling Suppliers should deliver food when staff have enough time to inspect it. Schedule deliveries at a time when they can be received correctly.

Staff needs Make specific staff responsible for receiving. Train them to follow food safety procedures, including checking items for correct temperatures, expired code dates, signs of thawing and refreezing, and pest damage. In the photo at right, a food handler is inspecting produce. Staff should be able to accept, reject, and sign for deliveries. Also, provide them with the tools they need, including purchase orders, temperature logs, thermometers, and scales. Then make sure that enough trained staff are available to receive and inspect food promptly.

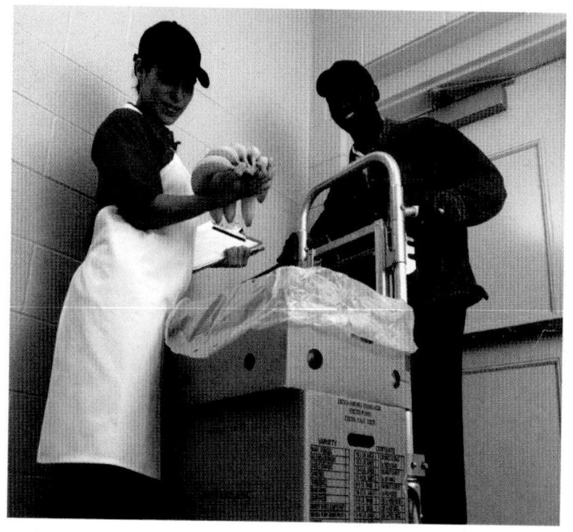

Good preparation Plan ahead for deliveries. Have clean hand trucks, carts, dollies, and containers ready. Also make sure there is enough space in dry-storage and walk-in areas for deliveries.

Timing and process for inspections Deliveries must be inspected immediately upon receipt. The process starts with a visual inspection of the delivery truck. Check it for signs of contamination. Inspect the overall condition of the vehicle. Look for signs of pests. If there are signs of problems, reject the delivery.

Continue with a visual inspection of food items. Look at each delivery right away to count quantities, check for damaged food, and look for items that might have been repacked or mishandled. Spot-check weights and take sample temperatures of all TCS food, as shown in the photo at right. Inspect and store each delivery before accepting another one. This will prevent temperature abuse in the receiving area.

Key Drop Deliveries

Some foodservice operations receive food after-hours when they are closed for business. This is often referred to as a **key drop delivery**. The supplier is given a key or other access to the operation to make the delivery. Products are then placed in coolers, freezers, and dry-storage areas. The delivery must be inspected once you arrive at the operation and must meet the following conditions:

- It is from an approved supplier.
- It was placed in the correct storage location to maintain the required temperature and was protected from contamination.
- It has not been contaminated.
- It is honestly presented.

Rejecting Deliveries

You can refuse any delivery that does not meet your standards. Staff should know how to reject an item or a shipment:

1. Set the rejected item aside from the items you are accepting.
2. Tell the delivery person exactly what is wrong with the item. Use your purchase order or invoice to support your decision.
3. Get a signed adjustment or credit slip from the delivery person before giving the item back to the delivery person.
4. Log the incident on the invoice or receiving document. Be specific about the action taken and the item involved.

Occasionally you may be able to recondition and use items that would have been rejected. For example, a shipment of cans with contaminated surfaces may be cleaned and sanitized, allowing them to be used. However, the same cans may not be reconditioned if they are damaged.

Recalls

Food items you have received may sometimes be recalled by the manufacturer. This may happen when food contamination is confirmed or suspected. It can also occur when items have been mislabeled or misbranded. Often food is recalled when food allergens have not been identified on the label. Most vendors will notify you of the recall. However, you should also monitor recall notifications made by the FDA and the USDA.

Follow these guidelines when notified of a recall:

- Identify the recalled food items by matching information from the recall notice to the item. This may include the manufacturer's ID, the time the item was manufactured, and the item's use-by date.

- Remove the item from inventory, and place it in a secure and appropriate location. That may be a cooler or dry-storage area. The recalled item must be stored separately from food, utensils, equipment, linens, and single-use items.
- Label the item in a way that will prevent it from being placed back in inventory. Some operations do this by including a "Do Not Use" and "Do Not Discard" label on recalled food items, as shown in the photo at right. Inform staff not to use the product.
- Refer to the vendor's notification or recall notice for what to do with the item. For example, you might be instructed to throw it out or return it to the vendor.

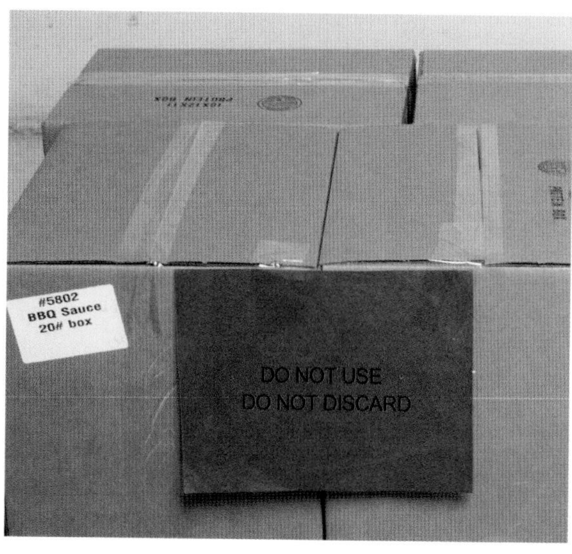

General Inspection Guidelines

When inspecting deliveries, focus on checking product temperatures, packaging, documentation, and the quality of the food. These can provide important evidence as to whether or not the food is safe.

Checking Temperatures

Use thermometers to check food temperatures. The following examples explain how to check the temperatures of various types of food.

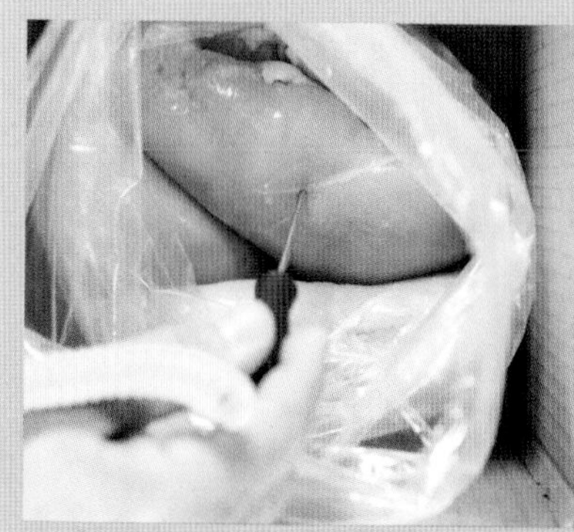

Meat, poultry, and fish

Insert the thermometer stem or probe directly into the thickest part of the food. The center is usually the thickest part.

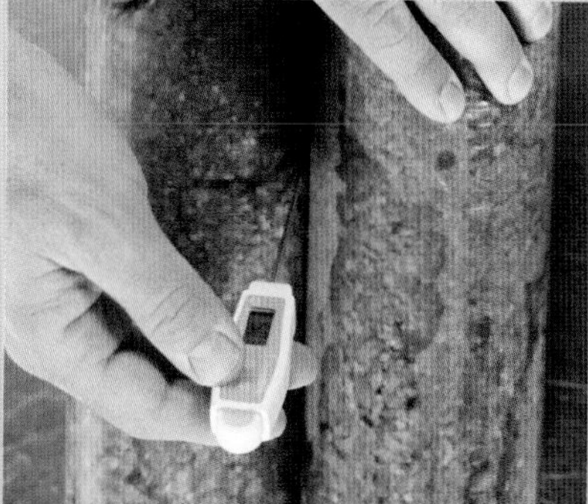

Reduced-oxygen packaging (ROP) food (modified atmosphere packaging [MAP], vacuum-packed, and sous vide food)

Insert the thermometer stem or probe between two packages. If the package allows, fold it around the thermometer stem or probe. Be careful **NOT** to puncture the package.

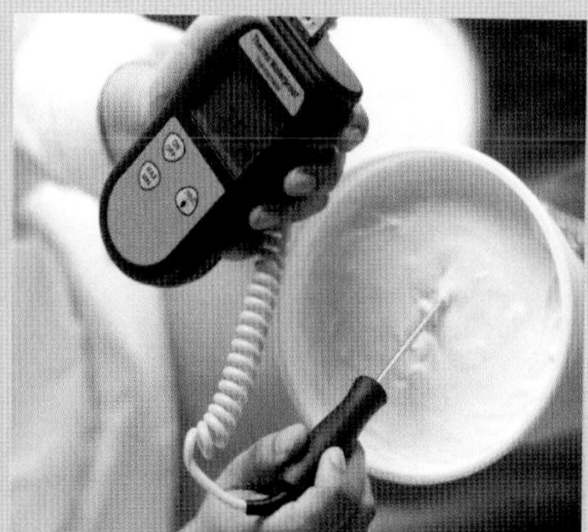

Other packaged food

Open the package and insert the thermometer stem or probe into the food. The sensing area must be fully immersed in the food. The stem or probe must **NOT** touch the package.

Temperature Requirements

Deliveries should be received at the temperatures indicated in Table 6.1.

Table 6.1: **Receiving Criteria for Food Deliveries**

	**Cold TCS food** • Receive at 41°F (5°C) or lower, unless otherwise specified.
	**Live shellfish (oysters, mussels, clams, and scallops)** • Receive at an air temperature of 45°F (7°C) and an internal temperature no greater than 50°F (10°C). • Cool the shellfish to 41°F (5°C) or lower in four hours.
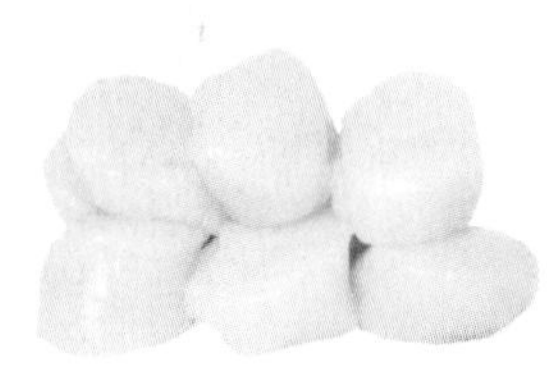	**Shucked shellfish** • Receive at 45°F (7°C) or lower. • Cool the shellfish to 41°F (5°C) or lower in four hours.
	**Milk** • Receive at 45°F (7°C) or lower. • Cool the milk to 41°F (5°C) or lower in four hours.
	**Shell eggs** • Receive at an air temperature of 45°F (7°C) or lower.

Table 6.1: **Receiving Criteria for Food Deliveries** *(continued)*

	**Hot TCS food** • Receive at 135°F (57°C) or higher.
	**Frozen food** • Frozen food should be frozen solid when received. **REJECT** frozen food for the following reasons: • Fluids or water stains appear in case bottoms or on packaging. • There are ice crystals or frozen liquids on the food or the packaging. This may be evidence of thawing and refreezing, which shows the food has been time-temperature abused.

Packaging

Both food items and nonfood items such as single-use cups, utensils, and napkins must be packaged correctly when you receive them. Items should be delivered in their original packaging with a manufacturer's label. The packaging should be intact and clean. It should protect food and food-contact surfaces from contamination.

Reject food and nonfood items if the packaging has any of the following problems.

Damage Reject items with tears, holes, or punctures in their packaging. Likewise, reject cans if they have any of these problems:

- Severe dents in the can seams, as shown in the photo at right
- Deep dents in the can body
- Missing labels
- Swollen or bulging ends
- Holes and visible signs of leaking
- Rust

All food packaged in a reduced-oxygen environment, such as vacuum-packed meat, must be rejected if the packaging is bloated or leaking, as show in the photo at right. Items with broken cartons or seals or with dirty or discolored packaging should also be rejected. Do **NOT** accept cases or packages that appear to have been tampered with.

Liquid Reject items with leaks, dampness, or water stains (which indicate the item was wet at some point). The flour bag shown at left has a water stain. Reject items if there are large ice crystals or frozen liquids on the packaging. This may be evidence of thawing and refreezing, which shows the food has been time-temperature abused.

Pests Reject items with signs of pests or pest damage.

Dates Food must be correctly labeled. Do **NOT** accept food that is missing a **use-by date** or **expiration date** from the manufacturer. This date is the recommended last date for the product to be at peak quality. Reject items that have passed their use-by or expiration dates. Some operations label food items with the date the item was received to help with stock rotation during storage.

You may see other dates on labels. A **sell-by date** tells the store how long to display the product for sale. A **best-by date** is the date by which the product should be eaten for best flavor or quality.

Documents and Stamps

Food items must be delivered with the correct documents. For example, shellfish must be received with a **shellstock identification tag**. These tags indicate when and where the shellfish were harvested. They also ensure that the shellfish are from an approved source. A shellstock tag is shown in the photo below.

ORIGINAL SHIPPER'S CERT. No. IF OTHER THAN ABOVE:MA10534SS
HARVEST DATE:12-8-18 SHIPPING DATE:12-8-18
HARVEST LOCATION:SC-47 MA
TYPE OF SHELLFISH: CHERRY STONE CLAMS WILD
PRODUCT OF: USA
QUANTITY OF SHELLFISH:50 ct
THIS TAG IS REQUIRED TO BE ATTACHED UNTIL CONTAINER IS EMPTY OR IS RETAGGED AND THEREAFTER KEPT ON FILE FOR 90 DAYS.

TO:	RESHIPPER'S CERT. No.	DATES RESHIPPED
RANDY'S SUPERMARKET		

Store shellfish in their original container. Do **NOT** remove the shellstock tag from the container until the last shellfish has been used. When the last shellfish is removed from the container, write the date on the shellstock tag. Then, keep the tag on file for 90 days from that date.

Fish that will be eaten raw or partially cooked must also be received with the correct documentation. These documents must indicate the fish was correctly frozen before you received it. Keep these documents for 90 days from the sale of the fish. If the fish was farm raised, it must have documentation that states the fish was raised to FDA standards. These documents must also be kept for 90 days from the sale of the fish.

Inspection and Grading Stamps

Meat must be purchased from plants inspected by the USDA or a state department of agriculture. Note that "inspected" does not mean that the product is free of pathogens; rather, it means that the product and the processing plant have met defined standards.

Carcasses and packages of meat that have been inspected will have an **inspection stamp** with abbreviations for "inspected and passed" by the inspecting agency, along with a number identifying the processing plant. An example of this stamp appears in the top illustration at right.

Poultry is inspected by the USDA or the state department of agriculture in much the same way as meat. An example of a poultry inspection stamp is shown in the bottom illustration at right.

Liquid, frozen, and dehydrated eggs must also have a USDA inspection mark. These types of eggs are required by law to be pasteurized.

Note that grading stamps might also appear on packages of eggs, meat, and poultry. Grading of these types of products is voluntary and paid for by processors and packers.

Food Quality

Poor food quality can be a sign that the food has been time-temperature abused and, therefore, may be unsafe. Work with your suppliers to define specific safety and quality criteria for the food items you typically receive. Reject food if it has any of the following problems.

Appearance Reject food that is moldy or has an abnormal color, as shown in the photo at right. Food that is moist when it should be dry, such as salami, should also be rejected. Do not accept any food item that shows signs of pests or pest damage. Reject frozen food that has large ice crystals on it. This may be evidence of thawing and refreezing.

Texture Reject meat, fish, or poultry that is slimy, sticky, or dry. Also reject it if it has soft flesh that leaves an imprint when you touch it.

Odor Reject food with an abnormal or unpleasant odor.

In addition to the guidelines above, you should always reject any item that does not meet your operation's standards for quality.

Inspecting Specific Types of Food

Certain types of food have specific criteria for accepting or rejecting them, as shown in Table 6.2.

Table 6.2: **Receiving Criteria for Specific Types of Food**

Fresh Fish

	Accept criteria	Reject criteria	
	**Color:** Bright red gills; bright shiny skin **Texture:** Firm flesh that springs back when touched **Odor:** Mild ocean or seaweed smell **Eyes:** Bright, clear, full **Packaging:** Product surrounded by crushed, self-draining ice	**Color:** Dull gray gills; dull dry skin **Texture:** Soft flesh that leaves an imprint when touched **Odor:** Strong fishy or ammonia smell **Eyes:** Cloudy, red-rimmed, sunken **Product:** Tumors, abscesses, or cysts on the skin	

Shellfish

	Accept criteria	Reject criteria	
	**Odor:** Mild ocean or seaweed smell **Shells:** Closed and unbroken, indicating that the shellfish are alive **Condition:** If fresh, they must be received alive	**Texture:** Slimy, sticky, or dry **Odor:** Strong fishy smell **Shells:** Excessively muddy or broken shells **Condition:** Dead on arrival (open shells that do not close when tapped)	

Crustaceans

	Accept criteria	Reject criteria	
	**Odor:** Mild ocean or seaweed smell **Condition:** Shipped alive, packed in seaweed, and kept moist	**Odor:** Strong fishy smell **Condition:** Dead on arrival	

Table 6.2: **Receiving Criteria for Specific Types of Food** *(continued)*

	Accept criteria	Reject criteria	
Meat			
 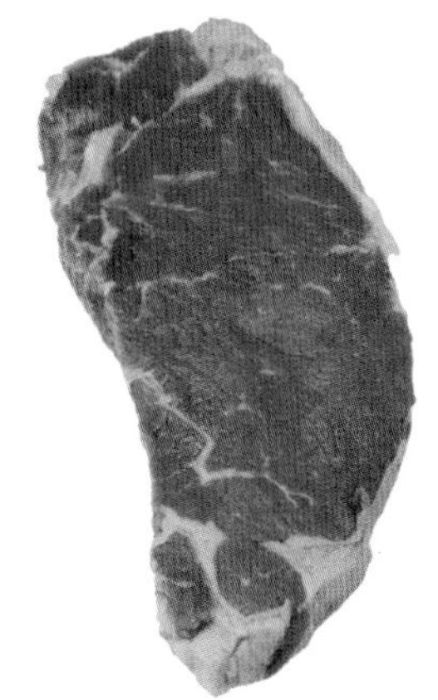	**Color:** • Beef: bright cherry red; aged beef may be darker; vacuum-packed beef will appear purplish • Lamb: light red • Pork: light pink meat; firm, white fat **Texture:** Firm flesh that springs back when touched **Odor:** No odor **Packaging:** Intact and clean	**Color:** • Beef: brown or green • Lamb: brown, whitish surface covering the lean meat • Pork: excessively dark color; soft or rancid fat **Texture:** Slimy, sticky, or dry **Odor:** Sour odor **Packaging:** Broken cartons; dirty wrappers; torn packaging; broken seals	 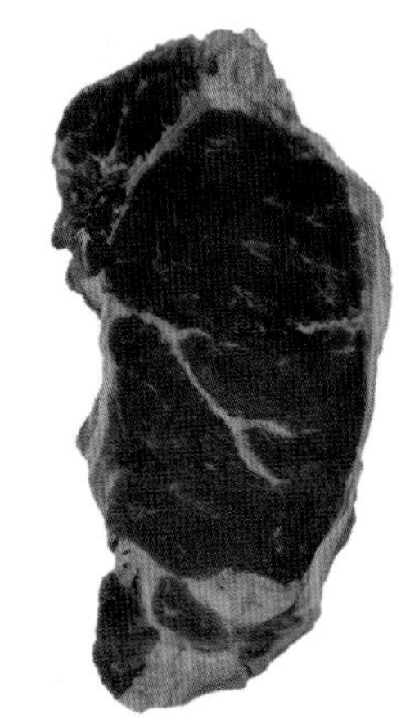
Poultry			
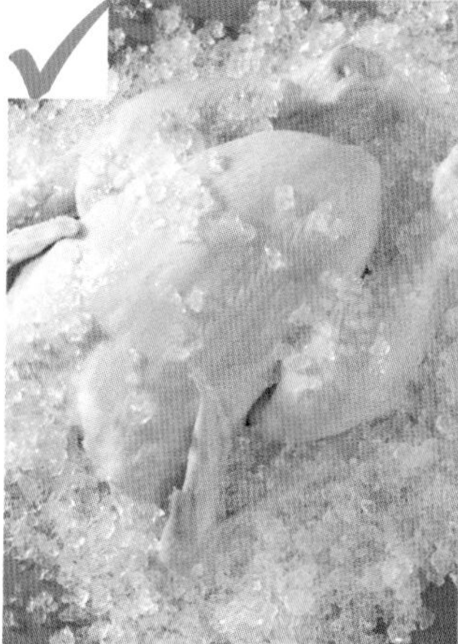	**Color:** No discoloration **Texture:** Firm flesh that springs back when touched **Odor:** No odor **Packaging:** Should be surrounded by crushed, self-draining ice	**Color:** Purple or green discoloration around the neck; dark wing tips (red are acceptable) **Texture:** Stickiness under the wings and around joints **Odor:** Abnormal, unpleasant odor	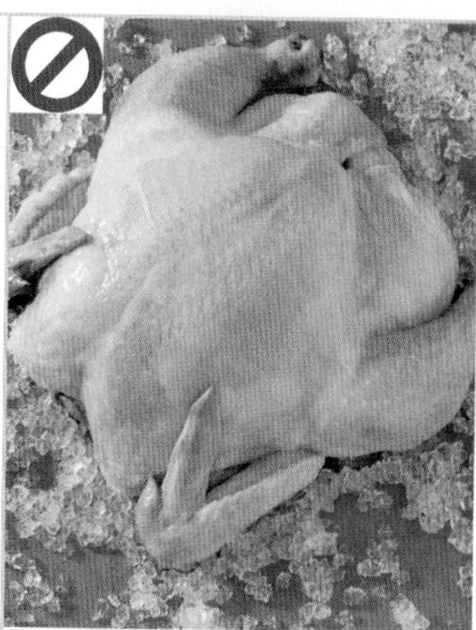
Shell eggs			
	**Odor:** No odor **Shells:** Clean and unbroken	**Odor:** Sulfur smell or off odor **Shells:** Dirty or cracked	

Table 6.2: **Receiving Criteria for Specific Types of Food** *(continued)*

Dairy products

	Accept criteria	Reject criteria	
	**Milk:** Sweetish flavor **Butter:** Sweet flavor; uniform color; firm texture **Cheese:** Typical flavor and texture; uniform color; clean and unbroken rind	**Milk:** Sour, bitter, or moldy taste; off odor; expired sell-by date **Butter:** Sour, bitter, or moldy taste; uneven color; soft texture; contains foreign matter **Cheese:** Abnormal flavor or texture; uneven color; unnatural mold; unclean or broken rind	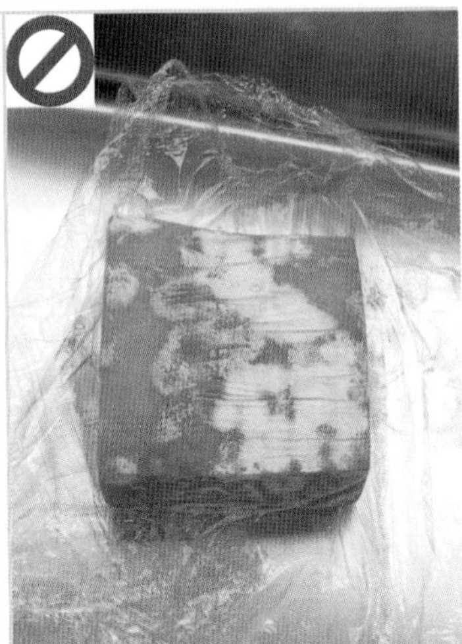

Fresh Produce

	Accept criteria	Reject criteria	
	**Temperature:** Varies according to the product **Condition:** Varies according to the product	**Condition:** Evidence of mishandling or insects (including insect eggs and egg cases) **Spoilage:** Mold, cuts, wilting, unpleasant odors, discoloration, etc. (will depend on the produce involved)	

Chapter Summary

- Purchase food only from approved, reputable suppliers. These suppliers must be inspected and meet applicable local, state, and federal laws.
- Deliveries must be immediately inspected by designated staff. The staff must be trained to follow food safety guidelines and should be given the proper tools. Start by inspecting the overall condition of the delivery trucks. Then inspect the food. Count quantities, check for damage, and look for items that might have been repacked or mishandled. Spot-check weights. Take sample temperatures of all TCS food.
- When inspecting food items, make sure food is received at safe temperatures. Receive cold TCS food at 41°F (5°C) or lower unless otherwise specified. Receive hot TCS food at 135°F (57°C) or higher. Frozen food should always be received frozen. Some items have other temperature requirements. Make sure items are labeled correctly and have the correct documentation and stamps. Packaging should protect food and food-contact surfaces from contamination and be intact and clean. Make sure food quality is acceptable and meets your operation's standards.
- Sometimes food items are recalled by the manufacturer. Identify these items, remove them from inventory, and secure them in an appropriate location. Mark them so that staff does not use or discard them.
- Key drop deliveries must be inspected as soon as staff arrive. These deliveries must be from an approved supplier, be placed in the correct storage location, be honestly presented, and not be contaminated.
- Poor food quality can be a sign that the food has been time-temperature abused and, therefore, may be unsafe. Work with your suppliers to define specific safety and quality criteria for the food regarding its appearance, texture, and odor.

Apply Your Knowledge

Use these questions to review the concepts presented in this chapter.

Discussion Questions

1 What are some general guidelines for receiving food safely?

2 What are some general guidelines for inspecting food?

3 What are the correct methods for checking the temperatures of fresh poultry delivered on ice and a carton of milk? What should the temperature be for each?

Apply Your Knowledge

4 What are three conditions that would result in rejecting a shipment of fresh poultry?

5 What types of external damage to cans are causes for rejection?

For answers, please turn to the Answer Key.

Apply Your Knowledge

Something to Think About

A Decision to Make

Two friends, who met in their senior year of hotel and restaurant management school, decided to become partners in a new fast-casual concept. The partners felt confident that their college and work experience had prepared them to open their new business—something they had been dreaming of for a long time.

All of the steps started to fall into place quickly. They identified a perfect location in a suburban strip mall, obtained financing, and developed a menu. The clock was ticking toward their projected opening date, yet they still had not selected their suppliers. Both partners turned their attention toward this important task.

1 What should the partners consider as they begin to select their suppliers?

For answers, please turn to the Answer Key.

Apply Your Knowledge

Something to Think About

Delivery Decision Could Cost Them

A large food delivery arrived at the Sunnydale Nursing Home during the busy lunch hour. It included cases of frozen ground beef patties, canned vegetables, frozen shrimp, fresh tomatoes, a case of potatoes, and fresh chicken.

Betty, the new assistant manager, thought the best thing to do was to put everything away and check it later, as she was very busy. She told Ed, who was in charge of receiving, to sign for the delivery and put the food in storage. Ed asked her if it would be better to ask the delivery driver to come back later. Because she needed the chicken for dinner, Betty asked Ed to accept the delivery now, and then she went back to the front of the house.

Ed put the frozen shrimp and ground beef patties in the freezer and the fresh chicken in the refrigerator. Then he put the fresh tomatoes, potatoes, and canned vegetables in dry storage. When he was finished, he went back to work in the kitchen.

1 What was done incorrectly and what is the risk to food safety?

For answers, please turn to the Answer Key.

Study Questions

Circle the best answer to each question.

1 **What is the most important factor in choosing a food supplier?**

A It has a HACCP program or other food safety system.

B It has documented manufacturing and packing practices.

C Its warehouse is close to the operation, reducing shipping time.

D It has been inspected and complies with local, state, and federal laws.

2 **What is the best method of checking the temperature of a delivery of fresh fish?**

A Feel the fish, making sure that it is cold to the touch.

B Insert a thermometer probe into the thickest part of the fish.

C Place a time-temperature indicator on the surface of the fish.

D Use an infrared thermometer to check the fish's temperature.

3 **What is the correct temperature for receiving cold TCS food?**

A 32°F (0°C) or lower

B 41°F (5°C) or lower

C 45°F (7°C) or lower

D 50°F (10°C) or lower

4 **Which item can be received at 45°F (7°C)?**

A Shell eggs

B Ground beef

C Bean sprouts

D Chopped tomatoes

5 **What causes large ice crystals to form on frozen food and its packaging?**

A Cross-contact

B Cross-contamination

C Time-temperature abuse

D Incorrect cleaning and sanitizing

Study Questions

6 **What is required when receiving fish that will be served raw or partially cooked?**

A It must be alive when received.
B It must be thawed in the microwave.
C It must be used within 24 hours of receiving.
D It must be correctly frozen before you receive it.

7 **How should the temperature of vacuum-packed meat be checked during receiving?**

A Lay the thermometer stem or probe on the surface of the top package.
B Place the thermometer stem or probe between two packages of product.
C Open a package and insert the thermometer stem or probe into the product.
D Insert the thermometer stem or probe through the package into the product.

8 **How should cartons of coleslaw be checked for the correct receiving temperature?**

A Touch the carton to see if it is cold.
B Place a thermometer against the outside of the carton.
C Check the interior air temperature of the delivery truck.
D Open a carton and insert a thermometer stem into the food.

9 **What should be done with an item that has been recalled?**

A Arrange for the vendor to pick up the item, notify staff, and document the recall.
B Recondition the item, heat it to its minimum internal temperature, or throw it out.
C Record the item's use-by date, place the item in storage, and note the loss for bookkeeping.
D Remove the item from inventory, put it in a secure location, and label it to keep it from being used or discarded.

10 **Which is a requirement for key drop deliveries?**

A The items are set apart from other inventory.
B The items are able to be reconditioned safely.
C The items are delivered just before staff arrive.
D The items are placed in the correct storage location.

For answers, please turn to the Answer Key.

Notes

Notes

Fatal Outbreak Linked to Incorrect Storage Practices

Two people died and 68 people became severely ill after dining at a family restaurant in the Midwest. An investigation revealed that several 10-pound packages of raw ground beef were incorrectly stored on the top shelf in a walk-in cooler. Authorities determined that the ground beef dripped onto fresh rolls and cartons of chocolate milk that were stored on the shelf below. Guests who had eaten the rolls or were served the cartons of chocolate milk got sick with *E. coli*. The operation, which had voluntarily closed for the investigation, never reopened.

1 **What should have been done differently at the operation to prevent the outbreak?**

For answers, please turn to the Answer Key.

7

The Flow of Food: Storage

Inside This Chapter

- General Storage Guidelines
- Storing Specific Food

Objectives

After completing this chapter, you should be able to identify the following:

- Requirements for labeling and date marking food
- How to rotate food using first-in, first-out (FIFO)
- Temperature requirements for food in storage
- Practices that can prevent temperature abuse during storage
- Practices that can prevent cross-contamination during storage
- Guidelines for storing specific types of food including meat, poultry, fish, shellfish, eggs, producce, and dry food

Key Terms

Date marking

First-in, first-out (FIFO) method

Reduced-oxygen packaged (ROP) food

General Storage Guidelines

When food is stored incorrectly and not used in a timely manner, quality and safety will suffer. The results can be serious.

In general, you must label and date mark your food correctly. You must also rotate food and store it at the correct temperature. Finally, you need to store items in a way that prevents cross-contamination.

Use the following general guidelines when storing food.

Labeling

Labeling food is important for many reasons. Illnesses have occurred when unlabeled chemicals were mistaken for food such as flour, sugar, and baking powder. Customers have also suffered allergic reactions when food was unknowingly prepped with a food allergen that was not identified on the label.

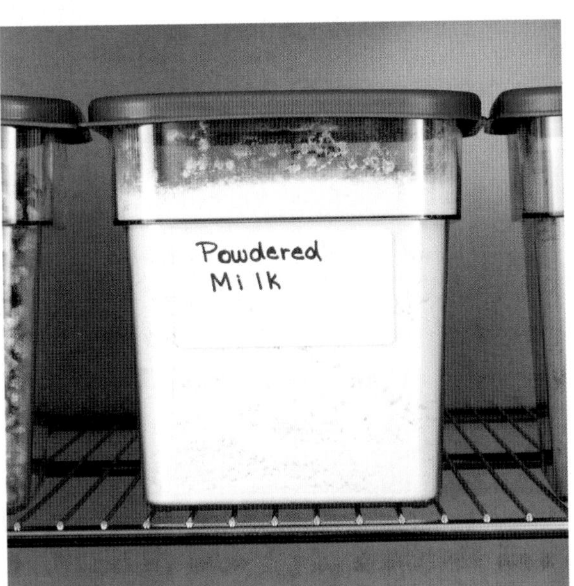

Labeling Food for Use On-Site

Any item not stored in its original container must be labeled. The label must include the common name of the food or a statement that clearly and accurately identifies it, as shown in the photo at left.

If a food is easily identifiable by sight and will not be mistaken for another item, it is not necessary to label the item. An example is dry pasta.

Labeling Food That Is Packaged On-site for Retail Sale

Food packaged in the operation that is being sold to customers for use at home, such as bottled salad dressing, must be labeled. The label must include the following information:

- Common name of the food or a statement that clearly identifies it.
- Quantity of the food.
- List of ingredients and subingredients in descending order by weight. This is necessary if the item contains two or more ingredients.

- List of artificial colors and flavors in the food.
- Chemical preservatives.
- Name and place of business of the manufacturer, packer, or distributor.
- Source of each major food allergen contained in the food. This is not necessary if the source is already part of the common name of the ingredient.

These labeling requirements do not apply to customers' leftover food items placed in carry-out containers.

Date Marking

Refrigeration slows the growth of most bacteria, but some types grow well at refrigeration temperatures. When food is refrigerated for long periods of time, these bacteria can grow enough to cause illness. For this reason, ready-to-eat TCS food must include **date marking** if it will be held for longer than 24 hours. The label must indicate when the food must be sold, eaten, or thrown out, as shown in the photo at right.

Ready-to-eat TCS food can be stored for only seven days if it is held at 41°F (5°C) or lower. After that date, the food must be discarded. The count begins on the day the food was prepared or a commercial container was opened. For example, a food handler who prepared and stored potato salad on October 1 would write a discard date of October 7 on the label.

Operations have a variety of systems for date marking. Some write the day or date the food was prepped on the label. Others write the use-by day or date on the label.

Commercially Processed Food

Sometimes commercially processed food will have a use-by date that is less than seven days from the date the container was opened. In this case, the container should be marked with this use-by date, as long as the date is based on food safety.

Combining Food

When combining food with different use-by dates in a dish, the discard date of the dish should be based on the earliest use-by date of any food items involved. Here is an example:

- A food handler is prepping jambalaya on December 4 using shrimp and sausage.
- The shrimp has a use-by date of December 8.
- The sausage has a use-by date of December 10.
- So, the use-by date of the jambalaya is December 8.

December						
Sunday	Monday	Tuesday	Wednesday	Thursday	Friday	Saturday
				1	2	3
4 Jambalaya Prep Date	5	6	7	8 Shrimp Use-By; Jambalaya Use-By	9	10 Sausage Use-By
11	12	13	14	15	16	17

Rotation

Food must be rotated while in storage to maintain quality and limit the growth of pathogens. Food items must be rotated so the items with the earliest use-by or expiration dates are used before those with later dates.

Many operations use the **first-in, first-out (FIFO) method** to rotate their refrigerated, frozen, and dry food during storage. Here is one way to use the FIFO method:

1. Identify the food item's use-by or expiration date.
2. Store items with the earliest use-by or expiration dates in front of items with later dates, as shown in the photo at left.
3. Once shelved, use those items stored in front first.
4. Throw out food that has passed its manufacturer's use-by or expiration date.

Temperatures

Pathogens can grow when food is not stored at the correct temperature. Follow these guidelines to keep food safe:

- Store TCS food at an internal temperature of 41°F (5°C) or lower, or 135°F (57°C) or higher. Randomly sample the internal temperature of stored food using a calibrated thermometer on a regular basis.
- Store meat, poultry, seafood, and dairy items in the coldest part of the unit away from the door.
- Store frozen food at temperatures that keep it frozen.
- Make sure storage units have at least one air-temperature measuring device. It must be accurate to within ±3°F or ±1.5°C. This device must be located in the warmest part of refrigerated units, and the coldest part of hot-holding units. The hanging thermometer in the photo at right is a common type of temperature measuring device used in coolers. Check cooler and freezer temperatures often.

- Do not overload coolers or freezers. Storing too many food items prevents good airflow and makes the units work harder to stay cold. Be aware that frequent opening of the cooler lets warm air inside, which can affect food safety.
- Consider using cold curtains in walk-in coolers and freezers to help maintain temperatures.
- Use open shelving. Do not line shelves with aluminum foil, sheet pans, or paper. This restricts the circulation of cold air in the unit.
- Monitor food temperatures in coolers regularly. Randomly sample the temperature of stored food to verify that the cooler is working. If the food is not at the correct temperature, throw it out.
- Defrost freezers regularly. They are more efficient when free of frost. Move food to another freezer while defrosting.

Preventing Cross-Contamination

Food and nonfood items must be stored in ways that prevent cross-contamination. Follow these guidelines.

Storage Location

Food should be stored in a clean, dry location away from dust and other contaminants. To prevent contamination, **NEVER** store food in these areas:

- Locker rooms or dressing rooms.
- Restrooms or garbage rooms.
- Mechanical rooms.
- Under unshielded sewer lines or leaking water lines.
- Under stairwells.

Damaged, Spoiled, or Incorrectly Stored Food

If you find expired, damaged, spoiled, or incorrectly stored food that has become unsafe, you should discard it. This includes food that is missing a date mark, ready-to-eat TCS food that has exceeded its date mark, and food that has exceeded time/temperature requirements.

If the food must be stored until it can be returned to the vendor, there is a risk of contaminating the food stored near it. To prevent this risk, follow these guidelines:

- Store the food away from other food and equipment.
- Label the food so food handlers do not use the product. The photo at left shows food that is properly labeled and stored until it can be returned to the vendor.

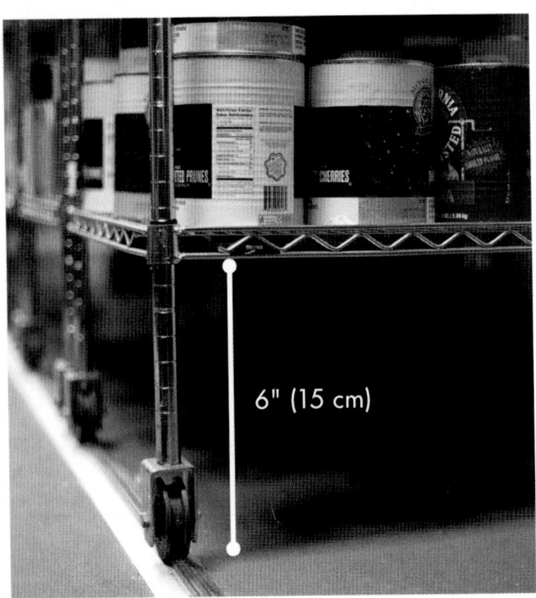

Supplies

- Store all items in designated storage areas.
- Store items away from walls and at least six inches (15 centimeters) off the floor, as shown in the photo at left.
- Store single-use items (e.g., sleeve of single-use cups, single-use gloves) in original packaging.

Containers

- Store food in containers intended for food.
- Use containers that are durable, leakproof, and able to be sealed or covered.
- **NEVER** use empty food containers to store chemicals. **NEVER** put food in empty chemical containers.
- Wrap or cover all food correctly. Leaving food uncovered can lead to cross-contamination.

Cleaning

Keep all storage areas clean and dry. Clean floors, walls, and shelving in coolers, freezers, dry-storage areas, and heated holding cabinets regularly. Clean up spills and leaks promptly to keep them from contaminating other food. Follow these guidelines:

- Clean dollies, carts, transporters, and trays often.
- Store food in containers that have been cleaned and sanitized.
- Store dirty linens away from food. Store them in clean, nonabsorbent containers. They can also be stored in washable laundry bags.

Storage Order

Safe food storage starts with wrapping or covering food. After that, how you store the food depends on the type of food and your options for storage.

- Store raw meat, poultry, and seafood separately from ready-to-eat food. If raw and ready-to-eat food cannot be stored separately, store ready-to-eat food above raw meat, poultry, and seafood, as shown below. This will prevent juices from raw food from dripping onto ready-to-eat food.
- Raw meat, poultry, and seafood can be stored with or above ready-to-eat food in a freezer if all of the items have been commercially processed and packaged. Frozen food that is being thawed in coolers must also be stored below ready-to-eat food.
- Store raw meat, poultry, and seafood in coolers in the following top-to-bottom order, as shown in the photo at right: seafood, whole cuts of beef and pork, ground meat and ground fish, whole and ground poultry. This order is based on the minimum internal cooking temperature of each food, with the food requiring the highest internal cooking temperature at the bottom.
- As an exception, ground meat and ground fish can be stored above whole cuts of beef and pork. To do this, make sure the packaging keeps out pathogens and chemicals. It also must not leak.

Storage Order, Top to Bottom	Minimum Internal Cooking Temperature
A Ready-to-eat food	N/A
B Seafood	145°F (63°C)
C Whole cuts of beef and pork	145°F (63°C)
D Ground meat and ground fish	155°F (68°C)
E Whole and ground poultry	165°F (74°C)

Storing Specific Food

The general storage guidelines apply to most food. However, certain types of food have special requirements. Table 7.1 shows some of these.

Table 7.1: **Additional Storage Requirements and Guidelines**

Meat

Temperature

- Fresh meat should be held at an internal temperature of 41°F (5°C) or lower.
- Frozen meat should be stored at a temperature that will keep it frozen.

Containers and location

- Immediately after delivery and inspection, store meat in its own storage unit or in the coldest part of the cooler.
- If meat is removed from its original packaging, wrap it in airtight, moisture-proof material or place it in clean and sanitized containers.
- Primal cuts, quarters, sides of raw meat, and slab bacon can be hung on clean and sanitized hooks or placed on sanitized racks.
- To prevent cross-contamination, do **NOT** store meat above other food.

Eggs

Temperature

- Store shell eggs at an air temperature of 45°F (7°C) or lower. Maintain constant temperature and humidity levels in coolers used to store shell eggs.
- Store frozen egg items at temperatures that will keep them frozen.
- Store liquid eggs according to the manufacturer's recommendations.
- Store dried egg items in a cool dry-storage area. Once they are reconstituted (mixed with water), store them in the cooler at 41°F (5°C) or lower.

Guidelines

- Do **NOT** wash shell eggs before storing them. They are washed and sanitized at the packing facility.
- Plan to use all shell eggs within four to five weeks of the packing date.
- Keep shell eggs in cold storage until the time they are used. Take out only as many eggs as are needed for immediate use.
- Do **NOT** reconstitute more dried egg items than needed for immediate use.

Table 7.1: **Additional Storage Requirements and Guidelines** *(continued)*

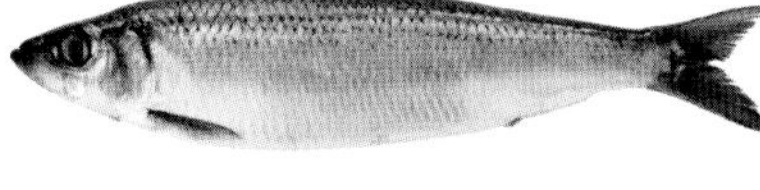

Fish

Fresh fish is very sensitive to time-temperature abuse. It can spoil quickly if handled incorrectly.

Temperature

- Store fresh fish at an internal temperature of 41°F (5°C) or lower.
- Store frozen fish at a temperature that will keep it frozen.

Containers

- Keep fillets and steaks in original packaging, or tightly wrap them in moisture-proof materials.
- Fresh, whole fish can be packed in flaked or crushed ice. Ice beds should be self-draining. Change the ice and clean and sanitize the container often.

Shellfish

Temperature

- Store shucked shellfish at an internal temperature of 41°F (5°C) or lower.
- Store live shellfish in its original container at an air temperature of 41°F (5°C) or lower.

Containers

- Do **NOT** remove the shellstock tag from the container until the last shellfish has been used. Keep shellstock identification tags on file for 90 days from the date the last shellfish was sold or served from the container.
- Live shellfish, such as clams, oysters, mussels, and scallops, can be stored in a display tank under one of two conditions:
  - The tank has a sign stating that the shellfish are for display only.
  - For shellfish to be served to customers, a variance has been obtained from the local regulatory authority that allows the shellfish to be served to customers.

  To obtain a variance, you will need to show the following:

  - Water from other tanks will not flow into the display tank.
  - Using the display tank will not affect food quality or safety.
  - Shellstock ID tags have been retained as required.

Table 7.1: **Additional Storage Requirements and Guidelines** *(continued)*

Fresh Produce

Temperature

- Cut melons, cut tomatoes, and cut leafy greens are TCS food. Store them at 41°F (5°C) or lower.
- Store whole citrus fruit, hard-rind squash, eggplant, and root vegetables—such as potatoes, sweet potatoes, rutabagas, and onions—in a cool dry-storage area. Temperatures of 60°F to 70°F (16°C to 21°C) are best.
- Other fruits and vegetables have various temperature requirements for storage. While many raw, whole fruits and vegetables can be stored at 41°F (5°C) or lower, not all can be stored at this temperature. Work with your produce supplier to determine the best storage temperature for the items you purchase.

Containers and location

- Raw, whole produce and raw, cut vegetables—such as celery, carrots, and radishes—delivered packed in ice can be stored as they are. Make sure the containers are self-draining. The ice should also be changed regularly.
- Make sure containers for whole citrus fruit, hard-rind squash, eggplant, and root vegetables—such as potatoes, sweet potatoes, rutabagas, and onions—are well ventilated.
- Store onions away from other vegetables that might absorb odor.

Guidelines

- Fruits and vegetables kept in the cooler can dry out quickly. Keep the relative humidity at 85 to 95 percent.
- Although most produce can be stored in the cooler, avocados, bananas, pears, and tomatoes ripen best at room temperature.
- Most produce should not be washed before storage. Moisture often promotes the growth of mold. Instead, wash produce before prepping or serving it.
- When soaking or storing produce in standing water or an ice-water slurry, do not mix different items or multiple batches of the same item.

Poultry

Temperature

- Store raw poultry at an internal temperature of 41°F (5°C) or lower.
- Frozen poultry should be stored at a temperature that will keep it frozen.

Containers

- If the poultry has been removed from its original packaging, place it in an airtight container or wrap it in airtight material.
- Ice-packed poultry can be stored in a cooler as is. Use self-draining containers. Change the ice and sanitize the container often.

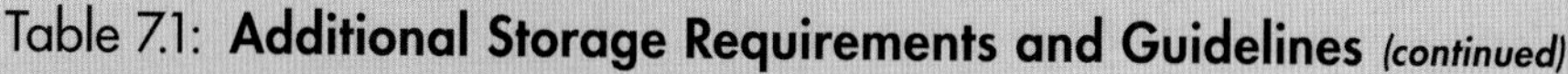

Table 7.1: **Additional Storage Requirements and Guidelines** *(continued)*

ROP Food

Temperature

- Always store **reduced-oxygen packaged (ROP) food** at temperatures recommended by the manufacturer or at 41°F (5°C) or lower. ROP food includes modified atmosphere packaged (MAP), vacuum-packed, and sous vide food.
- Frozen items should be stored at temperatures that will keep them frozen. Store and handle these items carefully.

Guidelines

- ROP items are especially susceptible to the growth of *Clostridium botulinum*. Throw the item away if the package shows any of the following characteristics:
  - It is torn or slimy.
  - It contains excessive liquid.
  - The food item bubbles, indicating the possible growth of *Clostridium botulinum*.
- Always check the expiration date before using ROP items. Labels should clearly list contents, storage temperature, prep instructions, and a use-by date.
- Operators who package food in-house using a ROP process need to follow specific rules for packaging and labeling. Consult your local regulatory authority for guidance.

UHT and Aseptically Packaged Food

Temperature

- Food that has been pasteurized at ultra-high temperatures (UHT) and aseptically packaged can be stored at room temperature.
- Once opened, store UHT and aseptically packaged food in the cooler at 41°F (5°C) or lower.
- Store UHT items that are not aseptically packaged at an internal temperature of 41°F (5°C) or lower.

Table 7.1: **Additional Storage Requirements and Guidelines** *(continued)*

Canned Goods

Temperature

Even canned food spoils over time. Higher storage temperatures may shorten shelf life.

Guidelines

- Acidic food, such as canned tomatoes, does not last as long as food that is low in acid. The acid can also form pinholes in the metal over time.
- Discard damaged cans.
- Keep dry-storage areas dry. Too much moisture will cause cans to rust.
- Wipe cans clean with a sanitized cloth before opening them. This will help prevent dirt from falling into the contents of the can.

Dry Food

Containers

Keep flour, cereal, and grain items, such as pasta or crackers, in airtight containers. These items can quickly become stale in a humid room. They can also become moldy with too much moisture.

Guidelines

- Before using dry food, check containers or packages for damage from insects or rodents. Cereal and grain items are often targets for these pests.
- If stored in the correct conditions, salt and sugar can be held almost indefinitely.

Chapter Summary

- Any item not stored in its original container must be labeled. The label must include the common name of the food or a statement that clearly and accurately identifies it.
- If TCS food was prepped in-house and will be stored longer than 24 hours, it must also be date marked. This food can be stored for only seven days if held at 41°F (5°C) or lower. After that, it must be discarded.
- Food packaged in the operation that is being sold to customers for use at home must be labeled with specific information. This includes the food name, quantity, ingredients, artificial colors and flavors, chemical preservatives, and major allergens. The label must also show the manufacturer's, packer's, or distributer's name and place of business.
- Food, linen, and single-use items should only be stored in designated storage areas. These items should be stored away from walls and at least six inches (15 centimeters) off the floor.
- Stored food items should always be rotated so that older items are used first.
- Store TCS food at an internal temperature of 41°F (5°C) or lower, or 135°F (57°C) or higher. Randomly sample the internal temperature of stored food. Follow storage and maintenance guidelines to ensure coolers and freezers can function properly.
- Store items to prevent cross-contamination. Store food only in containers intended for food. Keep raw meat, poultry, and seafood separate from ready-to-eat food. If raw and ready-to-eat food cannot be stored separately, store ready-to-eat food above raw meat, poultry, and seafood.
- Some food items may have special storage requirements. These items include meat, poultry, fish, shellfish, eggs, fresh produce, ROP food, UHT and aseptically packaged food, canned food, and dry food.

Apply Your Knowledge

Use these questions to review the concepts presented in this chapter.

Discussion Questions

1 What is the recommended top-to-bottom order for storing the following food in the same cooler: raw trout, an uncooked beef roast, raw chicken, pecan pie, and raw ground beef?

____

____

____

2 What are the requirements for storing live shellfish?

____

____

____

3 Explain the labeling requirements for food packaged on-site for retail sale.

____

____

____

4 Explain the FIFO method of stock rotation.

____

____

____

For answers, please turn to the Answer Key.

Apply Your Knowledge

Something to Think About

Storage Problems at Enrico's

A shipment was delivered to Enrico's Italian Restaurant. Alyce, who was in charge of receiving, inspected the shipment and immediately proceeded to store the items. First, she carried the bags of shrimp to the freezer. She wondered who had left the freezer without making sure the door was completely shut.

Alyce then loaded a case of sour cream on the dolly and wheeled it over to the reach-in cooler. When she opened the cooler, she noticed that it was tightly packed. However, she was able to squeeze the case into a spot on the top shelf.

Next, she wheeled several cases of fresh ground beef and fresh salmon over to the walk-in cooler. Alyce pushed through the cold curtains in the cooler and bumped into a stockpot of soup stored on the floor. She moved the soup to a storage shelf and then made a space for the ground beef on a shelf next to the door. Alyce was able to put the salmon on the shelf above the soup. Then she spent a few minutes talking to Mary, who had just cleaned the shelving in the unit and was lining it with new aluminum foil.

1 What storage errors occurred?

For answers, please turn to the Answer Key.

Apply Your Knowledge

Something to Think About

A Second Chance

Ginny's Bistro, a longtime fixture on the food scene just outside of a large Midwestern city, had finally completed a major renovation of its kitchen. The bistro had been open for 44 years and, except for some repairs along the way, not much had been done to improve the facilities in the back of the house. The kitchen staff was thrilled that the renovation work was nearly complete.

Chase, a young kitchen manager and Ginny's great-grandson, jumped at the chance to review how food storage should be done in the newly renovated space. He set out to do a complete food storage review. Chase and his staff were determined to start fresh and ensure that they followed good food storage guidelines as they prepared for the reopening of their kitchen.

1 List some things that Chase and his staff should consider as they conduct a review of the new storage area.

For answers, please turn to the Answer Key.

Study Questions

Circle the best answer to each question.

1 **What must be included on the label of TCS food that was prepped in-house?**

A Date that the food was received

B Name of each TCS ingredient included

C Date that the food should be thrown out

D List of all potential ingredients in the food

2 **How long can ready-to-eat TCS food that was prepped in-house be stored if it is held at 41°F (5°C) or lower?**

A 3 days

B 5 days

C 7 days

D 9 days

3 **An air-temperature measuring device used to measure the temperature in a cooler must be how accurate?**

A ±1°F or ±5°C

B ±2°F or ±1°C

C ±3°F or ±1.5°C

D ±4°F or ±3°C

4 **How far above the floor should food be stored?**

A At least 1 inch (3 centimeters)

B At least 2 inches (5 centimeters)

C At least 4 inches (10 centimeters)

D At least 6 inches (15 centimeters)

5 **What is the problem with storing raw ground turkey above raw ground pork?**

A Cross-contamination

B Poor personal hygiene

C Time-temperature abuse

D Cross-contact with allergens

Study Questions

6 **Due to an operation's space limits, ready-to-eat and uncooked food must be stored in the same cooler. How should food be stored, in top-to-bottom order?**

A According to the FIFO method, with oldest items on the top shelf and the newest items on the bottom

B According to preparation dates, with the earliest dates on the top shelf and the latest dates on the bottom

C According to minimum internal cooking temperatures, with ready-to-eat food on the top shelf and poultry on the bottom

D According to minimum acceptable storage temperatures, with food that can tolerate the warmest temperature on the top shelf and food needing the coldest temperature on the bottom

7 **When must you discard tuna salad that was prepped on July 19?**

A July 21

B July 23

C July 25

D July 27

8 **In top-to-bottom order, how should a fresh pork roast, fresh salmon, a container of lettuce, and a pan of fresh chicken breasts be stored in a cooler?**

A Lettuce, fresh salmon, fresh pork roast, fresh chicken breasts

B Fresh salmon, fresh pork roast, fresh chicken breasts, lettuce

C Lettuce, fresh chicken breasts, fresh pork roast, fresh salmon

D Fresh salmon, lettuce, fresh chicken breasts, fresh pork roast

9 **At what air temperature can you store shell eggs?**

A 41°F (5°C) or lower

B 45°F (7°C) or lower

C 60°F to 70°F (16°C to 21°C)

D Room temperature

10 **Where in a cooler should dairy products be stored?**

A Close to the door, in a clean and sanitized area

B Below meat products, in a covered container

C Away from ready-to-eat food, in a designated area

D Away from the door, in the coldest part of the cooler

For answers, please turn to the Answer Key.

Notes

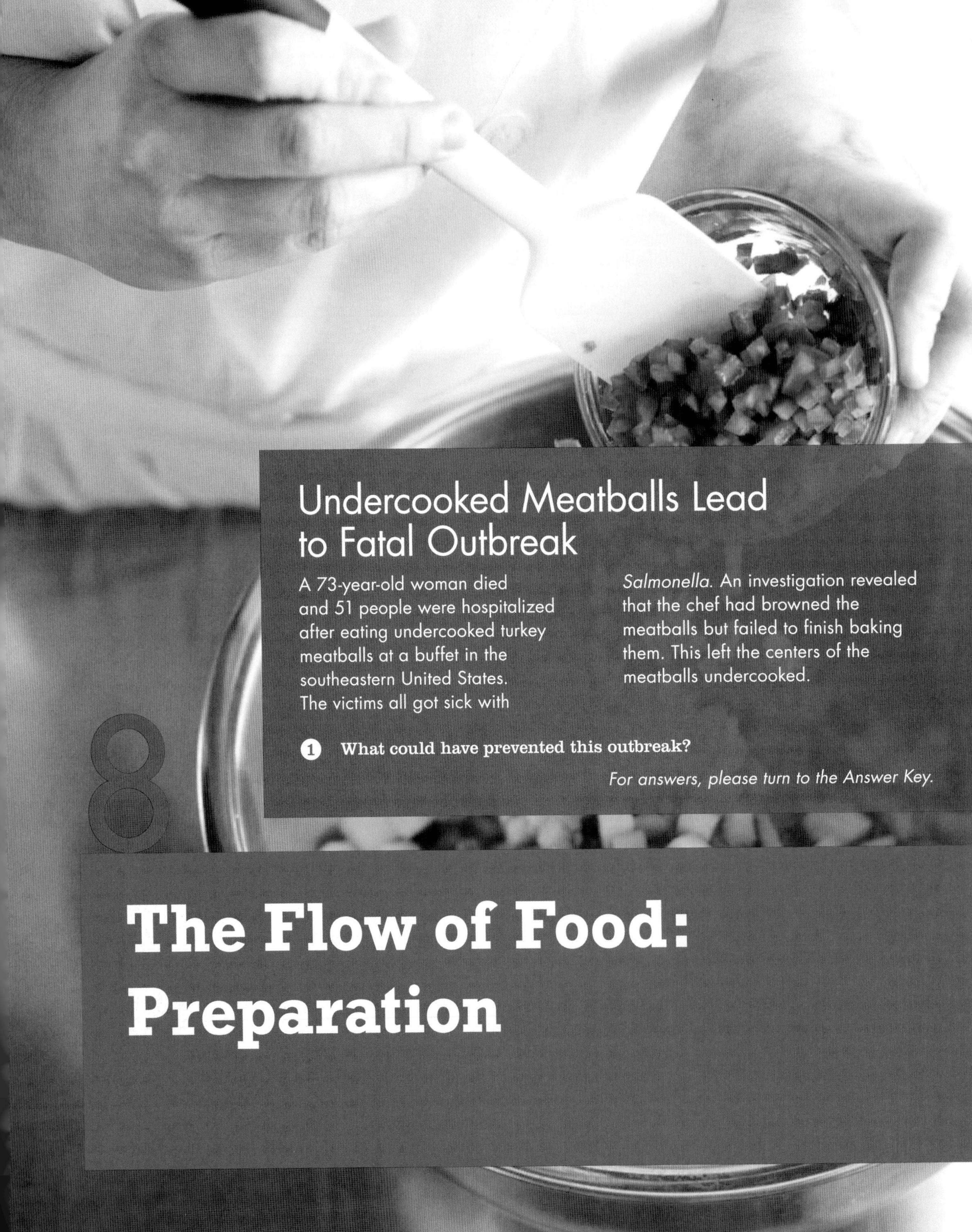

Undercooked Meatballs Lead to Fatal Outbreak

A 73-year-old woman died and 51 people were hospitalized after eating undercooked turkey meatballs at a buffet in the southeastern United States. The victims all got sick with *Salmonella*. An investigation revealed that the chef had browned the meatballs but failed to finish baking them. This left the centers of the meatballs undercooked.

1. **What could have prevented this outbreak?**

For answers, please turn to the Answer Key.

8

The Flow of Food: Preparation

Inside This Chapter

- Preparation
- Cooking Food
- Cooling and Reheating Food

Objectives

After completing this chapter, you should be able to identify the following:

- Correct ways for prepping food to prevent cross-contamination and time-temperature abuse
- Safe methods for thawing food
- The minimum internal cooking temperatures for TCS food
- The correct way to cook TCS food in a microwave oven
- The importance of informing consumers of risks when serving raw or undercooked food
- Requirements for partially cooking TCS food
- Methods and time-temperature requirements for cooling TCS food
- Time and temperature requirements for reheating TCS food

Key Terms

Slacking

Pooled eggs

Variance

Minimum internal temperature

Partial cooking (parcooking)

Preparation

General Preparation Practices

Cross-contamination and time-temperature abuse can happen easily when you are prepping food. You can prevent pathogens from spreading and growing by making good food-prep choices.

Equipment Make sure workstations, cutting boards, and utensils are clean and sanitized.

Quantity Only remove as much food from the cooler as you can prep in a short period of time. This keeps ingredients from sitting out for long periods of time. In the photo at left, the food handler has taken out too much meat and cheese.

Storage Return prepped food to the cooler, or cook it, as quickly as possible.

Additives If you use food or color additives when prepping food, follow these guidelines:

- Only use additives that have been approved by your local regulatory authority. **NEVER** use more than is allowed by law. **NEVER** use additives to alter the appearance of the food.
- Do **NOT** sell produce that was treated with sulfites before it was received in the operation. **NEVER** add sulfites to produce that will be eaten raw.

Presentation Food should be offered to guests in a way that does not mislead or misinform them. Guests must be able to judge the true appearance, color, and quality of food. Do **NOT** use the following to misrepresent the appearance of food:

- Food additives or color additives
- Colored overwraps
- Lights

Food also must be presented the way it was described. For example, if your menu offers "Fried Perch," you cannot substitute another fish for the perch.

Food that has not been honestly presented should be thrown out.

Corrective actions Food that has become unsafe should be thrown out unless it can be safely reconditioned. All food—especially ready-to-eat food—should be thrown out in the following situations:

- When it is handled by staff who have been restricted or excluded from the operation because of illness
- When it is contaminated by hands or bodily fluids; for example, from sneezing
- When it has exceeded the time and temperature requirements designed to keep food safe

Sometimes food can be restored to a safe condition. This is called reconditioning. For example, a hot food that has not been held at the correct temperature may be reheated if it has not been in the temperature danger zone for more than two hours. This can return food to a safe condition.

Thawing

When frozen food is thawed and exposed to the temperature danger zone, pathogens in the food will begin to grow. To reduce this growth, **NEVER** thaw food at room temperature.

For example, suppose a cook needs to thaw a 20-pound turkey. In a hurry, he places it on a prep table to thaw overnight. When the turkey begins to thaw, the skin and outer layers are exposed to the temperature danger zone even though the core of the turkey is still frozen. If there are pathogens on the turkey, they will grow to a level high enough to make the turkey unsafe.

General Guidelines for TCS Food

To prevent pathogen growth, thaw TCS food according to the methods and guidelines in Table 8.1.

Table 8.1: **Methods and Guidelines for Thawing TCS Food**

	**Refrigeration** Thaw food in a cooler, keeping its temperature at 41°F (5°C) or lower. This requires advance planning. Larger items, such as a turkey, can take several days to thaw completely in a cooler.
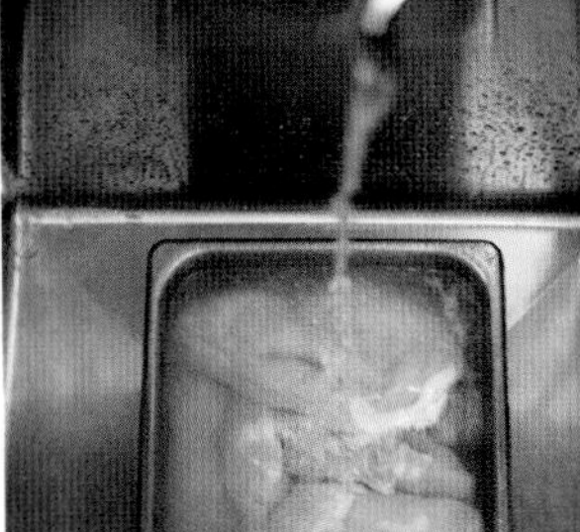	**Running water** • Submerge food under running, drinkable water at 70°F (21°C) or lower. The flow of the water must be strong enough to wash loose food bits into the drain. • Always use a clean and sanitized food-prep sink when thawing food this way. • **NEVER** let the temperature of the food go above 41°F (5°C) for longer than four hours. This includes the time it takes to thaw the food plus the time it takes to prep or cool it.
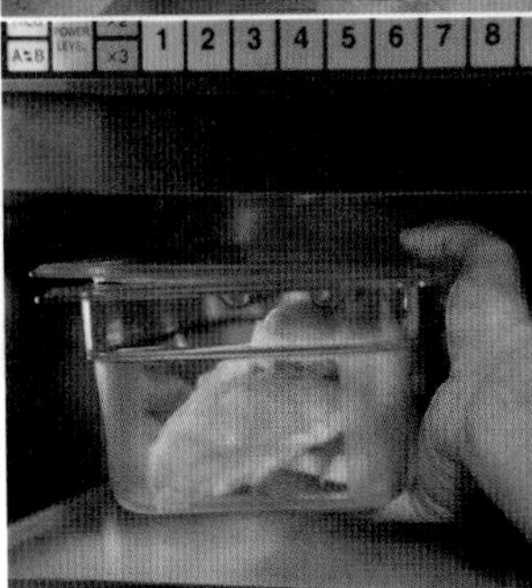	**Microwave** • Thaw food in a microwave oven if it will be cooked immediately after thawing. • The food must be cooked in conventional cooking equipment, such as an oven, once it is thawed.
	**Cooking** Thaw food as part of the cooking process. For example: • Frozen hamburger patties can go straight from the freezer onto a grill without first being thawed. • Frozen chicken can go straight into a deep fryer. These items cook quickly enough from the frozen state to pass through the temperature danger zone without harm. However, always verify the final internal cooking temperature with a thermometer.

Some frozen food may also be slacked before cooking. **Slacking** is the gradual thawing of frozen food to prep it for deep-frying. This allows even heating during cooking. For example, you might slack frozen breaded chicken breasts by having them warm from –10°F (–23°C) to 25°F (–4°C).

Slack food just before you cook it. Do not let it get any warmer than 41°F (5°C). If your regulatory authority allows slacking at room temperature, have a system that ensures the item does not exceed 41°F (5°C).

Thawing ROP Fish

Frozen fish may be supplied in reduced-oxygen packaging (ROP). This fish should usually remain frozen until ready for use. If this is stated on the label, the fish must be removed from the packaging at the following times:

- Before thawing it under refrigeration
- Before or immediately after thawing it under running water

Prepping Specific Food

Special care must be taken when handling meat, seafood, and poultry, as well as salads containing these items. Likewise, you will need to pay close attention when prepping eggs, batter and breading, and produce. Even ice needs special care.

Meat, Seafood, and Poultry

The sources of most cross-contamination in an operation are raw meat, poultry, and seafood. Your staff should follow specific procedures when handling these items.

Cleaning and sanitizing **Use clean and sanitized work areas, cutting boards, knives, and utensils. Prep raw meat, poultry, and seafood separately or at different times from fresh produce.**

Quantity **Only remove as much food from the cooler as you can prep in a short period of time. This keeps ingredients from sitting out for long periods of time. For example, if assembling pans of meat lasagna, remove only enough ingredients to prepare a few pans at a time. Then return the prepared pans of lasagna to the cooler before removing more ingredients.**

Prompt action **Return raw, prepped meat directly to the cooler, or cook it as quickly as possible. Store these items correctly to prevent cross-contamination.**

Salads Containing TCS Food

Chicken, tuna, egg, pasta, and potato salads have all been involved in foodborne-illness outbreaks. These salads are not usually cooked after prepping. This means you do not have a chance to reduce pathogens that may have gotten into the salad. Therefore, you must take a few extra steps. Follow these guidelines.

Prepping small batches Prep food in small batches so large amounts of food do not sit out at room temperature for long periods of time. The food handler in the photo at left has taken out a small amount of tuna salad to prep three sandwiches.

Using leftovers Leftover TCS food, such as pasta, chicken, and potatoes, should only be used to make salads if it has been cooked, held, cooled, and stored correctly.

Storing leftovers Do **NOT** use leftover TCS food that has been held for more than seven days. Check the use-by date of the stored TCS food before using it.

Chilling Consider chilling all ingredients and utensils before using them to make the salad. For example, tuna, mayonnaise, and mixing bowls can be chilled before making tuna salad.

Refrigeration Leave food in the cooler until all ingredients are ready to be mixed.

Eggs and Egg Mixtures

Historically the contents of whole, clean, uncracked shell eggs were considered bacteria-free.

However, specific species of nontyphoidal *Salmonella* can live within a laying hen. *Salmonella* can also be deposited in an egg before the shell is formed. Only a small number of eggs produced in the United States are likely to carry this type of bacteria. However, all untreated eggs are considered TCS food. They are able to support the rapid growth of bacteria.

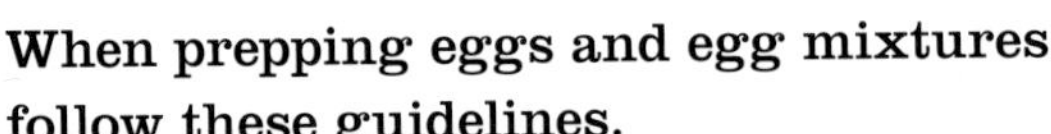

When prepping eggs and egg mixtures, follow these guidelines.

Pooled eggs **Pooled eggs** are eggs that are cracked open and combined in a common container, as shown in the photo at left. Handle them (if allowed) with special care because bacteria in one egg can be spread to the rest. Cook pooled eggs promptly after mixing or store them at 41°F (5°C) or lower. Clean and sanitize containers used to hold pooled eggs before using them for a new batch.

Pasteurized eggs Consider using pasteurized shell eggs or egg products for egg dishes requiring little or no cooking. Examples are hollandaise sauce, Caesar salad dressing, tiramisu, and mousse.

High-risk populations Operations that serve high-risk populations, such as hospitals and nursing homes, must take special care when using eggs. If you mainly serve these populations, use pasteurized eggs or egg products when dishes containing eggs will be served raw or undercooked. Shell eggs that are pooled must also be pasteurized. Unpasteurized shell eggs may be used if the dish will be cooked all the way through, such as in an omelet or a cake.

Cleaning and sanitizing Promptly clean and sanitize all equipment and utensils used to prep eggs.

Batters and Breading

Batters or breading prepped with eggs or milk, as shown in the photo at right, should be handled carefully. They run the risk of time-temperature abuse and cross-contamination. If you choose to make breaded or battered food from scratch, follow these guidelines.

Small batches Prepping batters in small amounts prevents time-temperature abuse of both the batter and the food being coated. Store what you do not need in a covered container at 41°F (5°C) or lower.

Prompt storage When breading food that will be cooked later, store it in the cooler as soon as possible.

Unused items Create a plan to throw out unused batter or breading after a set time. This might be after using a batch or at the end of a shift.

Thorough cooking The coating of battered and breaded food acts as an insulator that can prevent food from being thoroughly cooked. Cook this food all the way through. When deep-frying food, make sure the temperature of the oil recovers before loading each batch.

Overloading the basket when frying food also slows cooking time. This means items can be removed from the fryer before they are thoroughly cooked. Monitor oil and food temperatures using calibrated thermometers. Watch cooking time as well.

Fresh Juice

If you package fresh fruit and vegetable juice in-house for later sale, treat (e.g., pasteurize) the juice according to an approved HACCP plan. You will learn about HACCP plans in chapter 10.

As an alternative to manufacturing under a HACCP plan, the juice can be labeled with the following: Warning: *This product has not been pasteurized and, therefore, may contain harmful bacteria that can cause serious illness in children, the elderly, and people with weakened immune systems.* An example of a label is shown in the photo at left.

Produce

Handle fresh produce carefully to prevent foodborne illnesses. Viruses such as Hepatitis A, bacteria such as Shiga toxin-producing *E. coli*, and parasites such as *Cryptosporidium parvum* can survive on produce, especially cut produce. Follow these guidelines to minimize or eliminate the risk from these pathogens.

Prepping Make sure fruits and vegetables do **NOT** come in contact with surfaces exposed to raw meat, poultry, and seafood.

- Prep produce away from raw meat, poultry, and seafood, as well as from ready-to-eat food.
- Clean and sanitize the work space and all utensils that will be used before and after prepping produce.

Washing Wash fruits and vegetables thoroughly under running water to remove dirt and other contaminants. Do this before cutting, cooking, or combining the produce with other ingredients:

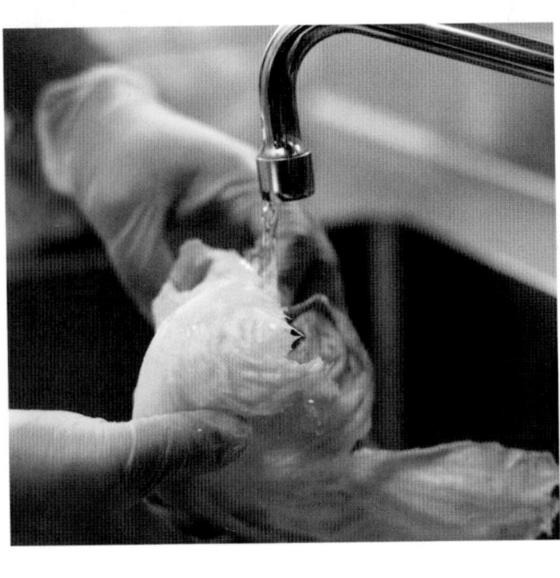

- The water should be slightly warmer than the temperature of the produce.
- Pay close attention to leafy greens, such as lettuce and spinach, as the food handler in the photo at left is doing. Remove the outer leaves. Pull lettuce and spinach completely apart and rinse thoroughly.
- Certain chemicals may be used to wash fruits and vegetables. Also, produce can be treated by washing it in water containing ozone. This treatment helps control pathogens. Your local regulatory authority can tell what is acceptable to use for this.

Soaking or storing When soaking or storing produce in standing water or an ice-water slurry, do **NOT** mix different items or multiple batches of the same item. Pathogens from contaminated produce can contaminate the water and the ice and can spread to other produce.

Refrigerating Refrigerate and hold cut melons, cut tomatoes, and cut leafy greens at 41°F (5°C) or lower. They are TCS food. Many operations hold other fresh-cut produce at this temperature as well.

High-risk populations If your operation primarily serves high-risk populations, do **NOT** serve raw seed sprouts.

Ice

People often forget that ice is a food and can become contaminated just as easily as any other food. Follow these guidelines to avoid contaminating ice in your operation.

Consumption Make ice from water that is safe to drink.

Cooling food **NEVER** use ice as an ingredient if it was used to keep food cold. For example, if ice is used to cool food on a salad bar, it cannot then be used in drinks.

Containers and scoops Use clean and sanitized containers and ice scoops to transfer ice from an ice machine to other containers. Also follow these guidelines:

- Store ice scoops outside of the ice machine in a clean, protected location, as shown in the photo at right.
- **NEVER** hold or carry ice in containers that have held raw meat, seafood, or poultry, or chemicals.
- **NEVER** touch ice with hands or use a glass to scoop ice.

Prepping Practices That Have Special Requirements

You will need a variance when prepping food in certain ways. A **variance** is a document issued by your regulatory authority that allows a regulatory requirement to be waived or changed. When applying for a variance, your regulatory authority may require you to submit a HACCP plan. The plan must account for any food safety risks related to the way you plan to prep the food item.

You will need a variance if your operation plans to prep food in any of the following ways:

- Packaging fresh juice on-site for sale at a later time unless the juice has a warning label that complies with local regulations.
- Smoking food as a way of preserving it (but not to enhance flavor).

- Using food additives or adding components such as vinegar to preserve or alter the food so that it no longer needs time and temperature control for safety.
- Curing food.
- Custom-processing animals for personal use. For example, a hunter brings a deer to a restaurant for dressing and takes the meat home for later use.
- Packaging food using a reduced-oxygen packaging (ROP) method. This includes MAP, vacuum-packed, and sous vide food, as shown in the photo at left.
- Sprouting seeds or beans.
- Offering live shellfish from a display tank.

Cooking Food

Minimum Internal Cooking Temperatures

The only way to reduce pathogens in food to safe levels is to cook it to its correct **minimum internal temperature**. The temperature is different for each food. Once reached, you must hold the food at this temperature for a specific amount of time.

The FDA recommends cooking food to the minimum internal temperatures listed in Table 8.2. However, your operation or regulatory authority might require different temperatures. Keep in mind that while cooking can reduce pathogens in food to safe levels, it will not destroy spores or toxins they may have produced. For this reason, it is critical to handle food correctly before it is cooked.

Table 8.2: **Minimum Internal Cooking Temperatures**

165°F (74°C) for 15 seconds

- Poultry—including whole or ground chicken, turkey, or duck
- Stuffing made with fish, meat, or poultry
- Stuffed meat, seafood, poultry, or pasta
- Dishes that include previously cooked TCS ingredients (raw ingredients should be cooked to their required minimum internal temperatures)

155°F (68°C) for 15 seconds

- Ground meat—including beef, pork, and other meat
- Injected meat—including brined ham and flavor-injected roasts
- Mechanically tenderized meat
- Ratites (mostly flightless birds with flat breastbones)—including ostrich and emu
- Ground seafood—including chopped or minced seafood
- Shell eggs that will be hot held for service

145°F (63°C) for 15 seconds

- Seafood—including fish, shellfish, and crustaceans
- Steaks/chops of pork, beef, veal, and lamb
- Commercially raised game
- Shell eggs that will be served immediately

145°F (63°C) for 4 minutes

- Roasts of pork, beef, veal, and lamb
- Roasts may be cooked to these alternate cooking times and temperatures depending on the type of roast and oven used:

Temperature	Time	Temperature	Time
130°F (54°C)	112 minutes	138°F (59°C)	18 minutes
131°F (55°C)	89 minutes	140°F (60°C)	12 minutes
133°F (56°C)	56 minutes	142°F (61°C)	8 minutes
135°F (57°C)	36 minutes	144°F (62°C)	5 minutes
136°F (58°C)	28 minutes		

Table 8.2: **Minimum Internal Cooking Temperatures** *(continued)*

	**135°F (57°C) (no minimum time)** • Fruit, vegetables, grains (e.g., rice, pasta), and legumes (e.g., beans, refried beans) that will be hot held for service
	**175°F (80°C)** • Tea **Automatic iced tea and automatic coffee machine equipment:** Tea leaves should remain in contact with the water for a minimum of one minute. **Traditional steeping method:** Tea leaves should be exposed to the water for about five minutes.

Cooking TCS Food in the Microwave Oven

Meat, seafood, poultry, and eggs that you cook in a microwave oven must be cooked to 165°F (74°C). In addition, follow these guidelines:

- Cover the food to prevent its surface from drying out.
- Rotate or stir it halfway through the cooking process so that the heat reaches the food more evenly.
- Let the covered food stand for at least two minutes after cooking to let the food temperature even out.
- Check the temperature in at least two places to make sure that the food is cooked through.

General Cooking Guidelines

Here are general guidelines to follow when cooking food.

Time and temperature Specify the cooking time and minimum internal temperature in all recipes.

Correct thermometer Use a thermometer with a probe that is the correct size for the food. Check the temperature in the thickest part of the food, as shown in the photo at left. Take at least two readings in different locations.

Overloading Avoid overloading ovens, fryers, and other cooking equipment. Overloading may lower the equipment or oil temperature, and the food might not cook fully.

Equipment temperature Let the cooking equipment's temperature recover between batches.

Consumer Advisories

You must cook TCS food to required minimum internal temperatures listed in this chapter unless a customer requests otherwise. This might happen often in your operation, particularly if you serve meat, eggs, or seafood.

Disclosure If your menu includes TCS items that are raw or undercooked, such as animal products, you must note it on the menu next to these items. This can also be done by placing an asterisk next to the item that points guests to a footnote at the bottom of the menu. The footnote must include a statement that indicates the item is raw or undercooked, or contains raw or undercooked ingredients. The menu in the photo at right shows an example of disclosure.

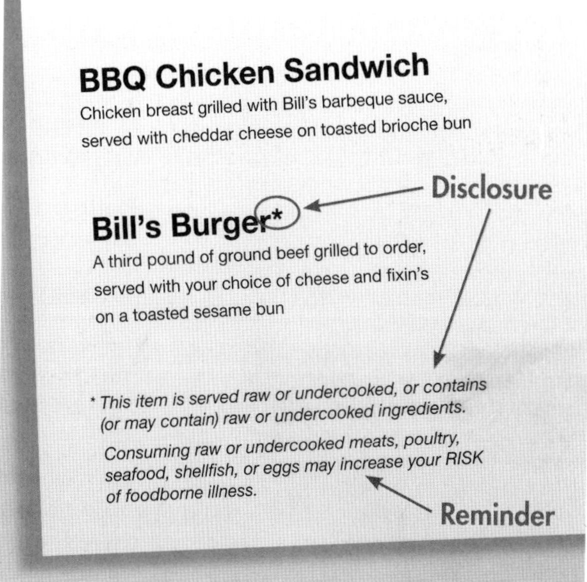

Reminder You must advise guests who order TCS food that is raw or undercooked, such as animal products, of the increased risk of foodborne illness. You can do this by posting a notice in your menu. You can also provide this information using brochures, table tents, signs, or other written methods. Check your local regulatory requirements. The menu at right also shows an example of a reminder statement below the disclosure.

Children's Menus

The Food and Drug Administration (FDA) advises against offering raw or undercooked meat, poultry, seafood, or eggs on a children's menu. This is especially true for undercooked ground beef, which may be contaminated with Shiga toxin-producing *E. coli* 0157:H7.

Operations That Mainly Serve High-Risk Populations

Operations that mainly serve a high-risk population, such as nursing homes or day-care centers, cannot serve certain items. **NEVER** serve these items:

- Raw seed sprouts.
- Raw or undercooked eggs (unpasteurized), meat, or seafood. Examples include over-easy eggs, raw oysters on the half shell, and rare hamburgers.
- Unpasteurized milk or juice.

Partial Cooking During Prepping

Some operations partially cook food during prep and then finish cooking it just before service. This is called **partial cooking**, or parcooking.

Follow the steps below if you plan to partially cook meat, seafood, poultry, or eggs, or dishes containing these items.

1 Do not cook the food for longer than 60 minutes during initial cooking.

2 Cool the food immediately after initial cooking.

3 Freeze or refrigerate the food after cooling it. If refrigerating the food, make sure it is held at 41°F (5°C) or lower. If the food will be refrigerated, store it away from ready-to-eat food.

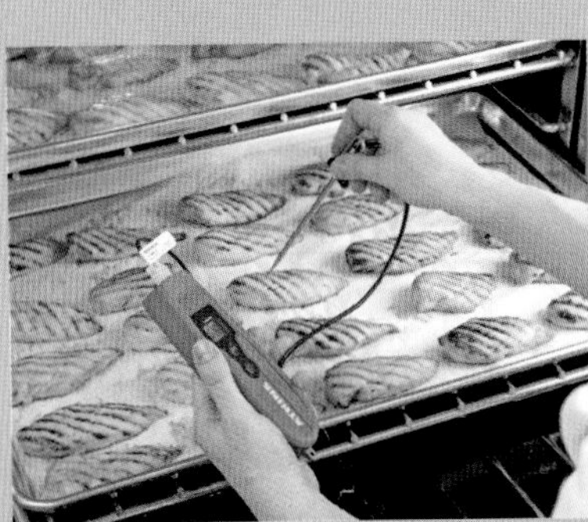

4 Heat the food to its required minimum internal temperature before selling or serving it.

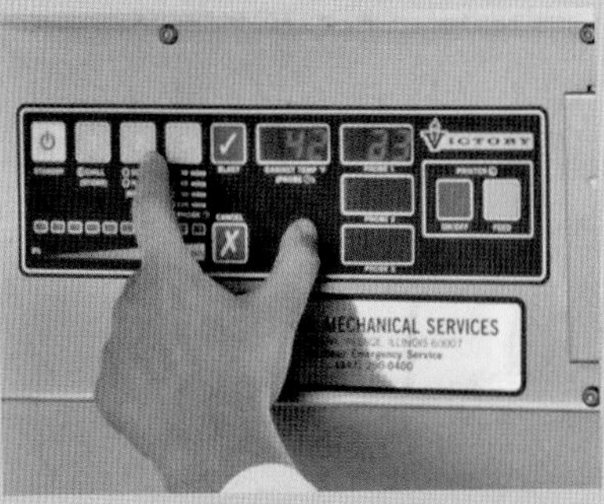

5 Cool the food if it will not be served immediately or held for service.

Your regulatory authority will require you to have written procedures that explain how the food cooked by this process will be prepped and stored. These procedures must be approved by the regulatory authority and describe the following:

- How the requirements will be monitored and documented
- Which corrective actions will be taken if requirements are not met
- How these food items will be marked after initial cooking to indicate they need further cooking
- How these food items will be separated from ready-to-eat food during storage, once initial cooking is complete

Cooling and Reheating Food

When you do not serve cooked food immediately, you must get it out of the temperature danger zone as quickly as possible. That means cooling it quickly. You also need to reheat it correctly, especially if you are going to hold it.

Temperature Requirements for Cooling Food

Pathogens grow well in the temperature danger zone. They grow even faster between 125°F and 70°F (52°C and 21°C). Food must pass through this temperature range quickly to reduce this growth.

Cool TCS food from 135°F to 41°F (57°C to 5°C) or lower within six hours.

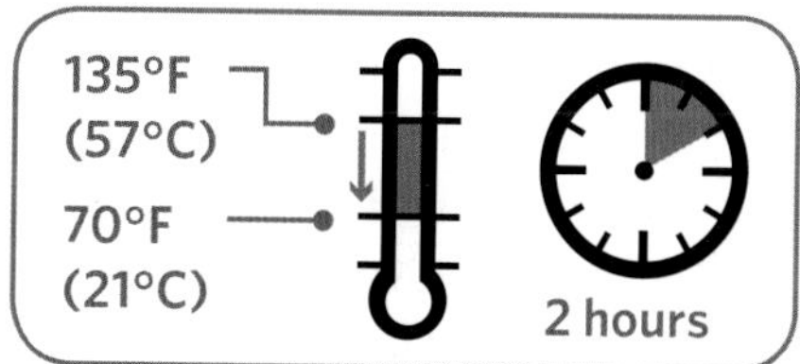

First, cool food from 135°F to 70°F (57°C to 21°C) within two hours.

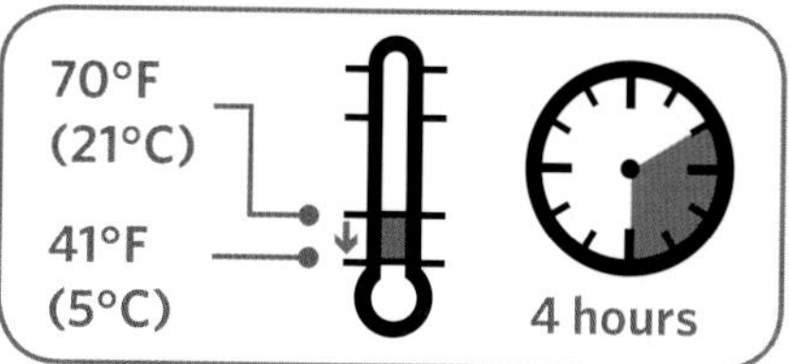

Then cool it from 70°F to 41°F (21°C to 5°C) or lower in the next four hours.

If food has not cooled to 70°F (21°C) within two hours, it must be reheated and then cooled again.

If you can cool the food from 135°F to 70°F (57°C to 21°C) in less than two hours, you can use the remaining time to cool it to 41°F (5°C) or lower. However, the total cooling time cannot be longer than six hours. For example, if you cool food from 135°F to 70°F (57°C to 21°C) in one hour, you have the remaining five hours to get the food to 41°F (5°C) or lower. Check your local regulatory requirements.

Cooling Food

The following factors and cooling methods affect how quickly food will cool.

Factors That Affect Cooling

Thickness or density of the food **The denser the food, the more slowly it will cool.**

Size of the food **Large food items cool more slowly than smaller items. To let food cool faster, you should reduce its size. Cut large food items into smaller pieces. Divide large containers of food into smaller containers or shallow pans, as shown in the photo at left.**

Storage container **The container in which food is stored also affects how fast it will cool. Stainless steel transfers heat away from food faster than plastic. Shallow pans disperse heat faster than deep ones.**

Methods for Cooling Food

NEVER cool large amounts of hot food in a cooler. Most coolers are not designed to cool large amounts of hot food quickly. Also, simply placing hot food in the cooler may not move it through the temperature danger zone fast enough. Here are some effective methods for cooling food quickly and safely.

Ice-water bath **After dividing food into smaller containers, place them into a clean prep sink or large pot filled with ice water, as shown in the photo at left. Stir the food often to cool it faster and more evenly.**

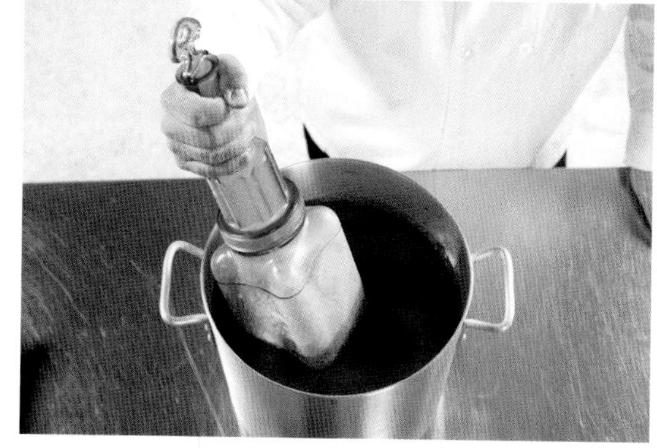

Ice paddle Ice paddles are plastic paddles that can be filled with ice or with water and then frozen. Food stirred with these paddles will cool quickly, as shown in the photo at right. Food cools even faster when placed in an ice-water bath and stirred with an ice paddle.

Blast or tumble chiller Blast chillers blast cold air across food at high speeds to remove heat. They are typically used to cool large amounts of food. Tumble chillers tumble bags of hot food in cold water. Tumble chillers work well on thick food, such as mashed potatoes.

Ice or cold water as an ingredient To cool soups or stews right away, the recipe is made with less water than required. Then, cold water or ice is added after cooking to cool the food and provide the remaining water.

Storing Food for Further Cooling

Loosely cover food containers before storing them. Food can be left uncovered if stored in a way that protects it from contaminants. Storing uncovered containers above other food, especially raw meat, seafood, and poultry, will help prevent cross-contamination.

Reheating Food

How you reheat food depends on how you intend to use the food. Follow these guidelines when reheating food.

Food reheated for immediate service You can reheat food that will be served immediately, such as beef for a beef sandwich, to any temperature. However, you must make sure the food was cooked and cooled correctly.

Food reheated for hot holding You must reheat TCS food for hot holding to an internal temperature of 165°F (74°C) for 15 seconds. Make sure the food reaches this temperature within two hours from start to finish. The food handler in the photo at right is reheating soup for hot holding. These guidelines apply to all reheating methods, such as ovens or microwave ovens.

Reheat commercially processed and packaged ready-to-eat food to an internal temperature of at least 135°F (57°C). This includes items such as cheese sticks and deep-fried vegetables.

Chapter Summary

- Prevent cross-contamination and time-temperature abuse when preparing food. General practices include prepping food in small batches; keeping workstations, cutting boards, and utensils clean and sanitized; only removing as much food from the cooler as you can prep in a short period; returning prepped food that is not going to be cooked immediately to the cooler; following guidelines for the use of additives; and thawing food correctly. Follow additional guidelines for prepping specific food items, when handling ice, and when using preparation practices that require a variance.
- Throw away food when it has become unsafe and cannot be safely reconditioned. Also throw it away if it has not been presented honestly.
- Thaw frozen food in the cooler, under running water, in a microwave oven, or as part of the cooking process. Never thaw food at room temperature.
- Some operations partially cook food during prep. Operations that parcook food must have written procedures to explain how food cooked this way will be prepped and stored. These procedures must be approved by the regulatory authority.
- Cook and reheat food to required minimum internal temperatures for a specific amount of time. Cooking temperatures and times vary from food to food. Reheat TCS food that will be hot held to an internal temperature of 165°F (74°C) for 15 seconds. Make sure the reheated food reaches this temperature within two hours.
- Meat, seafood, poultry, and eggs that you cook in a microwave oven must be cooked to 165°F (74°C). Cover the food, rotate or stir it halfway through the cooking process, let the food stand for at least two minutes, and check the temperature in at least two places.
- Your menu must tell guests when a TCS food is served raw or undercooked. You must also advise guests who order food that is raw or undercooked of the increased risk of foodborne illness. You can do this in different ways. The FDA advises against offering raw and undercooked food on children's menus. Operations that mainly serve high-risk populations should never serve raw seed sprouts; raw or undercooked eggs, meat, or seafood; or unpasteurized milk or juice.
- TCS food must be cooled from 135°F to 70°F (57°C to 21°C) within two hours. Then it must be cooled from 70°F to 41°F (21°C to 5°C) or lower in the next four hours.
- Food will cool faster if you reduce its size. Cut large food items into smaller pieces. Divide large containers of food into smaller ones. Use an ice-water bath, stir food with ice paddles, or use a blast or tumble chiller to cool food safely.

Apply Your Knowledge

Use these questions to review the concepts presented in this chapter.

Discussion Questions

1 What are the minimum internal cooking temperatures for poultry, fish, pork, and ground beef?

2 What are the four correct methods for thawing food?

3 What methods can be used to cool cooked food?

4 What are the rules for correctly cooking food in a microwave oven?

For answers, please turn to the Answer Key.

Apply Your Knowledge

Something to Think About

Something's Fishy

On Friday, John went to work at The Fish House knowing he had a lot to do. After changing clothes and punching in promptly at 7:30 a.m., he took a case of frozen raw shrimp out of the freezer. To thaw it quickly, he put the frozen shrimp into the prep sink under hot running water. While waiting for the shrimp to thaw, John took several fresh, whole salmon out of the walk-in cooler. He brought them back to the prep area and began to clean and fillet them.

Two hours later, he remembered the shrimp. He put the salmon aside and wiped off the worktable with a cloth towel. Then he rinsed off the boning knife and cutting board. Next, John transferred the shrimp from the sink to the worktable using a large colander. On the cutting board, he peeled, deveined, and butterflied the shrimp with the boning knife. He put the prepared shrimp in a covered container in the cooler.

John was surprised to see that it was already noon. He quickly returned to the salmon that he set aside. After cleaning and filleting the remaining fish, he put the fillets in a pan and returned them to the walk-in cooler.

1 What did John do wrong?

For answers, please turn to the Answer Key.

Apply Your Knowledge

Something to Think About

Chicken on the Fly

Aiden was a part-time line cook at Basil's Tavern, a popular meeting and drinking place in a small community. Happy hour was an extremely busy time, not just behind the bar, but in the kitchen as well. Basil's offered a huge variety of deep-fried appetizers and other small plates at reduced prices.

Aiden always worried about running out of batter for their famous signature onion rings and chicken tenders. So he decided to make a double batch of the egg-based batter the day before a happy hour. He prepared it in a large plastic tub and added it to batter that was left from the previous day. Aiden covered the batter and placed it in the walk-in cooler.

The next day during happy hour, things got crazy in the kitchen. Tickets for chicken fingers were lining up, and all three fryers were going full blast. In order to try to stay ahead, Aiden packed the fryer baskets with the battered chicken tenders and lowered the baskets quickly into the fryer. As each cooked batch came out of the fryer, a full basket of uncooked product was dropped in.

Plates started coming back almost as fast as they had left the kitchen. Guests were complaining that the chicken tenders were raw on the inside.

1 What did Aiden do wrong?

2 What should Aiden have done differently?

For answers, please turn to the Answer Key.

Study Questions

Circle the best answer to each question.

1 **What is the maximum water temperature allowed when thawing food under running water?**

A 70°F (21°C)
B 65°F (18°C)
C 60°F (16°C)
D 55°F (13°C)

2 **What must food handlers do to food immediately after thawing it in the microwave oven?**

A Hold it.
B Cook it.
C Cool it.
D Freeze it.

3 **Why must prep tables be cleaned and sanitized between uses?**

A To make space to work safely
B To prevent cross-contamination
C To reduce toxic-metal poisoning
D To avoid time-temperature abuse

4 **A food handler thaws several frozen turkeys on a prep table. What is the danger that this poses to the food?**

A Off flavors in food
B Cross-contamination
C Toxic-metal poisoning
D Time-temperature abuse

5 **A food handler pulled a hotel pan of tuna salad from the cooler and used it to prepare six tuna salad sandwiches. What is the potential problem with this situation?**

A Cross-contamination
B Poor personal hygiene
C Time-temperature abuse
D Poor cleaning and sanitizing

Study Questions

6 **Which food should not be offered on a children's menu?**

A Spaghetti with meat sauce
B Grilled cheese sandwich
C Fried chicken tenders
D Rare hamburger

7 **When partially cooking food for later service, what is the maximum amount of time that the food can be heated during the initial cooking step?**

A 60 minutes
B 70 minutes
C 80 minutes
D 90 minutes

8 **What is the minimum internal cooking temperature for ground beef?**

A 135°F (57°C) for 15 seconds
B 145°F (63°C) for 15 seconds
C 155°F (68°C) for 15 seconds
D 165°F (74°C) for 15 seconds

9 **A safe way to cool a stockpot of meat sauce is to put it into a**

A cooler.
B freezer.
C sink of ice water.
D cold-holding unit.

10 **What temperature must TCS food be reheated to if it will be hot held?**

A 135°F (57°C) for 15 seconds
B 145°F (63°C) for 15 seconds
C 155°F (68°C) for 15 seconds
D 165°F (74°C) for 15 seconds

For answers, please turn to the Answer Key.

Notes

Notes

9 The Flow of Food: Service

One Hundred Sickened by Norovirus Outbreak

A buffet attendant sickened over 100 guests at a large southwestern golf resort. Those who got sick had symptoms that included severe vomiting, diarrhea, and physical weakness. A food handler later tested positive for Norovirus. While the food handler was not experiencing symptoms at the time of the outbreak, he indicated that he had experienced vomiting and diarrhea the week before.

Local regulatory authorities determined that the food handler contaminated items on the buffet line as he worked. The food handler failed to wash his hands correctly before moving from buffet station to buffet station. Authorities believed that utensils used by the guests had become contaminated by the food handler. This led to the outbreak.

1. **What could have been done to prevent this situation from occurring in the first place?**

For answers, please turn to the Answer Key.

Inside This Chapter

- Holding Food for Service
- Serving Food Safely
- Off-Site Service

Objectives

After completing this chapter, you should be able to identify the following:

- Time and temperature requirements for holding hot and cold TCS food
- Ways of preventing time-temperature abuse and cross-contamination when displaying and serving food
- The requirements for using time rather than temperature as the only method of control when holding TCS food
- Ways of minimizing bare-hand contact with ready-to-eat food
- How to prevent staff from contaminating food during service
- How to prevent guests from contaminating self-service areas
- The possible hazards of transporting food and ways of preventing them
- The possible hazards of serving food off-site and ways of preventing them
- The possible hazards of vending food and ways of preventing them

Key Terms

Off-site service

Temporary units

Mobile units

Holding Food for Service

General Rules for Holding Food

To keep food safe during holding, consider the following.

Temperature **Hold TCS food at the correct internal temperature:**

- Hold hot food at an internal temperature of 135°F (57°C) or higher.
- Hold cold food at an internal temperature of 41°F (5°C) or lower.

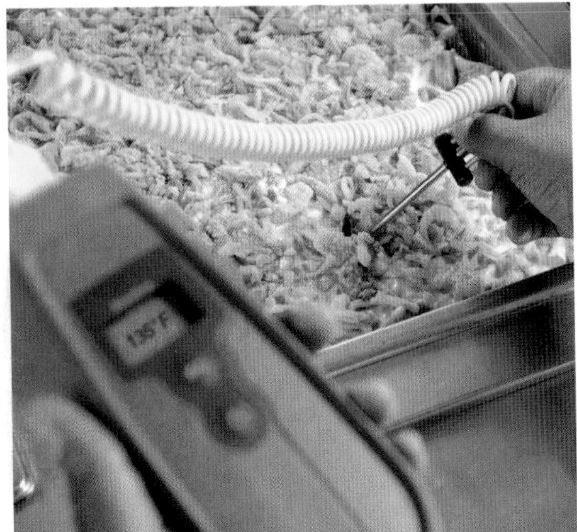

Thermometer Use a thermometer to check temperatures. **NEVER** use the temperature gauge on a holding unit to check the food's temperature. The gauge does not check the internal temperature of the food.

Time Check food temperatures at least every four hours, as shown in the photo at left. Follow these guidelines:

- Throw out food that is not being held at the correct temperature.
- You can also check the temperature every two hours. This will leave time for corrective action. For example, hot TCS food that has been held below 135°F (57°C) can be reheated and then placed back in the hot-holding unit.

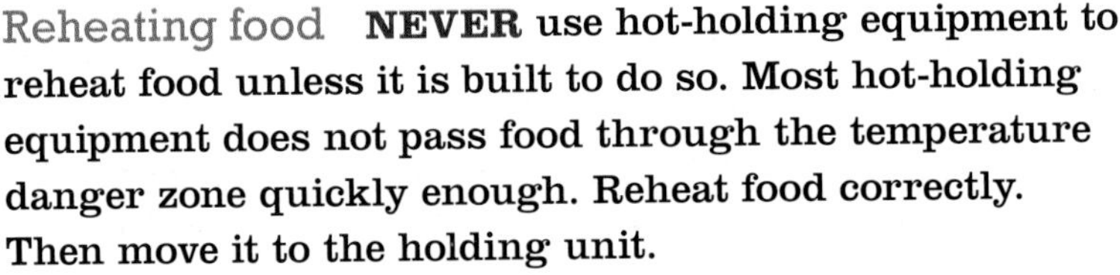

Reheating food **NEVER** use hot-holding equipment to reheat food unless it is built to do so. Most hot-holding equipment does not pass food through the temperature danger zone quickly enough. Reheat food correctly. Then move it to the holding unit.

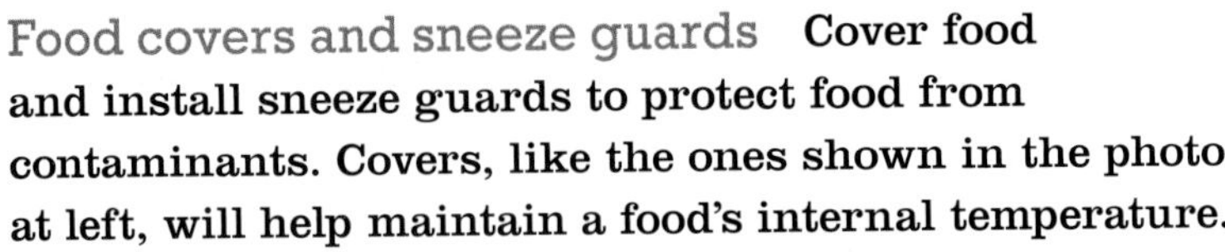

Food covers and sneeze guards Cover food and install sneeze guards to protect food from contaminants. Covers, like the ones shown in the photo at left, will help maintain a food's internal temperature.

Policies Create policies about how long the operation will hold food and when it will be thrown out.

Holding Food without Temperature Control

Your operation may want to display or hold TCS food without temperature control. However, if you primarily serve a high-risk population, **DO NOT** hold TCS food without temperature control.

Here are some examples of when food might be held without temperature control:

- When displaying food for a short time, such as at an off-site catered event, as shown in the photo at right.
- When electricity is not available to power holding equipment.

If your operation displays or holds TCS food without temperature control, it should do so under certain conditions. Also note that the conditions for holding cold food are different from those for holding hot food. Before using time as a method of control, check with your regulatory authority for specific requirements.

Cold Food

You can hold cold food without temperature control for up to six hours if you meet these conditions:

- Hold the food at 41°F (5°C) or lower before removing it from refrigeration.
- Label the food with the time you removed it from refrigeration and the time you must throw it out. The discard time on the label must be six hours from the time you removed the food from refrigeration, as shown in the photo at right. For example, if you remove potato salad from the cooler at 3:00 p.m. to serve at a picnic, the discard time on the label should be 9:00 p.m. This equals six hours from the time you removed it from refrigeration.
- Make sure the food temperature does not exceed 70°F (21°C) while it is being served. Throw out any food that exceeds this temperature.
- Sell, serve, or throw out the food within six hours.

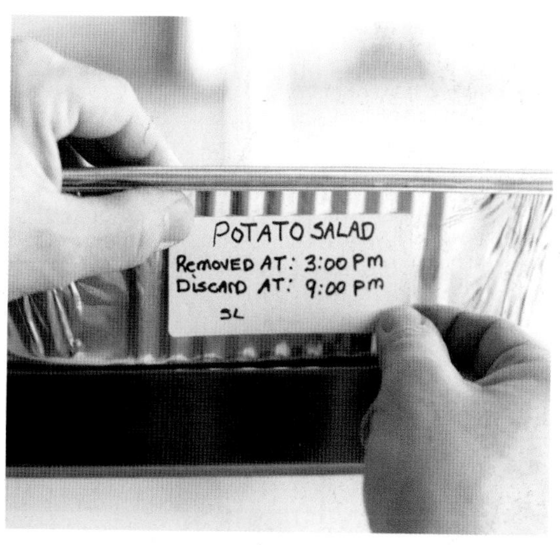

Hot Food

You can hold hot food without temperature control for up to four hours if you meet these conditions:

- Hold the food at 135°F (57°C) or higher before removing it from temperature control.
- Label the food with the time you must throw it out. The discard time on the label must be four hours from the time you removed the food from temperature control, as shown in the photo at right.
- Sell, serve, or throw out the food within four hours.

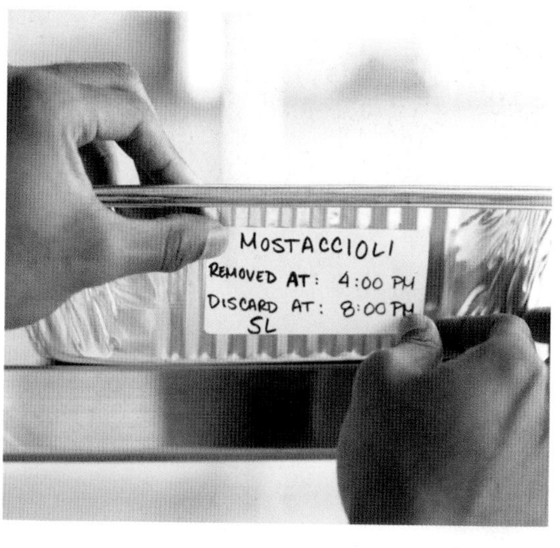

Serving Food Safely

Service Staff Guidelines

Service staff can contaminate food simply by handling the food-contact areas of glasses, dishes, and utensils. Service staff should use these guidelines when serving food.

- Hold dishes by the bottom or edge.
- Hold glasses by the middle, bottom, or stem.
- Do **NOT** touch the food-contact areas of dishes or glassware.

- Carry glasses in a rack or on a tray to avoid touching the food-contact surfaces.
- Do **NOT** stack glasses when carrying them.

- Hold flatware by the handle.
- Do **NOT** hold flatware by food-contact surfaces.
- Store flatware so that servers grasp handles, not food-contact surfaces.

- Avoid bare-hand contact with food that is ready to eat.

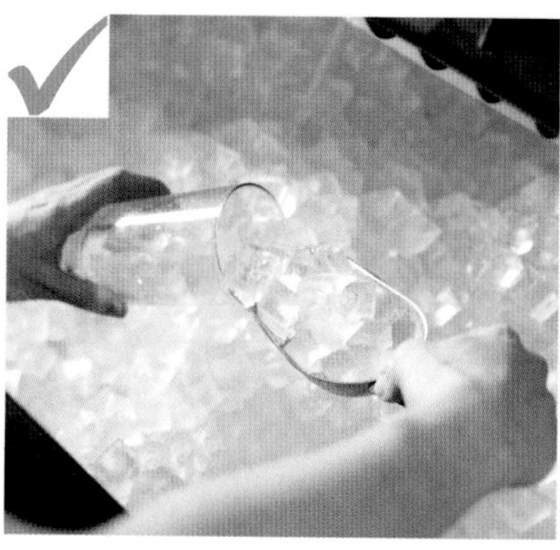

- Use ice scoops or tongs to get ice.
- **NEVER** scoop ice with your bare hands or a glass. A glass may chip or break.

Preset Tableware

If your operation presets tableware on dining tables, you must take steps to prevent it from becoming contaminated. This might include wrapping or covering the items, as shown in the photo at right.

Table settings do not need to be wrapped or covered if extra (or unused) settings meet these requirements:

- They are removed when guests are seated.
- If they remain on the table, they are cleaned and sanitized after guests have left.

Re-serving Food Safely

Service and kitchen staff should also know the rules about re-serving food that was previously served to another guest.

Returned menu items Do **NOT** re-serve food returned by a guest.

Plate garnishes **NEVER** re-serve plate garnishes such as fruit or pickles. Throw out served but unused garnishes.

Condiments Serve condiments in their original containers or in containers designed to prevent contamination. Offering condiments in individual packets or portions can also help keep them safe.

- **NEVER** re-serve uncovered condiments.
- Do **NOT** combine leftover condiments with fresh ones, as the food handler in the photo at left is doing.
- Throw away opened portions of condiments after serving them to guests. Salsa, butter, mayonnaise, and ketchup are examples.

Bread and rolls Do **NOT** re-serve uneaten bread or rolls to other guests. Change linens used in bread baskets after each guest.

Prepackaged food In general, you may re-serve only unopened, prepackaged food in good condition. This includes condiment packets and wrapped crackers. You may also re-serve bottles of ketchup, mustard, and other condiments. The containers must remain closed between uses.

Kitchen Staff Guidelines

Train your kitchen staff to serve food in these ways.

Bare-hand contact Food handlers must wear single-use gloves whenever handling ready-to-eat food. As an alternative, food can be handled with spatulas, tongs, deli sheets, or other utensils. The photo at left shows two ways to avoid bare-hand contact. Keep in mind that there are some situations where it may be acceptable to handle ready-to-eat food with bare hands, such as when a dish does not contain raw meat, seafood, or poultry and will be cooked to at least 145°F (63°C).

Serving utensils Use separate utensils for serving each food item. Clean and sanitize them after each serving task. If using utensils continuously, clean and sanitize them at least once every four hours.

Utensil storage Store serving utensils in the food with the handle extended above the rim of the container, as shown in the photo at left. Or if you are serving a non-TCS food item, you can also place them on a clean and sanitized food-contact surface. Spoons or scoops used to serve food, such as ice cream or mashed potatoes, can be stored under running water that is at least 135°F (57°C).

Refilling take-home containers Some jurisdictions allow food handlers to refill take-home containers brought back by a guest with food and beverages. Take-home containers can be refilled if they meet these conditions:

- They were designed to be reused.
- They were provided to the guest by the operation.
- They are cleaned and sanitized correctly.

Take-home beverage containers can also be refilled as long as the beverage is not a TCS food and the container will be refilled for the same guest. The container must also meet these conditions:

- It can be effectively cleaned at home and in the operation.
- It will be rinsed with fresh, hot water under pressure before refilling.
- It will be refilled by staff in the operation or by the guest using a process that prevents contamination.

Self-Service Areas

Self-service areas can be contaminated easily. Follow these guidelines to prevent contamination and time-temperature abuse.

Protection Food on display can be protected from contamination using sneeze guards, as shown in the photo at right. Food can also be protected by placing it in display cases or by packaging it to protect it from contamination. Whole, raw fruits and vegetables and nuts in the shell that require peeling or hulling before eating do not require the protection measures discussed above.

Labels Label food located in self-service areas. For example, place the name of the food, such as salad dressing, on ladle handles or signs, as shown in the photo at right.

Raw and ready-to-eat food Typically, raw unpackaged meat, poultry, and seafood cannot be offered for self-service. However, these items are an exception:

- Ready-to-eat food at buffets or salad bars that serve food such as sushi or raw shellfish.
- Ready-to-cook portions that will be cooked and eaten immediately on the premises, such as at Mongolian barbecues.
- Raw, frozen, shell-on shrimp or lobster.

Refills Do **NOT** let guests refill dirty plates or use dirty utensils at self-service areas. Assign a staff member to monitor guests. Post signs reminding guests not to reuse plates and utensils.

Utensils Stock food displays with the correct utensils for dispensing food. This might include tongs, ladles, or deli sheets.

Ice Ice used to keep food or beverages cold should **NEVER** be used as an ingredient.

Labeling Bulk Food

Label bulk food in self-service areas. The label must be in plain view of the guest. When labeling food, you can include the manufacturer or processor label provided with the food. As an alternative, you can provide this information using a card, sign, or other labeling method.

Bulk unpackaged food, such as bakery products and unpackaged food portioned for guests, does not need to be labeled if it meets these conditions:

- The product makes no claim regarding health or nutrient content.
- There are no laws requiring labeling.
- The food is manufactured or prepped on the premises.
- The food is manufactured or prepped at another food operation or processing plant owned by the same person. The operation must also be regulated.

Off-Site Service

Off-site service such as delivery, catering, mobile/temporary kitchens, and vending machines can present special challenges. Those who operate these services need to follow the same food safety rules as permanent operations. Food should be protected from contamination and time-temperature abuse. Facilities and equipment used to prep food need to be clean and safe. Menu items should contribute to safe service. Food needs to be handled correctly as well.

Delivery

Many operations prep food at one location and then deliver it to remote sites. The longer the time between preparation and consumption, the greater the risk that food will be exposed to contamination or time-temperature abuse.

When transporting food and items, follow these safety procedures.

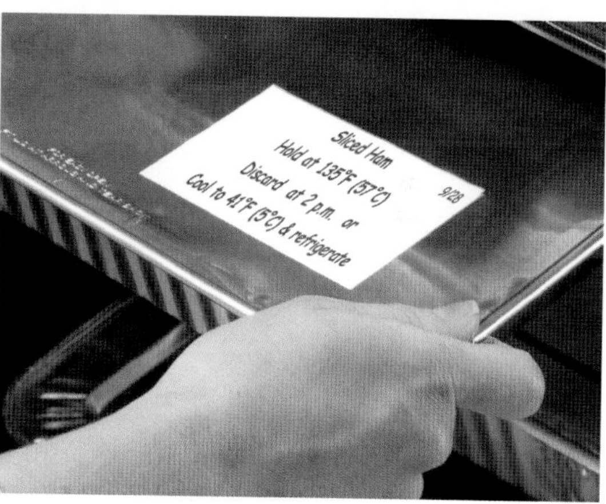

Containers Pack food in insulated, food-grade containers, as shown in the photo at right. They should be designed so food cannot mix, leak, or spill. At the service site, use appropriate containers or equipment to hold food at the correct temperature.

Labels Label food with a use-by date and time, and reheating and service instructions for staff at off-site locations. This is shown in the photo at right.

Delivery vehicles Clean the inside of delivery vehicles regularly.

Personal hygiene Practice good personal hygiene when distributing food.

Internal food temperatures Check internal food temperatures. If containers or delivery vehicles are not holding food at the correct temperature, reevaluate the length of the delivery route or the efficiency of the equipment being used.

Storage Store raw meat, poultry, and seafood separate from ready-to-eat items. For example, store raw chicken separate from ready-to-eat salads.

Catering

Caterers must follow the same food safety rules as permanent operations. Food must be protected from contamination and time-temperature abuse. Facilities must be clean and sanitary. Food must be prepared and served correctly, and staff must follow good personal hygiene practices.

Catering often presents unique challenges. Follow these guidelines to keep food safe.

Utilities Make sure the service site has the correct utilities:

- Safe water for cooking, dishwashing, and handwashing
- Garbage containers stored away from food-prep, storage, and serving areas

Insulated containers Use insulated containers to hold TCS food. Raw meat should be wrapped and stored on ice. Deliver milk and dairy products in a refrigerated vehicle or on ice.

Cold food Serve cold food in containers on ice or in chilled, gel-filled containers. If that is not desirable, the food may be held without temperature control according to the guidelines specified in this chapter.

Ready-to-eat food Store ready-to-eat food separate from raw food.

Leftovers If leftovers are given to guests, provide instructions on how they should be handled. Information such as a discard date and the food's storage and reheating instructions should be clearly labeled on the container.

Temporary Units

Temporary units typically operate in one location for less than 14 days. Foodservice tents or kiosks set up for food fairs, special celebrations, or sporting events may be temporary units. A temporary unit is shown in the photo at left.

In some areas, the definition also extends to units set up for longer periods. Temporary units usually serve prepackaged food or food requiring limited prepping, such as hot dogs. It is best to keep the menu simple to limit the amount of on-site food prep. Check with your regulatory authority for operating requirements.

Here are some additional guidelines:

- Temporary units should be constructed to keep out dirt and pests. If floors are made of dirt or gravel, cover them with mats or platforms to control dust and mud. Construct walls and the ceiling with materials that will protect food from weather and windblown dust.
- The safe-handling rules discussed throughout this book apply to food prep in temporary units.
- Safe drinking water also needs to be available for cleaning, sanitizing, and handwashing. Because dishwashing facilities will likely be limited too, it is best to use disposable, single-use items.

Mobile Units

Mobile units are portable facilities ranging from concession vans to elaborate field kitchens. Those serving only frozen novelties, candy, packaged snacks, and soft drinks need to meet basic sanitation requirements. However, mobile kitchens prepping and serving TCS food need to follow the same rules required of permanent foodservice kitchens. Both types of operations might be required to apply for a special permit or license from the regulatory authority.

Vending Machines

Vending operators should protect food from contamination and time-temperature abuse. This is especially important when prepping and packaging food and during transport and delivery. Follow these guidelines:

- Check product shelf life daily. Products often have an expiration or use-by date, such as that shown in the photo at right. If the date has expired, throw out the food immediately. Throw out refrigerated food prepped on-site if not sold within seven days of preparation.
- Keep TCS food at the correct temperature. It should be held at 41°F (5°C) or lower, or at 135°F (57°C) or higher. These machines must have controls that prevent TCS food from being dispensed if the temperature stays in the danger zone for a specified amount of time. This food must be thrown out.
- Dispense TCS food in its original container.
- Wash and wrap fresh fruit with edible peels before putting it in a machine.

Chapter Summary

- Your operation should have policies for holding and discarding food. Cover food or use sneeze guards. Hold TCS food at the correct temperature. Never use hot-holding equipment to reheat food unless it is built to do so.
- When holding TCS food for service, keep hot food at 135°F (57°C) or higher. Keep cold food at 41°F (5°C) or lower. Check the internal temperature of food at least every four hours. Throw food out if it is not at the correct temperature and cannot be restored to a safe condition.
- TCS food may be held without temperature control under certain conditions. Cold food must be held at 41°F (5°C) or lower before it is removed from refrigeration. Then, the food temperature must not get higher than 70°F (21°C). If it does, or if the food is not served or sold within six hours, the food must be thrown away. Hot food must be held at 135°F (57°C) or higher before it is removed from temperature control. Then it must be served, stored, or thrown away within four hours. Both cold and hot food must be labeled with the discard time. Operations that primarily serve high-risk populations should never hold food without temperature control.
- Staff should be trained to avoid bare-hand contact with ready-to-eat food. They should also be trained to use and maintain utensils correctly. Use separate utensils for different food items. Clean and sanitize them after each task and after four hours of continuous use. Store serving utensils correctly to avoid contamination. Follow guidelines for refilling take-home containers.
- Teach staff the correct ways for handling service items and tableware. Staff should also be trained on the rules for throwing away and re-serving food that was served to guests. This should address food returned by guests and unused condiments, bread, garnishes, and prepackaged food.
- Self-service areas can be contaminated by staff and guests. Protect food on display with sneeze guards, packaging, or other tools designed to keep food safe. Post self-service rules. Make it clear to guests that clean plates must be used for refills. Put the correct labels on displayed food and bulk food available for self-service. Make sure equipment holds food at the correct temperature.
- Catering, mobile units, temporary units, and vending machines pose their own challenges to food safety. Food served by these sources must be treated with the same care as any other food served to guests. Pack, label, reheat, hold, and store food properly. Make sure delivery vehicles are clean and holding equipment keeps food at the correct temperature. Practice good personal hygiene. Make sure the service site has the correct utilities. Temporary units must be built to keep food safe from weather, dirt, and pests. Mobile units may need to have a special permit or license to operate. Check the shelf life of food in vending machines daily. Learn and follow any regulatory requirements that may apply to your operation.

Apply Your Knowledge

Use these questions to review the concepts presented in this chapter.

Discussion Questions

1 What can be done to minimize contamination in self-service areas?

2 What hazards are associated with the transportation of food and how can they be prevented?

Apply Your Knowledge

3 What are the requirements for using time rather than temperature as the only method of control when holding TCS food?

4 What practices should be followed to serve catered food off-site?

For answers, please turn to the Answer Key.

Apply Your Knowledge

Something to Think About

In the Weeds

Jill, a line cook on the morning shift at Memorial Hospital, was busy helping the kitchen staff put food on display for lunch in the hospital cafeteria. Ann, the kitchen manager who usually supervised lunch in the cafeteria, was at an all-day seminar on food safety. Jill was also responsible for making sure meals were trayed and put into food carts for transport to the patients' rooms. The staff also packed two dozen meals each day for a neighborhood group that delivered them to homebound elderly people.

Knowing the delivery driver would arrive soon to pick up the meals, Jill looked for insulated food containers to hold them. When she could not find any, she loaded the meals into cardboard boxes she found near the back door. The cafeteria was busy, and the staff had many meals to tray and deliver.

As the lunch period was ending, Jill breathed a sigh of relief. She moved down the cafeteria serving line, checking food temperatures. One of the casseroles was at 130°F (54°C). Jill checked the water level in the steam table and turned up the thermostat. She then went to clean up the kitchen and finish her shift.

1 What did Jill do wrong?

____

____

____

____

2 What should she have done?

____

____

____

____

For answers, please turn to the Answer Key.

Apply Your Knowledge

Something to Think About

Megan's Day

Megan, a new server at The Fish House, reported for work 10 minutes early on Thursday. She was excited about her new job and wanted to make a good impression.

Her shift started off well. One of her guests ordered a menu item that Megan had not tried yet. When the order came up, Megan dipped her finger into the sauce at the edge of the plate for a taste. As the shift progressed, Megan's station got busier. When the hostess came to ask how soon one of Megan's tables could be cleared, Megan decided to do it herself. She took the dirty dishes to a bus station and then wiped down the table with a serving cloth she kept in her apron.

The buser, John, finished another task and came to help her set the table. While he put out silverware and linens, Megan filled water glasses with ice by scooping the glasses into the ice bin in the bus station. Only one slice of bread and one pat of butter were missing from the basket that had been on a previous guest's table, so she put that on a tray with the water glasses and brought it to the table.

The table was reset in record time, and Megan soon had more guests. While taking their orders, Megan reached up to scratch a sore on her neck. Then she went to the kitchen to turn in the order and pick up a dessert order for another table.

1 What errors did Megan make?

____

____

____

____

2 What should she have done?

____

____

____

____

Study Questions

For answers, please turn to the Answer Key. Circle the best answer to each question.

1 **Which part of the plate should a food handler avoid touching when serving guests?**

A Bottom
B Edge
C Side
D Top

2 **An operation has a self-service salad bar with 8 different items on it. How many serving utensils are needed to serve the items on the salad bar?**

A 2
B 4
C 6
D 8

3 **At what maximum internal temperature should cold TCS food be held?**

A 0°F (-18°C)
B 32°F (0°C)
C 41°F (5°C)
D 60°F (16°C)

4 **What item must guests take each time they return to a self-service area for more food?**

A Clean plate
B Extra napkins
C Hand sanitizer
D New serving spoon

5 **At what minimum temperature should hot TCS food be held?**

A 115°F (46°C)
B 125°F (52°C)
C 135°F (57°C)
D 145°F (63°C)

Study Questions

6 **An operation is located in a jurisdiction that allows it to hold TCS food without temperature control. How many hours can it display hot TCS food without temperature control before the food must be sold, served, or thrown out?**

A 2
B 4
C 6
D 8

7 **How often must you check the temperature of food that is being held with temperature control?**

A At least every 2 hours
B At least every 4 hours
C At least every 6 hours
D At least every 8 hours

8 **A pan of lasagna at 165°F (74°C) was packed in a heated cabinet for off-site delivery. What is the minimum information that should be on the pan label?**

A Use-by date and time and reheating and service instructions
B Use-by date and reheating and service instructions
C Use-by time and reheating and service instructions
D Use-by date and time and reheating instructions

9 **Which may be handled with bare hands?**

A Cooked pasta for salad
B Chopped tomatoes for soup
C Canned tuna for sandwiches
D Pickled watermelon for garnish

10 **When a utensil is stored in water between uses, what are the requirements?**

A Running water at any temperature, or a container of water at 70°F (21°C) or lower
B Running water at any temperature, or a container of water at 135°F (57°C) or higher
C Running water at 70°F (21°C) or lower, or a container of water at 70°F (21°C) or lower
D Running water at 135°F (57°C) or higher, or a container of water at 135°F (57°C) or higher

For answers, please turn to the Answer Key.

Notes

10 Food Safety Management Systems

Blue Skies Handles It Correctly

The calls started on a Thursday morning at Blue Skies Café, a small but well-liked diner in a busy city neighborhood. The callers complained of stomach cramps and diarrhea. The owner expressed concern and told the callers she would look into the situation. As she took each call, she filled out an incident report. After the first couple of calls, the owner realized that she might have a foodborne-illness outbreak on her hands. She immediately contacted the local regulatory authority.

"We were also getting calls, so we went to the café to see what happened," said the health inspector assigned to the case. "With the cooperation of the owner, we were able to identify the Caesar salad dressing as the source of the customers' illnesses." A batch of the dressing was made with contaminated eggs. It eventually made 30 people sick.

1. **What did the owner of the café do correctly when handling the situation?**

For answers, please turn to the Answer Key.

Inside This Chapter

- Food Safety Management Systems
- Active Managerial Control
- Crisis Management

Objectives

After completing this chapter, you should be able to identify the following:

- Methods for achieving active managerial control
- The public health interventions of the Food and Drug Administration (FDA)
- The seven HACCP principles for preventing foodborne illness
- Specialized processes that require a variance
- How to prepare for, respond to, and recover from a crisis
- How to respond to a foodborne-illness outbreak
- How to respond to imminent health hazards, including power outages, fire, flood, water interruption, and sewage

Key Terms

Food safety management system

Active managerial control

HACCP

HACCP plan

Critical control points (CCPs)

Imminent health hazard

Food Safety Management Systems

A **food safety management system** is a group of practices and procedures intended to prevent foodborne illness. It does this by actively controlling risks and hazards throughout the flow of food.

Having some food safety programs already in place gives you the foundation for your system. The principles presented in ServSafe are the basis of these programs. Here are some examples of the programs your operation needs:

Personal hygiene program

Food safety training program

Supplier selection and specification program

Quality control and assurance programs

Cleaning and sanitation program

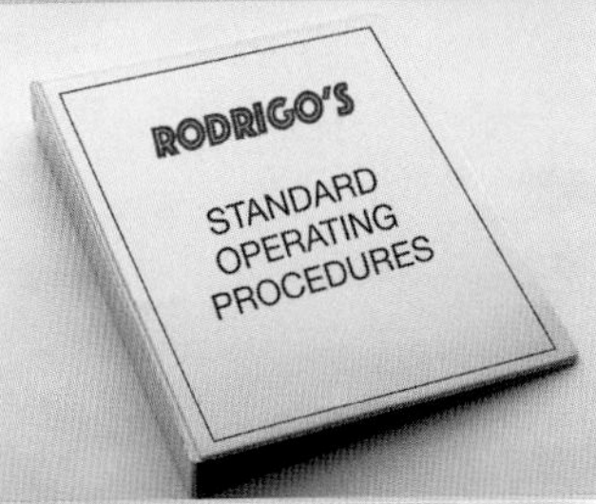

Standard operating procedures (SOPs)

Facility design and equipment maintenance program

Pest-control program

Active Managerial Control

Earlier, you learned that there are five common risk factors for foodborne illness:

1. Purchasing food from unsafe sources
2. Failing to cook food correctly
3. Holding food at incorrect temperatures
4. Using contaminated equipment
5. Practicing poor personal hygiene

It is the manager's responsibility to actively control these and other risk factors for foodborne illness. This is called **active managerial control**. It is important to note that active managerial control is proactive rather than reactive. You must anticipate risks and plan for them.

There are many ways to achieve active managerial control in the operation. According to the Food and Drug Administration (FDA), you can use simple tools such as training programs, manager supervision, and the incorporation of SOPs. Active managerial control can also be achieved through more complex solutions, such as a Hazard Analysis Critical Control Point (HACCP) program.

Managers should practice active managerial control throughout the flow of food. This includes anticipating potential foodborne-illness risk factors and then controlling or eliminating them. You might already do some of these things, such as purchasing food from approved suppliers. But, active managerial control also includes many of the other things you have learned; for example, making sure food is held at the proper temperature or cooking food to its required minimum internal cooking temperature. Monitoring the entire flow of food will help keep your guests and operation free from risk. You also must provide your staff with the proper tools, such as procedures and training, to make sure food is safe.

There are some important steps to take when implementing active managerial control in your operation.

1. Identify Risks Find and document the potential foodborne-illness risks in your operation. Then, identify the hazards that can be controlled or eliminated.

2 Monitor Food will be safe if managers monitor critical activities in the operation. So make note of where employees must monitor food safety requirements. This might include identifying when temperatures should be taken or how often sanitizer concentrations should be tested in a three-compartment sink. For example, the manager at left is monitoring a food handler as he carries out the critical task of reheating food correctly.

3 Corrective action Take the appropriate steps to correct improper procedures or behaviors. For example, if a sanitizer concentration level is too low when tested, the situation might be corrected by increasing the concentration level.

4 Management oversight Verify that all policies, procedures, and corrective actions are followed.

5 Training Ensure employees are trained to follow procedures and retrained when necessary.

6 Re-evaluation Periodically assess the system to make sure it is working correctly and effectively.

The FDA's Public Health Interventions

The FDA provides specific recommendations for controlling the common risk factors for foodborne illness. These are known as public health interventions. They are designed to protect public health.

Demonstration of knowledge As a manager, you must be able to show that you know what to do to keep food safe. Becoming certified in food safety is one way to show this.

Staff health controls Procedures must be put in place to make sure staff are practicing good personal hygiene. For example, staff must understand that they are required to report illnesses and illness symptoms to management.

Controlling hands as a vehicle of contamination Controls must be put in place to prevent bare-hand contact with ready-to-eat food. This might include requiring the use of tongs to handle ready-to-eat food, as shown in the photo at left.

Time and temperature parameters for controlling pathogens Procedures must be put in place to limit the time food spends in the temperature danger zone. Requiring food handlers to check the temperature of food being hot held every two hours is an example.

Consumer advisories Notices must be provided to guests if you serve raw or undercooked menu items. These notices must include a statement about the risks of eating this food.

HACCP

There are many systems you can implement to achieve active managerial control of foodborne-illness risk factors. A Hazard Analysis Critical Control Point (HACCP) program is one such system. A **HACCP** (pronounced HASS-ip) system is based on identifying significant biological, chemical, or physical hazards at specific points within a product's flow. Once identified, the hazards can be prevented, eliminated, or reduced to safe levels.

An effective HACCP system must be based on a written plan. This plan must be specific to each facility's menu, guests, equipment, processes, and operations. Because each **HACCP plan** is unique, a plan that works for one operation may not work for another.

The HACCP Approach

A HACCP plan is based on seven basic principles. They were created by the National Advisory Committee on Microbiological Criteria for Foods. These principles are the seven steps that outline how to create a HACCP plan.

The Seven HACCP Principles

Each HACCP principle builds on the information gained from the previous principle. You must consider all seven principles, in order, when developing your plan. Here are the seven principles:

1. Conduct a hazard analysis.
2. Determine critical control points (CCPs).
3. Establish critical limits.
4. Establish monitoring procedures.
5. Identify corrective actions.
6. Verify that the system works.
7. Establish procedures for record keeping and documentation.

In general terms, the principles break into three groups:

- Principles 1 and 2 help you identify and evaluate your hazards.
- Principles 3, 4, and 5 help you establish ways for controlling those hazards.
- Principles 6 and 7 help you maintain the HACCP plan and system and verify its effectiveness.

The next few pages provide an introduction to these principles. They also present an overview of how to build a HACCP program. A real-world example has also been included for each principle. It shows the efforts of Enrico's, an Italian restaurant, as it implements a HACCP program. The example will appear after the explanation of each principle.

Principle 1: Conduct a Hazard Analysis

First, identify and assess potential hazards in the food you serve. Start by looking at how food is processed in your operation. Many types of food are processed in similar ways. Here are some common processes:

- Prepping and serving without cooking (salads, cold sandwiches, etc.)
- Prepping and cooking for same-day service (grilled chicken sandwiches, hamburgers, etc.)
- Prepping, cooking, holding, cooling, reheating, and serving (chili, soup, pasta sauce with meat, etc.)

Look at your menu and identify items that are processed like this. Next, identify the TCS food. Determine where food safety hazards are likely to occur for each TCS food. They can come from biological, chemical, or physical contaminants.

Principle 1 Example

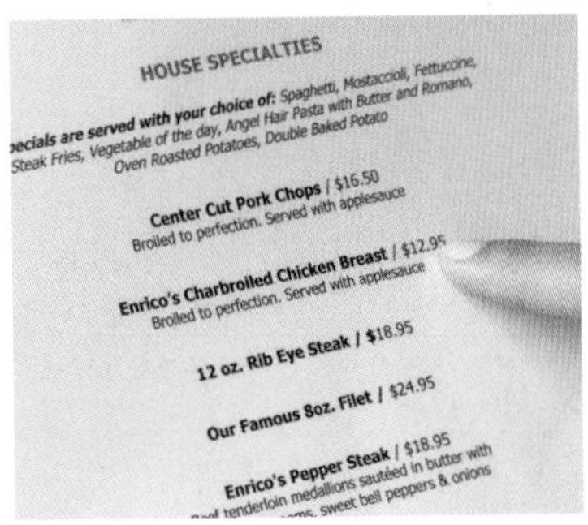

The management team at Enrico's decided to implement a HACCP program. They began by analyzing their hazards.

The team noted that many of their dishes were received, stored, prepared, cooked, and served the same day. The most popular of these items was the spicy charbroiled chicken breast.

The team determined that bacteria were the most likely hazard to food prepared this way.

Principle 2: Determine Critical Control Points (CCPs)

Find the points in the process where the identified hazard(s) can be prevented, eliminated, or reduced to safe levels. These are the **critical control points (CCPs)**. Depending on the process, there may be more than one CCP.

Principle 2 Example

Enrico's management identified cooking as the CCP for food prepared and cooked for immediate service. This included the chicken breasts.

These food items must be handled correctly throughout the flow of food. However, correct cooking is the only step that will eliminate or reduce bacteria to safe levels.

Because the chicken breasts were prepared for immediate service, cooking was the only CCP identified.

Principle 3: Establish Critical Limits

For each CCP, establish minimum or maximum limits. These limits must be met to prevent or eliminate the hazard, or to reduce it to a safe level.

Principle 3 Example

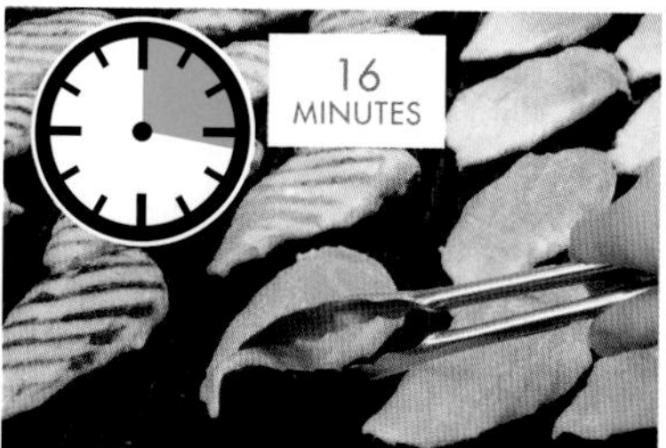

With cooking identified as the CCP for Enrico's chicken breasts, a critical limit was needed. Management determined that the critical limit would be cooking the chicken to a minimum internal temperature of 165°F (74°C) for 15 seconds.

They decided that the critical limit could be met by cooking chicken breasts in the broiler for 16 minutes.

Principle 4: Establish Monitoring Procedures

Once critical limits have been created, determine the best way for your operation to check them. Make sure the limits are consistently met. Identify who will monitor them and how often.

Principle 4 Example

At Enrico's, each charbroiled chicken breast is cooked to order. The team decided to check the critical limit by inserting a clean and sanitized thermocouple probe into the thickest part of each chicken breast.

The grill cook must check the temperature of each chicken breast after cooking. Each chicken breast must reach the minimum internal temperature of 165°F (74°C) for 15 seconds.

Principle 5: Identify Corrective Actions

Identify steps that must be taken when a critical limit is not met. These steps should be determined in advance.

Principle 5 Example

If the chicken breast has not reached its critical limit within the 16-minute cook time, the grill cook at Enrico's must keep cooking the chicken breast until it has reached it.

This and all other corrective actions are noted in the temperature log.

Principle 6: Verify That the System Works

Determine if the plan is working as intended. Evaluate it on a regular basis. Use your monitoring charts, records, hazard analysis, etc., and determine if your plan prevents, reduces, or eliminates identified hazards.

Principle 6 Example

Enrico's management team performs HACCP checks once per shift. They make sure that critical limits were met and appropriate corrective actions were taken when needed.

They also check the temperature logs on a weekly basis to identify patterns. This helps to determine if processes or procedures need to be changed. For example, over several weeks they noticed problems toward the end of each week. The chicken breasts often failed to meet the critical limit. The appropriate corrective action was being taken.

Management discovered that Enrico's received chicken shipments from a different supplier on Thursdays. This supplier provided a six-ounce chicken breast. Enrico's chicken specifications listed a four-ounce chicken breast. Management worked with the supplier to ensure they received four-ounce breasts. The receiving procedures were changed to include a weight check.

Principle 7: Establish Procedures for Record Keeping and Documentation

Maintain your HACCP plan and keep all documentation created when developing it. Keep records for the following actions:

- **Monitoring activities**
- **Taking corrective action**
- **Validating equipment (checking for good working condition)**
- **Working with suppliers (i.e., shelf-life studies, invoices, specifications, challenge studies, etc.)**

Principle 7 Example

Enrico's management team determined that time-temperature logs would be kept for three months. Receiving invoices would be kept for 60 days. The team used this documentation to support and revise their HACCP plan.

Another HACCP Example

The Enrico's example shows one type of HACCP plan. Another plan may look very different when it deals with food that is processed more simply. For example, food that is prepared and served without cooking needs a different approach.

Here is an example of the HACCP plan developed by The Fruit Basket. This fruit-only operation is known for its signature item—the Melon Medley Salad.

1 Analyzing hazards The HACCP team at The Fruit Basket decided to look at hazards for the Melon Medley. The salad has fresh watermelon, honeydew, and cantaloupe. The team determined that bacteria pose a risk to these fresh-cut melons.

2 Determining CCPs The melons are prepped, held, and served without cooking. The team determined that preparation and holding are CCPs for the salad. They decided that cleaning and drying the melons' surfaces during prep, as shown in the photo at right, would reduce bacteria. Holding the melon at the correct temperature could prevent the bacteria's growth. Receiving was ruled out as a CCP, because the operation only purchases melons from approved suppliers.

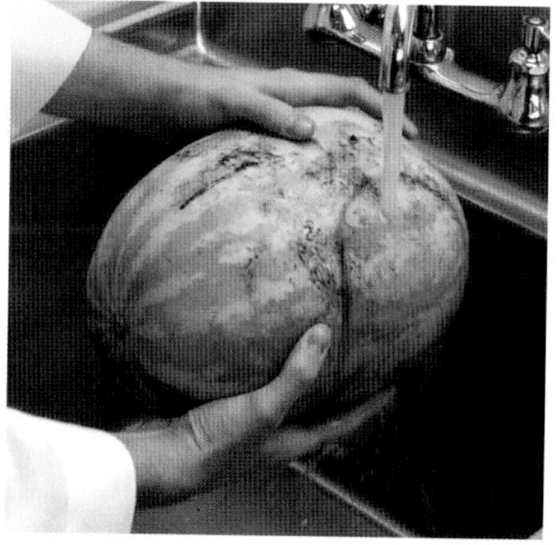

3 Establishing critical limits For the preparation CCP, the team decided the critical limit would be met by washing, scrubbing, and drying whole melons. They created an SOP with techniques for washing the melons. For the holding CCP, they decided that the salad must be held at 41°F (5°C) or lower, because it had cut melons.

4 Establishing monitoring procedures The team decided that the operation's team leader should monitor the salad's critical limits. The team leader must observe food handlers to make sure they are prepping the melons the correct way. Food handlers must remove all surface dirt from the washed melons. Then they must cut, mix, and portion the salad into containers. The finished salads are put in the display cooler. The team leader must then monitor the temperature of the held salads to make sure the holding critical limit is met. The internal temperature of the salads must be 41°F (5°C) or lower. It must be checked three times per day, as shown in the photo at right.

5 Identifying corrective actions Sometimes, after preparation, the melons still have surface dirt. The team had to determine a corrective action for this. They decided that the action would be to rewash the melons. Then the team leader must approve the melons before they are sliced.

To correct a holding temperature that is higher than 41°F (5°C), the team leader must check the temperature of every Melon Medley in the cooler. Any salad that is above 41°F (5°C) must be thrown out.

6 Verifying that the system works To make sure the system is working correctly, the team decided that the operation team leader must review the Manager Daily HACCP Check Sheet at the end of each shift. The team leader makes sure that each item was checked and initialed. The team leader also confirms that all corrective actions have been taken and recorded. The Fruit Basket also evaluates the HACCP system quarterly to see if it is working.

7 Establishing procedures for record keeping Because a foodborne illness associated with fresh produce can take as long as 16 weeks to emerge, the team determined that all HACCP records must be maintained for 16 weeks and kept on file.

Specialized Processing Methods and HACCP

Some food processes are highly specialized and can be a serious health risk if specific procedures are not followed. Typically these processes are carried out at processing plants:

- Smoking food as a method to preserve it (but not to enhance flavor).
- Using food additives or adding components, such as vinegar, to preserve or alter it so it no longer requires time and temperature control for safety.
- Curing food.
- Custom-processing animals. For example, this may include dressing deer in the operation for personal use.
- Packaging food using reduced-oxygen packaging (ROP) methods. This includes MAP, vacuum-packed, and sous vide food. *Clostridium botulinum* and *Listeria monocytogenes* are risks to food packaged in these ways.
- Packaging fresh juice on-site for sale at a later time, unless the juice has a warning label that complies with local regulations.
- Sprouting seeds or beans.
- Offering live shellfish from a display tank.

A variance from the regulatory authority will be required before processing food this way. A variance is a document that allows a requirement to be waived or changed.

A HACCP plan may also be required if the processing method carries a higher risk of causing a foodborne illness. There may also be dangers unique to these processes that are best addressed by a HACCP plan. For example, if not done correctly, reduced-oxygen packaging (ROP) has a very high risk of causing a foodborne illness. Because of this, a HACCP plan is required when a variance has not been requested.

Check with your local regulatory authority before using any of these specialized processing methods on-site.

Crisis Management

Putting the food safety principles you have learned into action can help keep food safe in your operation. However, despite your best efforts, a foodborne-illness outbreak or another type of crisis affecting food safety can still occur. How you respond can influence the outcome.

To handle these crises, you will need a crisis-management program. To be successful, the program needs to have a written plan that focuses on three phases: preparation, response, and recovery. For each phase, the plan should identify resources needed and procedures to be followed.

The time to prepare for a crisis is before one happens. There is no "off-the-shelf" disaster plan that works for everyone. Each plan needs to be customized to the operation.

A good way to ensure your plan works is to test it once it is complete. The results will help you identify potential gaps or problems. Testing the plan will also ensure it works as intended. You can do this yourself or hire a consulting firm with crisis-management experience. In either case, the test should simulate a crisis that will be as close as possible to what could happen.

Creating a Crisis-Management Team

To begin, create a crisis-management team. The size of the team will depend on the size of the operation. If your operation is large, the team may include representatives from the following departments:

- Senior management (president/CEO, etc.)
- Risk management (quality assurance, legal, etc.)
- Public relations
- Operations
- Finance
- Marketing
- Human resources

Smaller operations may include the chef, the general manager, and the owner/operator. Regardless of size, you should also consider using other external resources, such as your regulatory authority and experts from your suppliers and manufacturers.

Preparing for a Crisis

Your crisis-management team should consider the following when preparing for a crisis.

Emergency contact list Create an emergency contact list and post it by phones. It should include the names and numbers of all crisis-management team members; the media spokesperson; management or headquarters personnel; and outside resources such as testing labs, subject-matter experts, the police and fire departments, and the regulatory authority.

Crisis-communication plan Develop a crisis-communication plan that includes the following:

- List of media responses or a question-and-answer sheet suggesting what to say for each crisis.
- Sample press releases that can be tailored quickly to each incident.
- List of media contacts to call for press conferences or news briefings. Include a media-relations plan with "dos and don'ts" for dealing with the media.
- Plan for communicating with staff during the crisis. Possibilities include shift meetings, email, a telephone tree, etc.

Several guides are available to help you develop a crisis-communication plan.

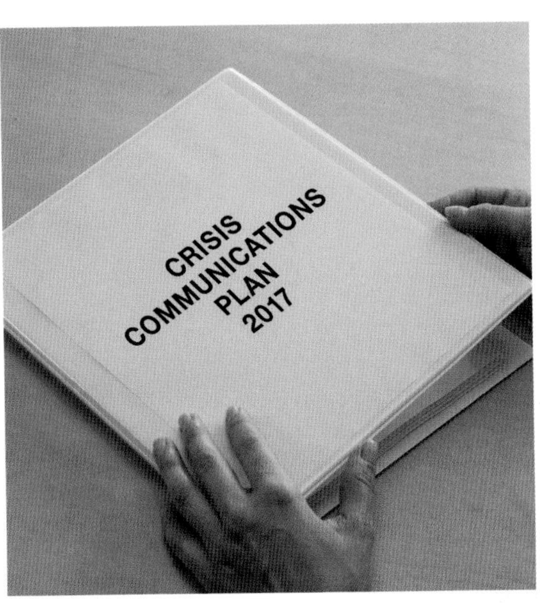

You must appoint a single spokesperson to handle all media queries and communications. This usually results in more consistent messages. It also allows you to control media access to your staff. Crisis situations can be very stressful, and training will enable your spokesperson to handle it better. The spokesperson should also have interview skills, so that he or she knows what to expect and how to respond.

Make sure your staff knows who the spokesperson is. Instruct them to direct questions to that person.

Crisis kit Assemble a crisis kit for the operation. It can be a three-ring binder or notebook enclosing the plan's materials. Keep the kit in an accessible place, such as the manager's or chef's office, as shown in the photo at left.

Preparing for a Foodborne-Illness Outbreak

The greatest threat to your guests is foodborne illness. To prevent an outbreak, you need a food safety program. You also need to train your staff on policies and procedures that will keep the food you serve safe.

In the event of an outbreak, it will be critical to gather accurate information. To prepare for this, you should develop a foodborne-illness incident report form, and train staff to complete it.

Develop the form with legal guidance and include all critical information. The form may contain the following:

- What and when the guest ate at the operation
- When the guest first got sick, what the symptoms were, and how long the guest experienced them
- When and where the guest sought medical attention, what the diagnosis was, and what treatment was received
- What other food was eaten by the guest

Crisis Response

A crisis-management plan should include response procedures to help manage a crisis more effectively. When a crisis occurs, gather your crisis-management team to implement your plan. Direct the team to collect information, plan courses of action, and manage events as they unfold.

Good communication is critical when handling a crisis. Consider the following to keep the situation under control.

Media relations Work with the media. Make sure your spokesperson is fully informed before arranging a press conference. Contacting the media before they contact you also helps you control what they report. Stick to the facts and be honest. If you do not have all the facts, say so. Let the media know you will communicate with them as soon as you do have all the facts. Keep calm and do not be defensive. The easiest way to worsen a crisis is to deny, lie, misinform, or change your story.

Direct communication Communicate information directly to your key audiences. Do not depend on the media to relay all of the facts. Tell your side of the story to staff, guests, stockholders, and the community. Use newsletters, a website, flyers, and newspaper or radio advertising.

Solution Fix the problem. Then communicate to both the media and your customers what you have done. Each time you take a step to resolve the problem, let the media know. Hold briefings when you have news. Go into each briefing or press conference with an agenda. Take control rather than simply responding to questions.

Responding to a Foodborne-Illness Outbreak

In the event of a foodborne-illness outbreak, you may be able to avoid a crisis by acting quickly. Table 10.1 shows how to respond to certain situations.

Table 10.1: **Foodborne-Illness Outbreak Responses**

If	Then
A customer calls to report a foodborne illness.	• Take the complaint seriously and express concern. Do not admit responsibility or accept liability. • Ask for general contact information. Ask about the food that was eaten and when the person first became sick. Ask the person to describe symptoms. • Complete a foodborne-illness incident report form.
There are similar customer complaints of foodborne illness.	• Contact the crisis-management team. • Identify common food items to determine the potential source of the complaint. • Contact the regulatory authority to assist with the investigation if an outbreak is suspected.
The suspected food is still in the operation.	• Set aside the suspected product and identify it to prevent further sale. Include a label with "Do Not Use" and "Do Not Discard." • Log information about the product, including a description, product date, and lot number. The sell-by date and pack size should also be recorded. • If possible, obtain samples of the suspect food from the customer.
The suspected outbreak is caused by a sick staff member.	• Maintain a list of food handlers scheduled at the time of the suspected contamination. Interview them about their health status. • Exclude the suspect staff member from the operation following requirements.
The regulatory authority confirms your operation is the source of the outbreak.	• Cooperate with the regulatory authority to resolve the crisis. Provide appropriate documentation, including temperature logs, HACCP documents, staff files, etc.

Crisis Recovery and Assessment

The final step in a crisis-management plan is developing procedures for recovering from a crisis. Determine what you need to do to ensure both the operation and the food are safe. This is critical for getting your operation running again.

To recover from a foodborne-illness outbreak, you will need to take several steps. They should be planned in advance and include the following:

- Working with the regulatory authority to resolve issues.
- Cleaning and sanitizing all areas of the operation.
- Throwing out all suspect food, as seen in the photo at right.
- Investigating to find the cause of the outbreak.
- Reviewing food handling procedures to identify if standards are not being met or procedures are not working. Establish new procedures or revise existing ones based on the investigation results.
- Developing a plan to reassure guests that the food you serve is safe.

Imminent Health Hazards

In addition to foodborne-illness outbreaks, other crises can affect the safety of the food you serve. Among these are power outages, fire, and flood. Water interruption and sewage backup are also a concern. These are considered by the regulatory authority to be imminent health hazards. An **imminent health hazard** is a significant threat or danger to health that requires immediate correction or closure to prevent injury. If there is a significant risk to the safety or the security of your food, service must be stopped. Then the local regulatory authority must be notified. Spoiled or contaminated food must be thrown out, along with food in packaging that is not intact.

Power Outage

Power failures and refrigeration breakdowns can threaten your ability to control the temperature of TCS food. This can result in the growth of pathogens. Consider the following when planning ahead in case of a power outage:

- Arrange access to an electrical generator and a refrigerated truck that you can use in the event of an emergency.
- Prepare a menu with items that do not require cooking to use in the event of an emergency.
- Develop a policy that addresses when cooler doors should be opened.

To manage your response to a power outage, consider the steps in Table 10.2.

Table 10.2: **Power Outage Responses**

If	Then
Refrigeration equipment stops working.	• Write down the time of the power outage. • Check and record food temperatures periodically. • Keep cooler and freezer doors closed. • Pack TCS food in ice bought from an approved, reputable supplier.
Ventilation hoods or fans stop working.	• Stop all cooking.
Hot-holding equipment stops working.	• Write down the time of the power outage. • Throw out all TCS food held below 135°F (57°C) for more than four hours. • Food can be reheated if the power outage was less than four hours.

You also need to plan for the recovery from a power outage. For example, refrigeration units will need to be checked often after the power has been restored to ensure the equipment can maintain product temperatures. TCS food will also have to be thrown out if it has been in the temperature danger zone for more than four hours.

Water Service Interruption

Broken water mains and breakdowns at water treatment facilities are a risk to the safety of food. Consider the following when planning for a water service interruption:

- Prepare a menu with items that require little or no water to be used in the event of an emergency.
- Keep a supply of single-use items.
- Keep a supply of bottled water. Also have a supplier who can provide bottled water in an emergency.
- Have a supplier who can provide ice in an emergency.
- Have emergency-contact information for your regulatory authority, plumber, and water department.
- Develop procedures that minimize water use during the emergency (e.g., use single-use items for service).
- Work with your regulatory authority to develop an emergency handwashing procedure for use during water service interruptions.

To manage your response to a water service interruption, consider the steps identified in Table 10.3.

Table 10.3: **Water Service Interruption Responses**

If	Then
Hands cannot be washed.	• Implement an emergency handwashing procedure.
Toilets do not flush.	• Find other restrooms for staff use during operating hours. • Stop operations if restrooms are not available.
Drinking water is not available or is contaminated.	• Use bottled water. • Use water from an approved, reputable supplier. • Keep water in a covered, sanitized container during hauling or storage.
Food items that require water during preparation cannot be made.	• Throw out any ready-to-eat food made with water before the contamination was discovered. • Use bottled or boiled water for ready-to-eat food.
Water is not available for food preparation and cooking.	• Use water from an approved, reputable supplier. • Use the emergency menu. • Use prewashed, packaged produce or frozen or canned fruits and vegetables. • Thaw food only in the cooler or microwave or as a part of the cooking process.
Ice cannot be made.	• Throw out existing ice. • Use ice from an approved, reputable supplier.
Equipment, utensils, and facility cannot be cleaned or sanitized.	• Use single-use items. • Use bottled water or water from an approved source to clean and sanitize.
Beverages made with water cannot be prepared.	• Stop using the drink machines that require water, such as the auto-fill coffee maker, etc.

When water is restored or the regulatory authority has lifted any boiled-water advisory, you should plan on taking these actions:

- Clean and sanitize equipment with water line connections, such as spray misters, coffee or tea urns, ice machines, etc. Follow manufacturers' instructions.
- Flush water lines as required by the regulatory authority.
- Work with your regulatory authority to resume normal operations.

Fire

Consider the following when planning ahead in case of a fire:

- Have emergency-contact information for the fire and police departments, the regulatory authority, and management or headquarters personnel.
- Post the fire department phone number by each phone so it is easy to see.

If a fire occurs, you must stop operating until the fire is out and you can again prep food safely. Block off areas and do not use equipment, utensils, and other items affected by the fire. Take the following into account when recovering from a fire:

- Throw out all food affected by the fire.
- Throw out all damaged utensils, linens, or items that cannot be cleaned and sanitized.
- Clean and sanitize the operation.
- If needed, hire a janitorial service that specializes in cleaning up areas exposed to fires.
- Check water lines. The use of fire hoses may have lowered water pressure in the area. This could cause backflow and water contamination.

Flood

Consider the following when planning ahead in case of a flood:

- Have a plan to monitor and maintain flood-control equipment: plumbing, storm drains, sump pumps, etc.
- Have emergency-contact information for the regulatory authority, the plumber, utility companies, etc.
- Keep a supply of bottled water.

To manage your response to a flood, consider the steps identified in Table 10.4.

Table 10.4: **Flood Responses**

If	Then
A water line leaks or water builds up on the floor, but food, utensils, etc., are not affected.	• Keep people away from the wet floor. • Repair the leak. • Block off areas, equipment, utensils, and other items affected by the flood.
A flood affects or damages food, utensils, etc.	• Stop all operations.
The flood is the result of a sewage backup in the prep area.	• Close the affected area right away. • Correct the problem. • Clean the area thoroughly.

Take the following into account when planning recovery from a flood:

- Throw out all damaged utensils, linens, or items that cannot be cleaned and sanitized.
- Throw out any food or food packaging that made contact with the water.
- Clean and sanitize the facility, utensils, equipment surfaces, floors, or other affected areas.
- If needed, hire a janitorial service that specializes in cleaning up areas exposed to floods.

Chapter Summary

- A food safety management system is a group of procedures and practices intended to prevent foodborne illness. It does this by actively controlling risks and hazards throughout the flow of food.
- It is the manager's responsibility to actively control the risk factors for foodborne illness. This is called active managerial control. It can be achieved by incorporating specific actions and procedures into the operation to prevent foodborne illness.
- The FDA provides specific recommendations for controlling the common risk factors for foodborne illness. These are known as public health interventions. They are designed to protect public health.
- HACCP is based on identifying significant biological, chemical, or physical hazards at specific points within a product's flow. Once identified, the hazards can be prevented, eliminated, or reduced to safe levels.
- A HACCP plan is based on seven basic principles. These principles are the seven steps that outline how to create a HACCP plan.
- Some food processes are highly specialized and can be a serious health risk if specific procedures are not followed. This includes processing methods such as curing food or smoking food to extend shelf life. Always check with your local regulatory authority before using specialized processing methods on-site.
- Prepare for a crisis before one occurs. Start with a written plan that focuses on preparation, response, and recovery. For each of these phases, the plan should identify resources needed and procedures to be followed.
- Each crisis management plan needs to be customized to the operation. A good way to ensure your plan achieves what you need is to test it once it is complete. The results will help you identify potential gaps or problems.

Apply Your Knowledge

Use these questions to review the concepts presented in this chapter.

Discussion Questions

1 What types of food safety programs must be in place as a foundation for a food safety management system?

2 What are some ways to achieve active managerial control?

3 List the seven HACCP principles in order.

4 What specialized food prep processes require a variance from the regulatory authority?

For answers, please turn to the Answer Key.

Apply Your Knowledge

Something to Think About

Trouble at Nathan's

Bryce, a restaurant owner, opened his morning paper and almost fell off his chair. He was shocked to see an article about foodborne illness at his friend Nathan's restaurant. Even though Nathan had a HACCP program in place and had passed a recent health inspection with flying colors, 23 people got sick after eating dinner at the restaurant. The regulatory authority closed the restaurant temporarily until the cause of the outbreak could be determined.

The article went on to say that even though the paper had called the restaurant several times to find out more about the outbreak, the restaurant manager did not return the calls. Direct calls to Nathan were also not returned. When interviewed, several staff members stated that they did not know what was going on and they had not heard anything from the owner or manager about the outbreak.

1 What is wrong with how Nathan handled the crisis?

2 What should have been done differently?

For answers, please turn to the Answer Key.

Apply Your Knowledge

Something to Think About

Maria's Challenge

Maria, an owner/operator of a local family restaurant, realized that she needed to do more to keep her place safe. That meant taking charge of food safety in a more formal way than before. It was time to develop a food safety management system. Although she had not had any formal training in HACCP, she wanted to develop a HACCP plan for her operation.

Maria began by reviewing her menu to try and identify CCPs for each menu item. Most dishes on the menu were grilled items that were prepared, cooked, and then served. Maria determined that risks to these items could best be controlled through cooking, so she identified cooking as the CCP. Next, she identified critical limits for each CCP. For grilled hamburgers, she determined that cooking them to 150°F (66°C) for 15 seconds would reduce pathogens to a safe level. For grilled chicken, she knew it was necessary to cook it to 165°F (74°C) for 15 seconds.

Maria decided to monitor the critical limits by having cooks press on the meat with their fingertips to check for doneness. As an additional safeguard, she required cooks to cut into the meat to check the color for doneness. Maria knew she needed to identify a corrective action for products that had not been cooked enough. She decided that if the meat did not feel right or if the color inside was not correct, cooks needed to keep cooking the meat. Maria knew that record keeping was often part of a HACCP program, but she was not sure what types of records to keep. She ended up deciding that for her operation, this record keeping was not really necessary.

1 What did Maria do wrong?

____

____

____

2 What should she have done differently?

____

____

____

For answers, please turn to the Answer Key.

Study Questions

Circle the best answer to each question.

1 The temperature of a roast is checked to see if it has met its critical limit of 145°F (63°C) for 4 minutes. This is an example of which HACCP principle?

A Verification
B Monitoring
C Record keeping
D Hazard analysis

2 The temperature of a pot of beef stew is checked during holding. The stew has not met the critical limit and is thrown out according to house policy. Throwing out the stew is an example of which HACCP principle?

A Monitoring
B Verification
C Hazard analysis
D Corrective action

3 A deli serves cold sandwiches in a self-serve display. Which step in the flow of food would be a critical control point?

A Storage
B Cooling
C Cooking
D Reheating

4 A chef sanitized a thermometer probe and then checked the temperature of minestrone soup being held in a hot-holding unit. The temperature was 120°F (49°C), which did not meet the operation's critical limit of 135°F (57°C). The chef recorded the temperature in the log and reheated the soup to 165°F (74°C) for 15 seconds within 2 hours. Which was the corrective action?

A Reheating the soup
B Checking the critical limit
C Sanitizing the thermometer probe
D Recording the temperature in the log

Study Questions

5 **What is the purpose of a food safety management system?**

A To keep all areas of the facility clean and pest-free

B To identify, tag, and repair faulty equipment within the facility

C To identify and control possible hazards throughout the flow of food

D To identify, document, and use the correct methods for receiving food

6 **Reviewing temperature logs and other records to make sure that the HACCP plan is working as intended is an example of which HACCP principle?**

A Monitoring

B Verification

C Hazard analysis

D Record keeping

7 **What is the first step in developing a HACCP plan?**

A Identify corrective actions.

B Conduct a hazard analysis.

C Establish monitoring procedures.

D Determine critical control points.

8 **What does an operation that wants to smoke food as a method of preservation need to have before processing food this way?**

A A food safety certificate

B A crisis-management plan

C A master cleaning schedule

D A variance from the regulatory authority

For answers, please turn to the Answer Key.

Notes

Notes

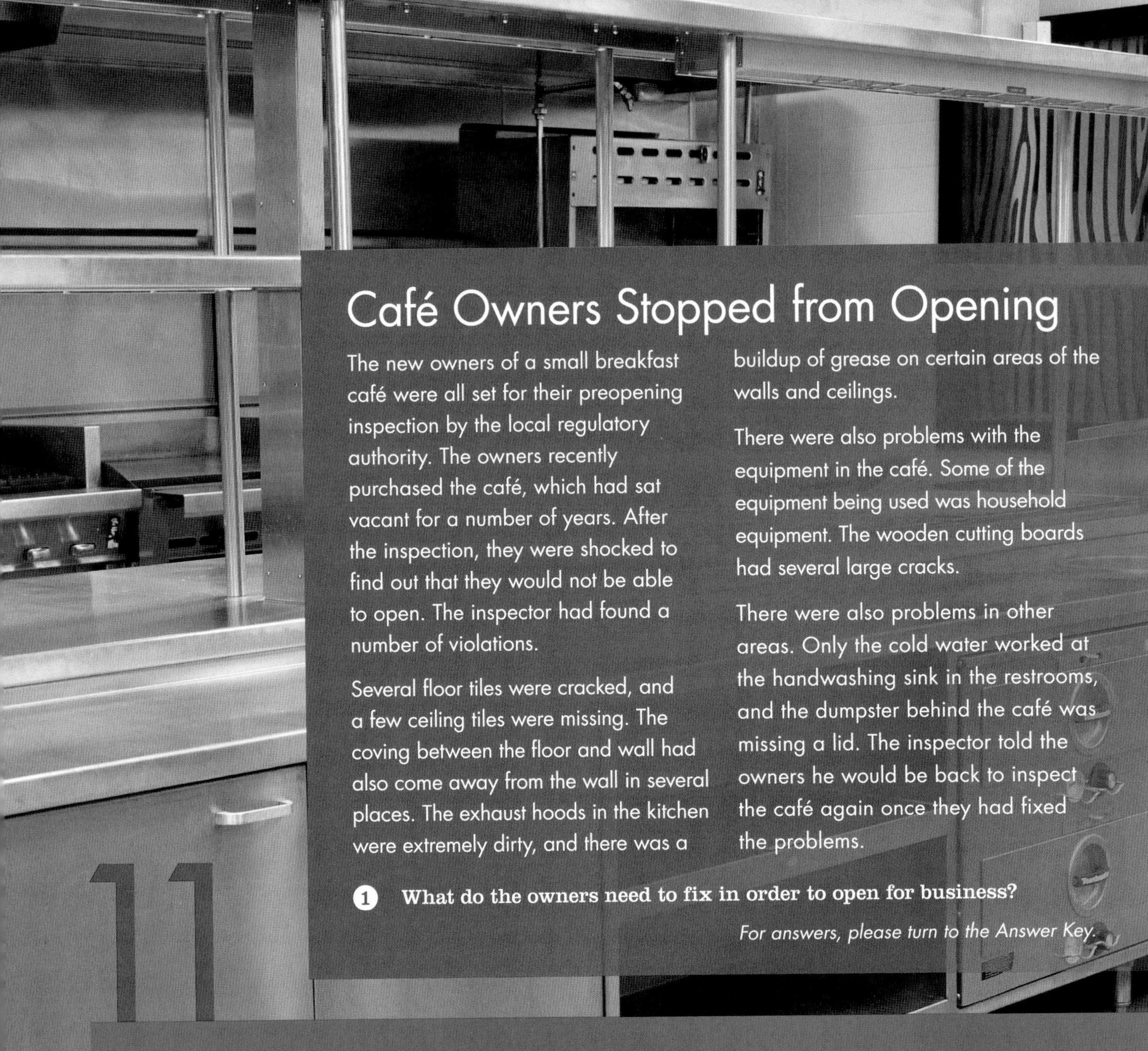

Café Owners Stopped from Opening

The new owners of a small breakfast café were all set for their preopening inspection by the local regulatory authority. The owners recently purchased the café, which had sat vacant for a number of years. After the inspection, they were shocked to find out that they would not be able to open. The inspector had found a number of violations.

Several floor tiles were cracked, and a few ceiling tiles were missing. The coving between the floor and wall had also come away from the wall in several places. The exhaust hoods in the kitchen were extremely dirty, and there was a buildup of grease on certain areas of the walls and ceilings.

There were also problems with the equipment in the café. Some of the equipment being used was household equipment. The wooden cutting boards had several large cracks.

There were also problems in other areas. Only the cold water worked at the handwashing sink in the restrooms, and the dumpster behind the café was missing a lid. The inspector told the owners he would be back to inspect the café again once they had fixed the problems.

1 What do the owners need to fix in order to open for business?

For answers, please turn to the Answer Key.

11

Safe Facilities and Equipment

Inside This Chapter

- Designing a Safe Operation
- Considerations for Other Areas of the Facility
- Equipment Selection
- Installing and Maintaining Kitchen Equipment
- Utilities

Objectives

After completing this chapter, you should be able to identify the following:

- When a review of the construction plan is required
- Characteristics of correct flooring and interior finishes, including doors, walls, and ceilings
- Requirements for restrooms
- Requirements for handwashing stations
- Requirements for food-contact surfaces
- Organizations that certify equipment that meets sanitation standards
- Requirements for dishwashing facilities
- Requirements for installing equipment
- Approved water sources and testing requirements
- Methods for preventing cross-connection and backflow
- The correct response to a wastewater overflow
- Lighting-intensity requirements for different areas of the operation
- Ways of preventing lighting sources from contaminating food
- Ways of preventing ventilation systems from contaminating food and food-contact surfaces
- Requirements for handling garbage, including correct storage and removal
- The importance of keeping physical facilities in good repair

Key Terms

Porosity
Resiliency
Coving
NSF
Potable
Booster heater
Cross-connection
Backflow
Backsiphonage
Vacuum breaker
Air gap

Designing a Safe Operation

When designing or remodeling a facility, consider how both the building and its equipment will be kept clean. Poorly designed areas are generally harder to clean and can become a breeding ground for pathogens. Food passing through these areas runs a much higher risk of contamination.

This chapter focuses on four topics related to the safe layout and design of equipment and facilities:

- Designing and arranging equipment and fixtures to comply with sanitation standards.
- Selecting wall, floor, and ceiling materials that are easier to clean.
- Designing utilities to prevent contamination and make cleaning easier.
- Managing garbage correctly to avoid contaminating food and attracting pests.

Construction Plan Review

Before starting any new construction or a large remodeling project, you must check with your regulatory authority. You will need approval of your construction plans before construction begins. This mandatory regulatory review of the plans has several benefits:

- It ensures the design meets regulatory requirements.
- It ensures a safe flow of food.
- It may save time and money.
- It assures that contractors are constructing the facility correctly and approved equipment is being used.

In addition to submitting your construction plans to the regulatory authority, you should also check with your local building department to see what is required.

Layout

A well-designed kitchen will address the following factors.

Work flow Establish a work flow that will minimize the time food spends in the temperature danger zone. It should also minimize the number of times food is handled. For example, locate storage areas near the receiving area, as shown in the illustration below, to prevent delays in storing food. Locate prep tables near coolers and freezers for the same reason.

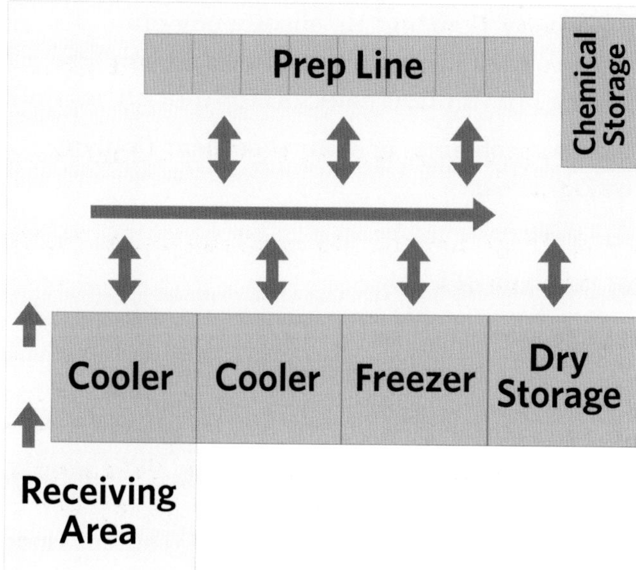

Contamination A good layout will minimize the risk of cross-contamination. Place equipment in a way that will prevent splashing or spilling from one piece of equipment onto another. For example, avoid placing the dirty-utensil table next to the salad-prep sink.

Equipment accessibility Hard-to-reach areas are less likely to be cleaned. A well-planned layout will ensure that equipment is accessible for cleaning.

Materials for Interior Construction

When selecting materials for interior construction, the most important consideration is how easy the operation will be to clean and maintain. Sound-absorbent surfaces that resist grease and moisture and reflect light will probably create an environment acceptable to your regulatory authority.

Flooring

Each area of your operation has its own flooring needs. Flooring should be smooth, durable, nonabsorbent, and easy to clean. This makes cleaning easier. It should also resist wear and help prevent slips. Once installed, flooring should be kept in good condition and be replaced if damaged or worn. If standing water occurs due to spraying or flushing the floors when cleaning, remove it as quickly as possible.

The flooring's porosity is another important factor. **Porosity** is the extent to which a material will absorb liquids. Avoid high-porosity flooring. Its absorbency often makes it ideal for pathogen growth. High-porosity flooring can also cause people to slip or fall. It often deteriorates quickly as well.

To prevent these problems, use nonabsorbent flooring in the following areas:

- Walk-in coolers
- Prep and food-storage areas
- Dishwashing areas
- Restrooms
- Dressing and locker rooms

Nonporous, Resilient Flooring

In most areas of the operation, nonporous, resilient flooring is the best choice. **Resiliency** means a material can react to a shock without breaking or cracking.

Nonporous, resilient materials, such as vinyl or rubber tiles, are relatively inexpensive. They are also easy to clean and maintain, as shown in the photo at left. If individual tiles break, they can be easily replaced. They can also handle heavy traffic and resist grease and alkalis.

However, this type of flooring does have disadvantages. Sharp objects can easily damage it. It also tends to be slippery when wet. It is usually a poor choice for dining rooms or public areas. It is more practical for break rooms, staff dressing rooms, and foodservice offices. See Table 11.1 for characteristics and recommended uses of nonporous, resilient flooring.

Table 11.1: **Characteristics of Nonporous, Resilient Flooring**

	Where to Use	Durability	Advantages	Disadvantages
Rubber tile	Kitchens; restrooms	Less durable and less resistant to grease and alkalis	Nonslip; resilient; easy to clean	Can only be used in moderate-traffic areas
Vinyl sheet	Offices; kitchens; corridors	Less resistant to grease and alkalis	Very resilient; easy to clean	Can only be used in light- or moderate-traffic areas
Vinyl tile	Offices; staff restrooms	Wears out quickly with high traffic	Very resilient; easy to clean	Requires waxing and machine buffing

Hard-Surface Flooring

Because it is durable and nonabsorbent, hard-surface flooring is often used in foodservice operations. These types of flooring—especially quarry and ceramic tile—are excellent for public restrooms or high-dirt areas.

Still, these flooring materials have their disadvantages. They may crack or chip if heavy objects are dropped on them. They do not absorb sound, and they are expensive to install and maintain. Finally, hard-surface flooring is somewhat difficult to clean.

While most hard-surface floors, especially marble, can be slippery, unglazed tiles can provide a hard, slip-resistant surface. See Table 11.2 for characteristics and recommended uses of hard-surface flooring.

Table 11.2: **Characteristics of Hard-Surface Flooring**

	Where to Use	Durability	Advantages	Disadvantages
Marble; terrazzo	Public corridors; dining rooms; public restrooms	Wear resistant	Nonporous; good appearance	Nonresilient; heavy; expensive; requires special care; difficult to install
Quarry tile	Kitchen; service, dishwashing, and receiving areas; offices; restrooms; dining rooms	Wear resistant	Nonporous	Nonresilient; heavy; expensive; slippery when wet unless an abrasive is added
Wood	Offices; dining rooms	Durable in lower-traffic areas	Good appearance and sound absorption	Requires frequent polishing and periodic refinishing to maintain surface qualities

Carpeting

Carpeting is a popular choice for certain areas, such as dining rooms, because it absorbs sound. However, it is not recommended in high-dirt areas such as waitstaff service areas, tray and dish drop-off areas, beverage stations, and major traffic aisles.

Carpet can be maintained by simple vacuuming. Areas prone to heavy traffic and moisture will require routine cleaning. You can also purchase special carpet for areas where sanitation, dirt, moisture, and fire safety are concerns.

Special Flooring Needs

Use nonslip surfaces in traffic areas. Nonslip surfaces are ideal for the entire kitchen as well, because slips and falls are a potential hazard.

For safety reasons, rubber mats are allowed in areas where standing water may occur, such as in the dish room. When scrubbing floors, pick up rubber mats and clean them separately.

Coving is required in operations using resilient or hard-surface flooring materials. **Coving** is a curved, sealed edge placed between the floor and the wall to eliminate sharp corners or gaps that would be impossible to clean. An example is shown in the photo at left. The coving tile or strip should adhere tightly to the wall. This will help eliminate hiding places for insects. It will also prevent moisture from deteriorating the wall.

Finishes for Interior Walls and Ceilings

Interior finishes are the materials used on the surface of an operation's walls and ceilings. As with flooring, these finishes need to be smooth, nonabsorbent, durable, and easy to clean.

Consider the location when selecting finishes for walls and ceilings. A material that might be suitable in one area may be a poor choice for another. Walls and ceilings in prep areas should be light in color to distribute light and to make it easier to spot dirt when cleaning. They should also be kept free of cracks, holes, and peeling paint.

The best wall finish in cooking areas is ceramic tile, as shown in the photo at left. However, it needs to be monitored for grout loss and regrouted when needed. Stainless steel is used occasionally because it is durable and moisture resistant.

The most common ceiling materials are acoustic tile, painted drywall, painted plaster, and exposed concrete.

Wall and ceiling support structures (studs, joists, and rafters) as well as pipes should not be exposed unless finished and sealed for cleaning.

Flexible materials such as paper, vinyl, and thin wood veneers are often used for walls and ceilings. Vinyl wall coverings are popular because they are attractive, relatively inexpensive, easy to clean, and durable. They are also rated for flammability by testing agencies.

Plaster or cinder-block walls that have been sealed and painted with oil-resistant, easy-to-wash, glossy paints are appropriate for dry areas of the facility.

Considerations for Other Areas of the Facility

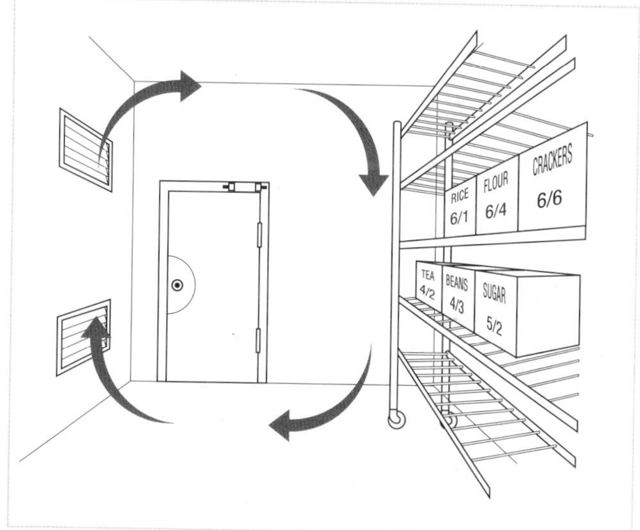

Dry Storage

Construct dry-storage areas with easy-to-clean materials that allow good air circulation, as seen in the illustration at right. Shelving, tabletops, and bins for dry ingredients should be made of corrosion-resistant metal or food-grade plastic.

Any windows in the dry-storage area should have frosted glass or shades. Direct sunlight can increase the area's temperature and affect food quality.

Steam pipes, water lines, and other conduits do not belong in a well-designed dry-storage area. Dripping condensation or leaks in overhead pipes can promote pathogen growth in such normally stable items as crackers, flour, and baking powder. Leaking overhead sewer lines can also contaminate food. Hot-water heaters or steam pipes can raise the area's temperature to levels that allow foodborne pathogens to grow as well.

Dry food is also susceptible to attack by insects and rodents. Cracks and crevices in floors or walls should therefore be filled. Doors leading to the building's exterior should be self-closing. Screens for windows and doors should be 16 mesh to the inch without any tears or holes.

Handwashing Stations

Handwashing stations should be put in areas that make it easy for staff to wash their hands often. Handwashing stations are required:

- In restrooms or directly next to them
- In areas used for food prep, service, and dishwashing

Handwashing sinks must be used only for handwashing and not for any other purpose. And, to prevent cross-contamination, make sure adequate barriers, as seen in the photo at left, are present on handwashing sinks, or that there is adequate distance between handwashing sinks and food and food-contact surfaces, so that water cannot splash on these items.

Make sure these stations work correctly and are well stocked and maintained. They must also be available at all times. This means that handwashing stations cannot be blocked by portable equipment or stacked full of dirty kitchenware, as shown in the photo below.

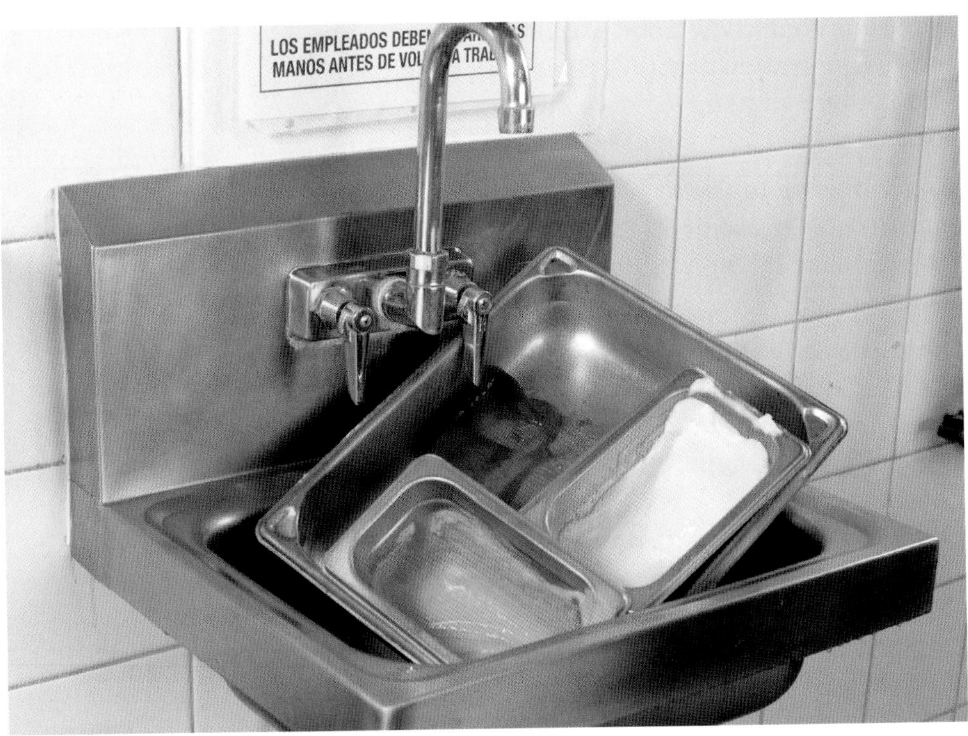

See Table 11.3 for requirements at a handwashing station.

Some jurisdictions allow the use of automatic handwashing facilities in an operation. Check with your local regulatory authority for more information.

Table 11.3: **Requirements at a Handwashing Station**

Hot and cold running water
The water must be drinkable and meet temperature and pressure requirements.

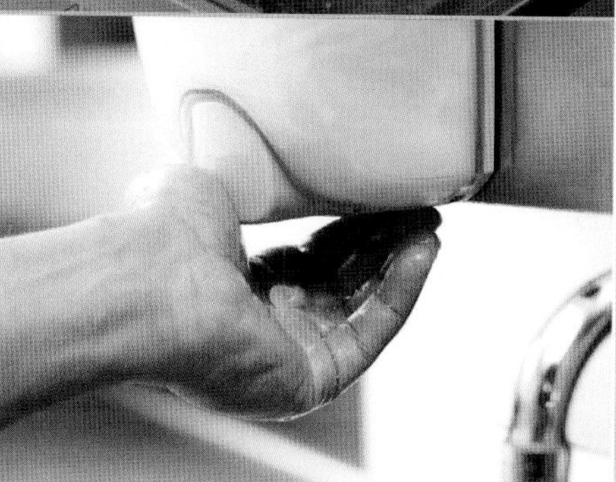

Soap
The soap can be liquid, bar, or powder.

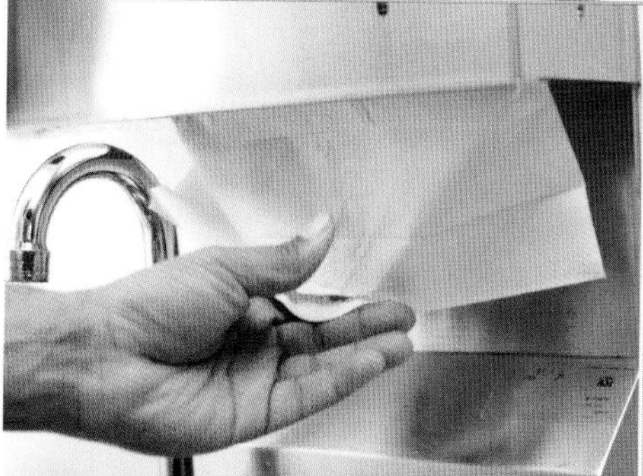

A way to dry hands
Disposable paper towels or a continuous towel system that supplies the user with a clean towel can be used. Hands can also be dried with a hand dryer using either warm air or room-temperature air delivered at high velocity.

Garbage container
Garbage containers are required if disposable paper towels are used.

Signage
A clearly visible sign or poster must tell staff to wash hands before returning to work.

Sinks

To prevent cross-contamination, staff must use each sink in an operation for its intended purpose. Handwashing sinks are for handwashing. Prep sinks are for prepping food. Service sinks are for cleaning mops and disposing of wastewater. At least one service sink or curbed drain area is required for disposing of dirty water, as shown in the photo at left.

Restrooms

If possible, provide separate restrooms for staff and guests. If this is not possible, the operation must be designed so patrons do not pass through prep areas to reach the restroom. Otherwise, they could contaminate food or food-contact surfaces.

Restrooms should be convenient, sanitary, and have self-closing doors. They must be adequately stocked with toilet paper. Garbage containers must be provided if disposable paper towels are used. Women's restrooms also need covered garbage containers for disposing of sanitary supplies.

Dressing Rooms and Lockers

Dressing rooms are not required. If available, they should not be used for prepping food, storage, or utensil washing. Lockers should be located in a separate room or one where food, equipment, utensils, linens, and single-service items cannot be contaminated.

Premises

Parking lots and walkways should be angled so standing pools of water do not form. They should also be surfaced to minimize dirt and blowing dust.

Concrete and asphalt are recommended for walkways and parking lots. Gravel, while acceptable, is not recommended.

Guest traffic through prep areas is prohibited, although guided tours are allowed. Do not allow the premises to be used for living or sleeping quarters.

Equipment Selection

Equipment Standards

Foodservice equipment must meet certain standards if it will come in contact with food. **NSF** is an organization that creates these national standards. NSF is accredited by the American National Standards Institute (ANSI). NSF/ANSI standards for food equipment require that it be nonabsorbent, smooth, and corrosion resistant. Food equipment must also be easy to clean, durable, and resistant to damage. The NSF mark, shown at right, will appear on equipment that meets these standards.

Only commercial foodservice equipment should be used in operations. Household equipment is not built to withstand heavy use.

Dishwashing Machines

Dishwashing machines vary widely by size, style, and method of sanitizing. High-temperature machines sanitize with extremely hot water. Chemical-sanitizing machines use a chemical solution.

The following machines are common in foodservice operations.

Single-tank, stationary-rack machine with doors

This machine holds a stationary rack of tableware and utensils. Items are washed by detergent and water from below, and sometimes from above, the rack. The wash cycle is followed by a hot-water or chemical-sanitizer final rinse.

Conveyor machine With this machine, a conveyor moves racks of items through the various cycles of washing, rinsing, and sanitizing. The machine may have a single tank or multiple tanks.

Carousel or circular-conveyor machine This multiple-tank machine moves tableware and utensils on a peg-type conveyor or in racks.

Flight type This is a high-capacity, multiple-tank machine with a peg-type conveyor. It may also have a built-in dryer.

Batch-type, dump This stationary-rack machine combines the wash and rinse cycles in a single tank. Each cycle is timed. The machine automatically dispenses both the detergent and the sanitizing chemical or hot water. Wash and rinse water are drained after each cycle.

Recirculating, door-type, non-dump machine

This stationary-rack machine is not fully drained of water between cycles. The wash water is diluted with fresh water and reused from cycle to cycle.

Dishwasher Selection and Installation Guidelines

Consider these guidelines when selecting and installing dishwashers.

Installation Dishwashers must be installed so that they are reachable and conveniently located. That installation must also keep utensils, equipment, and other food-contact surfaces from becoming contaminated. The machine should be raised at least six inches (15 centimeters) off the floor to permit easy cleaning beneath. Always follow the manufacturer's instructions when installing, operating, and maintaining a dishwasher.

Plumbing Water pipes to the dishwashing machine should be as short as possible to prevent the loss of heat.

Chemicals Use detergents and sanitizers approved by the regulatory authority.

Settings Purchase dishwashers that can measure the following:

- Water temperature
- Water pressure
- Cleaning and sanitizing chemical concentration

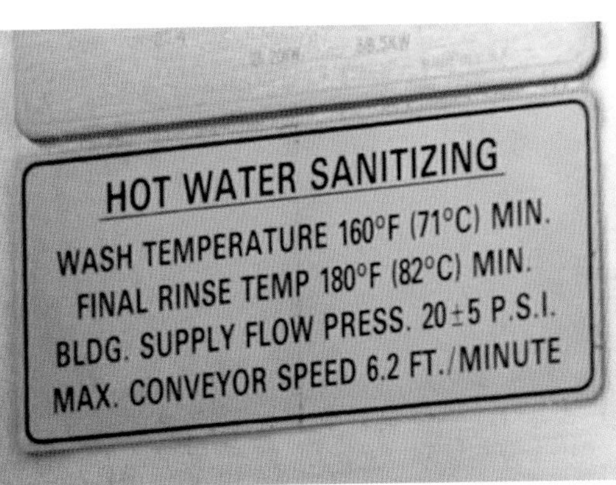

HOT WATER SANITIZING
WASH TEMPERATURE 160°F (71°C) MIN.
FINAL RINSE TEMP 180°F (82°C) MIN.
BLDG. SUPPLY FLOW PRESS. 20±5 P.S.I.
MAX. CONVEYOR SPEED 6.2 FT./MINUTE

Information about the correct settings should be posted on the machine. The label in the photo at left shows an example.

Thermometer The machine's thermometer should be located so it is readable, with a scale in increments no greater than 2°F (1°C).

Cleaning Dishwashers should be easy to clean. They should be cleaned as often as necessary. Follow the manufacturer's recommendations and local regulatory requirements.

Three-Compartment Sinks

Many operations use three-compartment sinks to clean and sanitize items manually in the operation. Purchase sinks that can accommodate large equipment and utensils. Have other ways of cleaning these items as well, such as cleaning a large piece of equipment in place.

Coolers and Freezers

There are several types of cooler and freezer units. The two most common are walk-in and reach-in coolers and freezers. The doors should withstand heavy use and close with a slight nudge.

A drain must be provided and maintained for disposal of condensation and defrost water as well. A correctly plumbed, indirect drain can be used in the walk-in cooler. You can minimize any excess condensation by maintaining a flush-fitting floor sweep (gasket) under the door.

Considerations When Purchasing Coolers or Freezers

In addition to the sanitation standards discussed in this chapter, consider these factors when purchasing a cooler or freezer unit.

Installation Make sure walk-in units can be sealed to the floor and wall. They should offer no access to moisture or rodents.

Reach-ins Purchase reach-in cooler or freezer units with legs that elevate them six inches (15 centimeters) off the floor. Otherwise, mount and seal them on a masonry base. Caster wheels are often preferred or required by regulatory authorities, as shown in the photo at right. They make it easier to move the unit for cleaning.

Temperature Make sure the unit meets the temperature requirements of the food you store. Built-in thermometers should be easy to locate and read. They should also be accurate to within ±3°F or ±1.5°C.

Blast Chillers and Tumble Chillers

Blast chillers cool food quickly. Many can cool food from 135°F to 37°F (57°C to 3°C) within 90 minutes. A blast chiller is shown in the photo at right. Most units allow the operator to set target chill temperatures and monitor the temperature of food throughout the chill cycle. Once chilled to safe temperatures, the food can then be stored in conventional coolers or freezers.

Tumble chillers cool food quickly as well. Prepackaged hot food is placed into a drum that rotates inside a reservoir of chilled water. The tumbling action increases the effectiveness of the chilled water in cooling the food.

Cook-Chill Equipment

Some operations prep food using a cook-chill system. By this method, food is partially cooked, rapidly chilled, and then held in refrigerated storage. When needed, the food is simply reheated. A cook-chill unit is an integrated piece of equipment that can cook, cool, and reheat food.

Cutting Boards

Many regulatory authorities allow the use of either wooden or synthetic cutting boards. If the regulatory authority allows wooden cutting boards and baker's tables, they need to be made from a nonabsorbent hardwood, such as maple or oak. They need to be nontoxic and free of cracks and seams as well.

Installing and Maintaining Kitchen Equipment

Stationary equipment should be easy to clean and easy to clean around. In the photo at left, the dishwasher is installed so that the floor underneath can be cleaned easily.

Installing Kitchen Equipment

Follow the manufacturer's directions when installing equipment. Also check with your regulatory authority for requirements.

In general, stationary equipment should be installed as follows.

Floor-mounted equipment Put floor-mounted equipment on legs at least six inches (15 centimeters) high. Another option is to seal it to a masonry base.

Tabletop equipment Put tabletop equipment on legs at least four inches (10 centimeters) high, or seal it to the countertop.

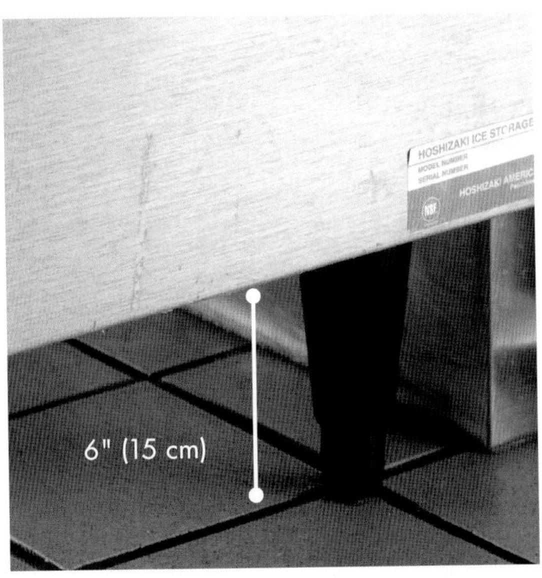

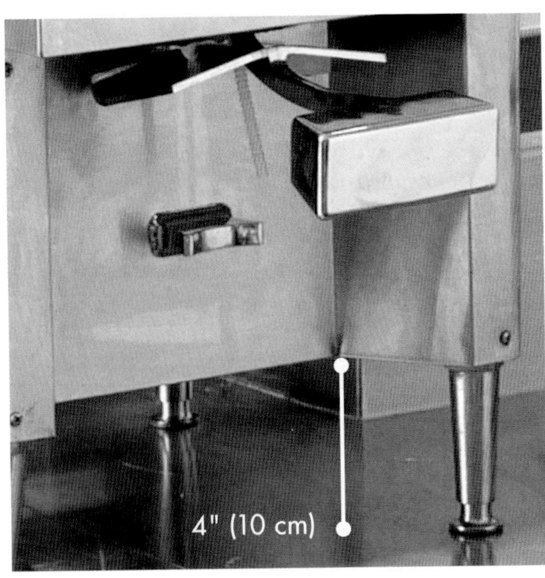

Also seal all cracks or seams to prevent food buildup or pests. However, do not use sealant to cover wide gaps from faulty construction or repairs. Any gaps should be correctly repaired before equipment is installed.

Maintaining Equipment

Once you have installed equipment, make sure it is maintained regularly by qualified people. Also set up a maintenance schedule with your supplier or manufacturer. Check equipment regularly to be sure it is working correctly.

Utilities

An operation uses many utilities and building systems. Utilities include water, electricity, gas, sewage, and garbage disposal. Building systems include plumbing, lighting, and ventilation. There must be enough utilities to meet the needs of the operation. In addition, the utilities and systems must work correctly. If they do not, the risk of contamination is greater.

Water Supply

Each regulatory authority establishes standards for water in its jurisdiction. Only water that is drinkable can be used for prepping food and come in contact with food-contact surfaces. Drinkable water is called **potable** water. This water may come from the following sources:

- Approved public water mains
- Private water sources that are regularly tested and maintained
- Closed, portable water containers
- Water transport vehicles

If your operation uses a private water supply, such as a well, rather than an approved public source, check with your regulatory authority for information on inspections, testing, and other requirements. Nonpublic water systems should be tested at least each year. The report should also be kept on file in the operation.

Regardless of where your water comes from, you should know how to prevent plumbing issues that can affect food safety.

If your operation has an on-site septic system, make sure it is properly tested and maintained.

Hot Water

Providing a continuous supply of hot water can be a problem for many operations serving the public. Evaluate water heaters often to make sure they can meet peak demands. Consider how quickly the heater produces hot water as well. Also take into account the size of the holding tank and the heater's location in relation to sinks or dishwashing machines.

Most general-purpose water heaters will not heat water to temperatures required for hot-water sanitizing. You might then need a **booster heater** to maintain water temperature. Many dishwashing machines now come with booster heaters.

Plumbing

Incorrectly installed or poorly maintained plumbing has been implicated in outbreaks of typhoid fever, Hepatitis A, Norovirus, and other illnesses. For this reason, only licensed plumbers should install and maintain plumbing.

Cross-Connections

The greatest challenge to water safety comes from cross-connections. A **cross-connection** is a physical link between safe water and dirty water, which can come from drains, sewers, or other wastewater sources.

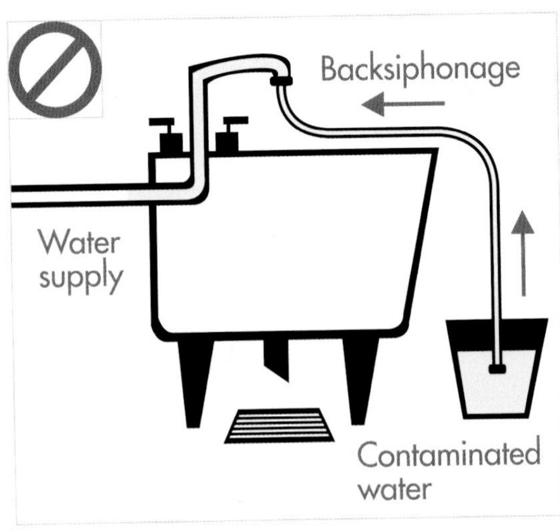

A cross-connection is dangerous because it can let backflow occur. **Backflow** is the reverse flow of contaminants through a cross-connection into a drinkable water supply. Backflow can be the result of pressure pushing contaminants back into the water supply. It can also happen when high water use in one area of an operation creates a vacuum in the plumbing system that sucks contaminants back into the water supply. This is called **backsiphonage**. A running faucet below the flood rim of a sink is an example of a cross-connection that can lead to backsiphonage. A running hose in a mop bucket is another example, as shown in the illustration at left.

Backflow Prevention

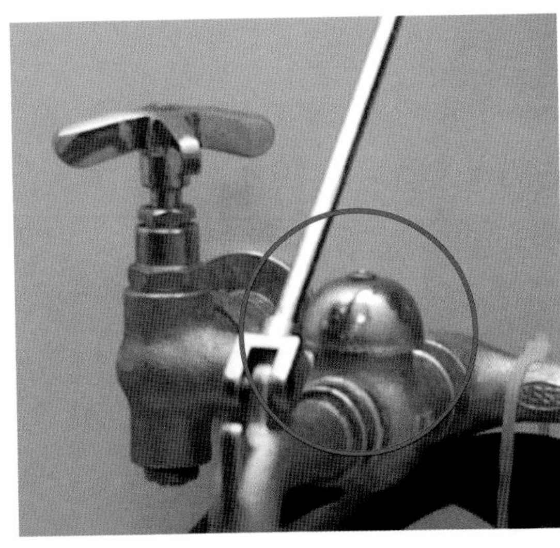

The best way to prevent backflow is to avoid creating a cross-connection. Some ways to do this include:

- **DO NOT** attach a hose to a faucet unless a backflow prevention device, such as a vacuum breaker, is attached. A **vacuum breaker** is a mechanical device that prevents backsiphonage, as seen in the photo at left. It does this by closing a check valve and sealing the water supply line shut when water flow is stopped.
- Other mechanical devices are used to prevent backflow. These include double-check valves and reduced-pressure-zone backflow preventers. These devices include more than one check valve for sealing off the water supply. They also provide a way to determine if the check valves are operational.

Backflow prevention devices must be checked periodically to make sure they are working correctly. This must be done by a trained and certified technician. And, the work must be documented. Always follow local requirements and manufacturers' recommendations.

The only sure way to prevent backflow is to create an air gap. An **air gap** is an air space that separates a water supply outlet from a potentially contaminated source. A sink that is correctly designed and installed usually has two air gaps, as shown in the illustration at right. One is between the faucet and the flood rim of the sink. The other is between the drainpipe of the sink and the floor drain of the operation.

Grease Condensation and Leaking Pipes

Grease condensation in pipes is another common problem in plumbing systems. Grease traps are often installed to prevent the buildup of grease from creating a drain blockage. An example is shown in the photo at right. If used, grease traps must be easily accessible. They must also be installed by a licensed plumber and cleaned periodically according to the manufacturer's recommendations. If traps are not cleaned or are not cleaned correctly, a backup of wastewater could lead to odor and contamination.

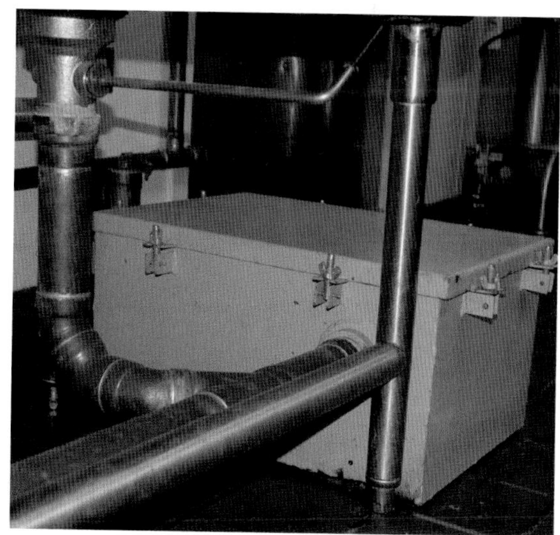

Overhead wastewater pipes or fire-safety sprinkler systems can also leak and become a source of contamination. Even overhead lines carrying drinkable water can be a problem. Water can condense on the pipes and drip onto food. Check all pipes often to ensure they appear in good condition and do not leak. They should be serviced immediately when leaks occur.

Sewage

Sewage and wastewater contain pathogens, dirt, and chemicals. It is absolutely essential to prevent them from contaminating food or food-contact surfaces.

If there is a backup of raw sewage in the operation, the affected area should be closed right away. Then the problem must be corrected and the area thoroughly cleaned. If the backup is a significant risk to the safety of food, service must be stopped. Then the local regulatory authority must be notified.

The facility must have adequate drainage to handle all wastewater. Any area subjected to heavy water exposure should have its own floor drain. The drainage system should be designed to prevent floors from flooding.

Lighting

Lighting intensity—how bright the lights are in the operation—is usually measured in units called foot-candles or lux. Different areas of the facility have different lighting-intensity requirements. Regulatory authorities usually require prep areas to be brighter than other areas. This allows staff to recognize the condition of food. It also helps staff identify items that need cleaning. Lighting intensity requirements are shown in Table 11.4. Contact the regulatory authority for requirements in your jurisdiction.

Table 11.4: **Minimum Lighting Intensity by Area**

Minimum Lighting Intensity	Area
50 foot-candles (540 lux)	• Prep areas
20 foot-candles (215 lux)	• Handwashing or dishwashing areas • Buffets and salad bars • Displays for produce or packaged food • Utensil-storage areas • Wait stations • Restrooms • Inside some pieces of equipment (e.g., reach-in refrigerators)
10 foot-candles (108 lux)	• Inside walk-in coolers and freezer units • Dry-storage areas • Dining rooms (for cleaning)

Once the correct level of lighting has been installed in each area, you need to monitor it. Replace any bulbs that have burned out. Make sure they are the correct size as well. All lights should have shatter-resistant light bulbs or protective covers. These products prevent broken glass from contaminating food or food-contact surfaces.

Ventilation

Ventilation improves the air inside an operation. It removes heat, steam, and smoke from cooking lines. It also eliminates fumes and odors. If ventilation systems are not working correctly, grease and condensation will build up on walls and ceilings.

To prevent this, clean and maintain ventilation systems according to the manufacturer's recommendations and/or your local regulatory requirements.

Mechanical ventilation must be used in areas for cooking, frying, and grilling. Ventilation must be designed so that hoods, fans, guards, and ductwork do not drip onto food or equipment. Hood filters or grease extractors need to be tight fitting and easy to remove. They should be cleaned often. The hood and ductwork should be cleaned periodically by professionals as well.

Garbage

Garbage can attract pests and contaminate food, equipment, and utensils if not handled correctly. To control contamination from garbage, consider the following.

Garbage removal

Garbage should be removed from prep areas as quickly as possible to prevent odors, pests, and possible contamination. Staff must be careful when removing garbage so they do not contaminate food or food-contact surfaces. The food handler in the photo at right has not been careful and may contaminate the prep table.

Cleaning of containers

Clean the inside and outside of garbage containers frequently. This will help prevent the contamination of food and food-contact surfaces. It will also reduce odors and pests. Do not clean garbage containers near prep or food-storage areas.

Indoor containers

These must be leakproof, waterproof, and pestproof. They also should be easy to clean. Containers must be covered when not in use.

Designated storage areas

Waste and recyclables must be stored separately from food and food-contact surfaces. The storage of these items must not create a nuisance or a public health hazard.

Outdoor containers

Place garbage containers on a surface that is smooth, durable, and nonabsorbent. Asphalt and concrete are good choices, as shown in the photo at right. Make sure the containers have tight-fitting lids and are kept covered at all times. Keep their drain plugs in place.

Chapter Summary

- Plans for new construction or extensive remodeling must be reviewed and approved by the local regulatory authority and the local building department.
- Choose flooring, wall, and ceiling materials that are smooth and durable. This will make cleaning easier. Replace and maintain these materials when necessary.
- Make sure equipment that will come in contact with food is smooth, nonabsorbent, and easy to clean. Floor-mounted equipment must be put on legs at least six inches high or sealed to a masonry base. Tabletop equipment must be put on legs at least four inches high or sealed to the countertop.
- Dishwashing machines must be installed so that they prevent contamination of utensils, equipment, and other food-contact surfaces.
- Handwashing stations are required in areas used for food prep, service, and dishwashing. They must be used only for handwashing and should never be blocked for use.
- Handwashing stations should include hot and cold running drinkable water, soap, and a way to dry hands. They should also include a garbage container if paper towels are provided, and signage reminding staff to wash hands before returning to work.
- Plumbing must always be installed and maintained by a licensed plumber. This will help prevent cross-connections from occurring. A cross-connection is dangerous because it can let backflow occur. Backflow is the reverse flow of contaminants through a cross-connection into a drinkable water supply.
- The best way to prevent backflow is to avoid creating a cross-connection. Vacuum breakers, double-check valve backflow preventers, and reduced-pressure-zone backflow preventers can all be used to prevent backflow. However, an air gap is the best way to prevent backflow.
- Garbage must be removed from prep areas as quickly as possible to prevent odors, pests, and possible contamination. Garbage containers must be leakproof, waterproof, and pestproof. They must be cleaned, inside and out, frequently. Facilities must also be regularly maintained. Clean them on a regular basis, and make sure there are no leaks, holes, or cracks in the floors, foundation, or ceilings.

Apply Your Knowledge

Use these questions to review the concepts presented in this chapter.

Discussion Questions

1 What is one of the most important considerations when choosing flooring for food-preparation areas?

2 What action must be taken in the event of a backup of raw sewage in an operation?

3 What can be done to prevent backflow in an operation?

4 What are some approved water sources for an operation? What are the testing requirements for nonpublic water systems?

5 What are the requirements of a handwashing station? In what areas of an operation are handwashing stations required?

6 What are the requirements for installing stationary equipment?

For answers, please turn to the Answer Key.

Apply Your Knowledge

Something to Think About

Go or No-Go

A food handler walked to the ingredient prep area in the back of the gourmet sandwich shop where he worked. He was shocked to see a small puddle of sewage that had formed around a floor drain. He watched the drain closely, but nothing else backed up. He quickly told a manager, who evaluated the situation. Because it appeared the sewage had not contaminated food or equipment, the manager decided to remain open. However, no new sandwich ingredients were prepared. Instead the shop sold sandwiches made from remaining ingredients. When they had used these up, they sold premade sandwiches from the display case. The manager assigned one of the staff members to clean up the spill. She then contacted the building management, who quickly sent out a licensed plumber.

1 Did the manager handle the situation correctly? Why or why not?

For answers, please turn to the Answer Key.

Apply Your Knowledge

Something to Think About

Where There's Smoke

A regional manager for a small quick-service chain had stopped to check in on one of her stores. Unfortunately, she had not visited the store for several months. As the manager walked around, she noticed that there was a buildup of grease on the kitchen walls and ceilings. She also noticed condensation dripping from these areas.

1 What is the problem?

2 What should the regional manager do to fix it?

For answers, please turn to the Answer Key.

Study Questions

Circle the best answer to each question.

1 **What are the most important food safety features to look for when selecting flooring, wall, and ceiling materials?**

A Absorbent and durable
B Hard and durable
C Porous and durable
D Smooth and durable

2 **What organization creates national standards for foodservice equipment?**

A CDC
B EPA
C FDA
D NSF

3 **When installing tabletop equipment on legs, the space between the base of the equipment and the tabletop must be at least**

A 2 inches (5 centimeters).
B 4 inches (10 centimeters).
C 6 inches (15 centimeters).
D 8 inches (20 centimeters).

4 **Besides information on chemical concentration and water temperature, what other machine setting information should be posted on dishwashing machines?**

A Water pH
B Water salinity
C Water pressure
D Water hardness

Study Questions

5 **Signage posted at a handwashing station must include a reminder to staff to**

A wash hands before returning to work.
B use hot running water when washing.
C scrub hands and arms for 10 to 15 seconds.
D avoid touching faucet handles after washing.

6 **What is the most reliable method for preventing backflow?**

A Air gap
B Ball valve
C Cross-connection
D Vacuum breaker

7 **A food handler drops the end of a hose into a mop bucket and turns the water on to fill it. What has the food handler done wrong?**

A Created a cross-connection
B Created an air gap separation
C Prevented backflow
D Prevented atmospheric vacuuming

8 **Which area of the operation is usually required to be the brightest?**

A Dry storage
B Preparation
C Refrigerated storage
D Service

Study Questions

9 **An operation has a buildup of grease and condensation on the walls and ceiling. What is the most likely problem?**

A The ventilation system is not working correctly.

B The cleaning chemicals are not being used correctly.

C The staff are not cleaning the walls correctly.

D The grill is not being operated at a high-enough temperature.

10 **An operation received a violation in the outside area of the facility. The manager reviewed the area and saw that the dumpster was placed on a freshly graveled drive. The lids were closed, and the drain plug was in place to prevent the dumpster from draining. What was the problem?**

A The dumpster lids should have been open to allow it to air out.

B The drain plug should have been removed to allow the dumpster to drain correctly.

C The surface underneath the dumpster should have been paved with concrete or asphalt.

D The dumpster should have been freshly painted so that food debris would not stick to surfaces.

11 **A broken water main has caused the water in an operation to appear brown. What should the manager do?**

A Boil the water for 1 minute before use.

B Contact the local regulatory authority before use.

C Use the water for everything except dishwashing.

D Use the water for everything except handwashing.

For answers, please turn to the Answer Key.

Notes

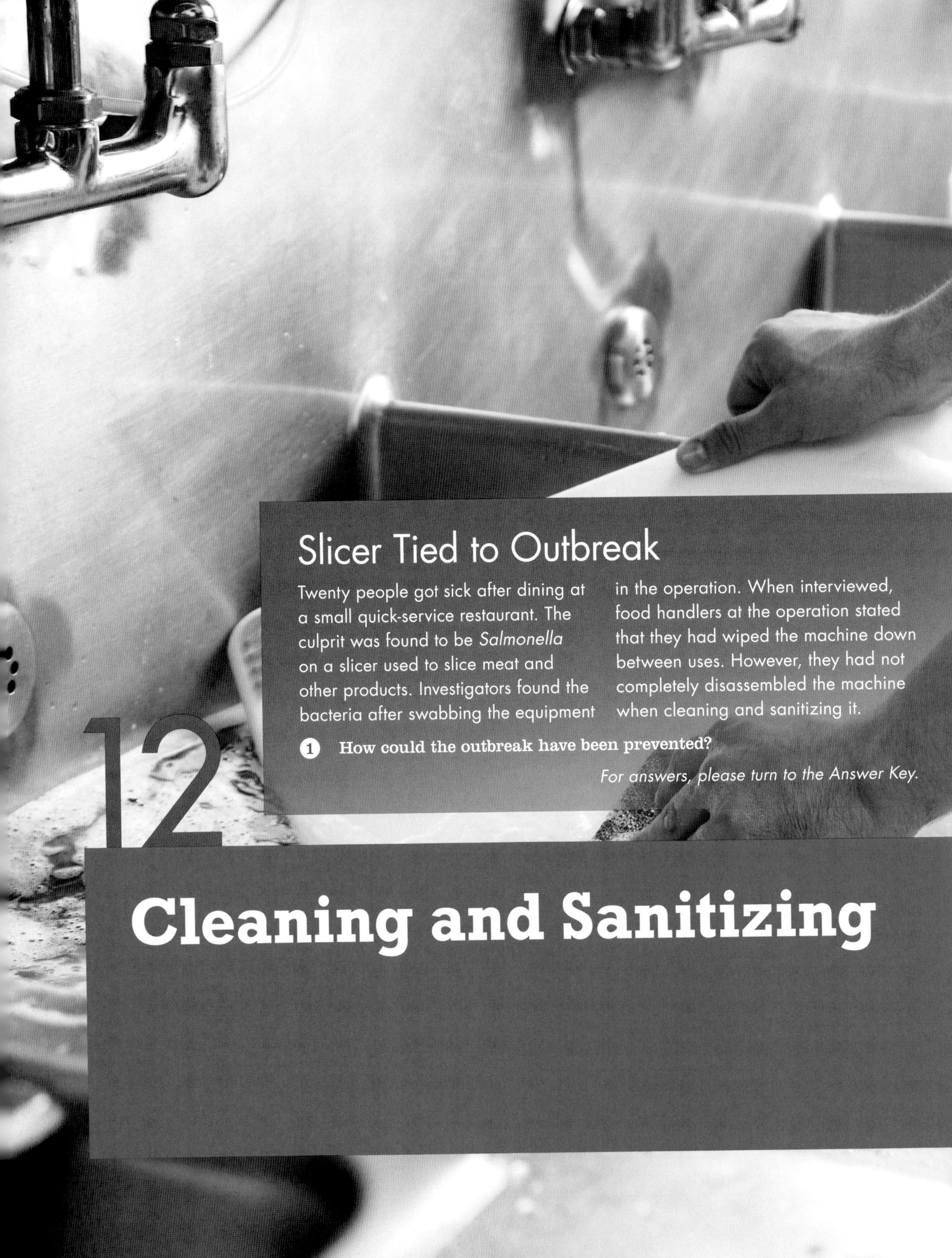

Slicer Tied to Outbreak

Twenty people got sick after dining at a small quick-service restaurant. The culprit was found to be *Salmonella* on a slicer used to slice meat and other products. Investigators found the bacteria after swabbing the equipment in the operation. When interviewed, food handlers at the operation stated that they had wiped the machine down between uses. However, they had not completely disassembled the machine when cleaning and sanitizing it.

1 **How could the outbreak have been prevented?**

For answers, please turn to the Answer Key.

12 Cleaning and Sanitizing

Inside This Chapter

- Cleaning
- Sanitizing
- Dishwashing
- Cleaning the Premises
- Developing a Cleaning Program

Objectives

After completing this chapter, you should be able to identify the following:

- Correct cleaners for specific tasks
- Methods of sanitizing and requirements for their effective use (e.g., contact time, water temperature, concentration, water hardness, pH)
- How and when to clean and sanitize food-contact surfaces
- Guidelines for using dishwashing machines
- How to clean and sanitize items in a three-compartment sink
- How to clean nonfood-contact surfaces
- How to store clean and sanitized tableware and equipment
- Storage requirements for chemicals and cleaning tools
- How to develop a cleaning program

Key Terms

Cleaning
Detergents
Degreasers
Delimers
Abrasive cleaners
Sanitizing
Concentration
Water hardness
Nonfood-contact surfaces

Cleaning

If you do not keep your facility and equipment clean and sanitary, food can easily become contaminated.

Factors That Affect Cleaning

Everything in your operation must be kept clean. **Cleaning** removes food and other dirt from a surface. There are several factors that affect the cleaning process.

Type and condition of the dirt Certain types of dirt require special cleaning methods. The condition of the dirt also affects how easily it can be removed. For example, dried or baked-on dirt will be more difficult to remove.

Water hardness Cleaning is more difficult in hard water. Minerals react with the detergent and decrease how effective it is. Hard water can also cause scale or lime deposits to build up on equipment. This can require the use of lime-removal cleaners, as shown in the photo at left.

Water temperature In general, the hotter the water, the better it dissolves detergent and loosens dirt.

Surface Different surfaces call for different cleaners. Some cleaners work well in one situation but not in another. The wrong cleaner might even damage equipment.

Agitation or pressure Scouring or scrubbing a surface helps remove the outer layer of dirt. This allows the cleaner to penetrate deeper.

Length of treatment The longer dirt on a surface is exposed to a cleaner, the easier the dirt is to remove.

Types of Cleaners

Cleaners are chemicals that remove food, dirt, rust, stains, minerals, or other deposits. They must be stable, noncorrosive, and safe to use. Ask your supplier to help you pick cleaners that meet your needs.

To use cleaners correctly, follow these guidelines:

- Follow manufacturers' instructions carefully, as the manager in the photo at left is doing. If not used the correct way, cleaners may not work and can even be dangerous.
- Only use cleaners for their intended purpose. **NEVER** use one type of cleaner in place of another unless the intended use is the same.

Cleaners are divided into four categories, each with a different purpose. These include detergents, degreasers, delimers, and abrasive cleaners. Some categories may overlap. For example, most abrasive cleaners and some delimers contain detergents. Some detergents may also contain degreasers.

Detergents

Different **detergents** are used for different cleaning tasks. However, all detergents contain surfactants (surface acting agents) that reduce surface tension between the dirt and the surface being cleaned. These allow the detergent to quickly penetrate and soften the dirt.

General-purpose detergents are mildly alkaline cleaners that remove fresh dirt from floors, walls, ceilings, prep surfaces, and most equipment and utensils. Heavy-duty detergents are highly alkaline cleaners that remove wax, aged or dried dirt, and baked-on grease. Dishwashing detergents, for example, are highly alkaline.

Degreasers

Degreasers are detergents that contain a grease-dissolving agent. These cleaners work well in areas where grease has been burned on, such as grill backsplashes, oven doors, and range hoods. A degreaser is being used in the photo at right.

Delimers

Delimers are used on mineral deposits and other dirt that other cleaners cannot remove. They are often used to remove scale in dishwashing machines and on steam tables. Follow the instructions carefully and use delimers with caution.

Abrasive Cleaners

Abrasive cleaners contain a scouring agent that helps scrub hard-to-remove dirt. These cleaners are often used to remove baked-on food in pots and pans. Use abrasives with caution because they can scratch surfaces.

Sanitizing

Sanitizing reduces pathogens on a surface to safe levels. Food-contact surfaces must be sanitized after they have been cleaned and rinsed. This can be done by using heat or chemicals.

Heat Sanitizing

One way to sanitize items is to soak them in hot water. For this method to work, the water must be at least 171°F (77°C). The items must be soaked for at least 30 seconds. You may need to install a heating device to maintain this temperature. Another way to sanitize items with heat is to run them through a high-temperature dishwasher.

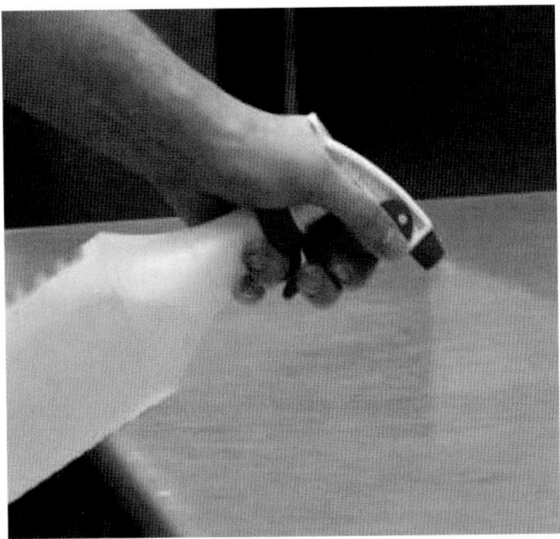

Chemical Sanitizing

Tableware, utensils, and equipment can be sanitized by soaking them in a chemical sanitizing solution. Or you can rinse, swab, or spray them with sanitizing solution, as shown in the photo at left.

Three common types of chemical sanitizers are chlorine, iodine, and quaternary ammonium compounds, or quats. Chemical sanitizers are regulated by state and federal environmental protection agencies.

In some cases, you can use detergent-sanitizer blends to sanitize. Operations that have two-compartment sinks often use these. If you use a detergent-sanitizer blend, use it once to clean, and then use it a second time to sanitize.

Sanitizer Effectiveness

Several factors influence the effectiveness of chemical sanitizers. The most critical include concentration, water temperature, contact time, water hardness, and pH.

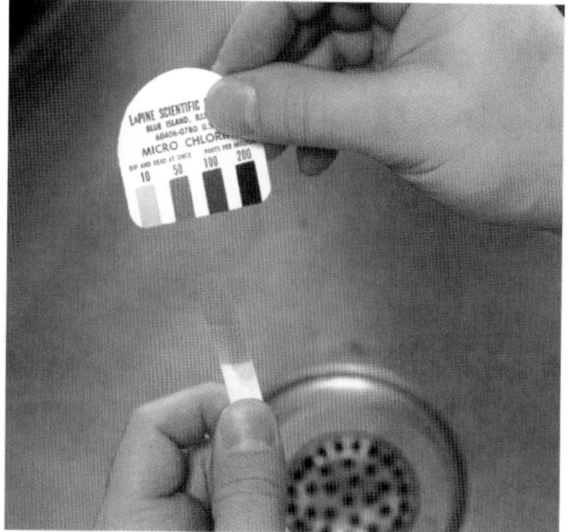

Concentration Sanitizing solution is a mix of chemical sanitizer and water. The **concentration** of this mix—the amount of sanitizer for a given amount of water—is critical. Too little sanitizer may make the solution weak and useless. Too much sanitizer may make the solution too strong and unsafe. It can also leave a bad taste on items or corrode metal.

Concentration is measured in parts per million (ppm). To check the concentration of a sanitizing solution, use a test kit, as shown in the photo at right. Make sure it is made for the sanitizer being used. These kits are usually available from the chemical manufacturer or supplier. Make sure they are available at all times and easily accessible to employees.

Hard water, food bits, and leftover detergent can reduce the solution's effectiveness. Change the solution when it looks dirty or its concentration is too low. Check the concentration often.

Temperature The water in a sanitizing solution must be the correct temperature. Follow manufacturers' recommendations.

Contact time For a sanitizing solution to kill pathogens, it must make contact with the object being sanitized for a specific amount of time. This is called contact time. For example, the bain in the photo at right is being sanitized in an iodine sanitizing solution. The bain must be in contact with the solution for at least 30 seconds.

Water hardness **Water hardness** can affect how well a sanitizer works. Water hardness is determined by the amount of minerals in your water. Find out what your water hardness is from your municipality. Then work with your supplier to identify the correct amount of sanitizer to use for your water.

pH Water pH can also affect a sanitizer. Find out what the pH of your water is from your municipality. Then work with your supplier to find out the correct amount of sanitizer to use for your water.

Table 12.1 summarizes some guidelines for using different types of sanitizers.

Table 12.1: **General Guidelines for the Effective Use of Chlorine, Iodine, and Quats**

	Chlorine		Iodine	Quats
Water temperature	≥100°F (38°C)	≥75°F (24°C)	68°F (20°C)	75°F (24°C)
Water pH	≤10	≤8	≤5 or as per manufacturer's recommendation	As per manufacturer's recommendation
Water hardness	As per manufacturer's recommendation		As per manufacturer's recommendation	≤500 ppm or as per manufacturer's recommendation
Sanitizer concentration	50–99 ppm	50–99 ppm	12.5–25 ppm	As per manufacturer's recommendation
Sanitizer contact time	≥7 seconds	≥7 seconds	≥30 seconds	≥30 seconds

How and When to Clean and Sanitize

Surfaces that do not touch food only need to be cleaned and rinsed to prevent the accumulation of dirt. However, any surface that touches food must be cleaned, rinsed, and sanitized.

How to Clean and Sanitize

To clean and sanitize a surface, follow the steps detailed here. If surfaces have not been cleaned and sanitized properly, take corrective action immediately.

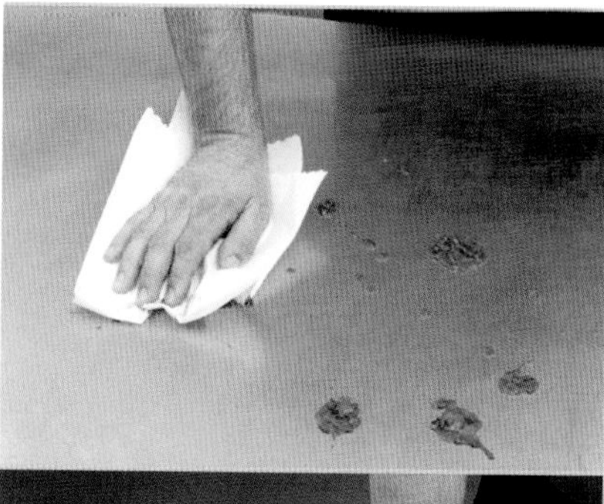

1 Scrape or remove food bits from the surface.
- Use the correct cleaning tool, such as a nylon brush or pad or a cloth towel.

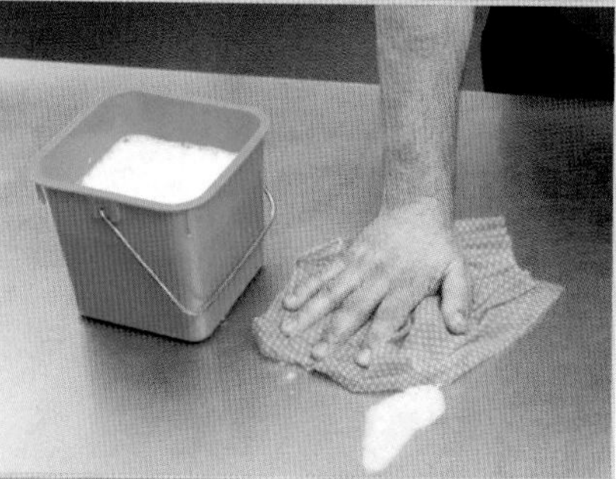

2 Wash the surface.
- Prepare the cleaning solution with an approved cleaner.
- Wash the surface with the correct cleaning tool, such as a cloth towel.

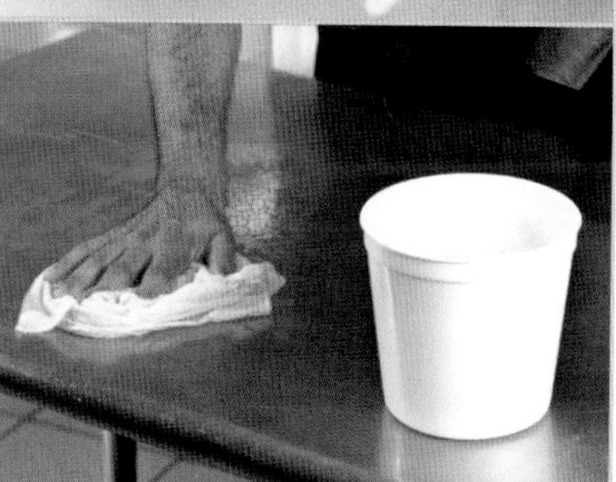

3 Rinse the surface.
- Use clean water.
- Rinse the surface with the correct cleaning tool, such as a cloth towel.

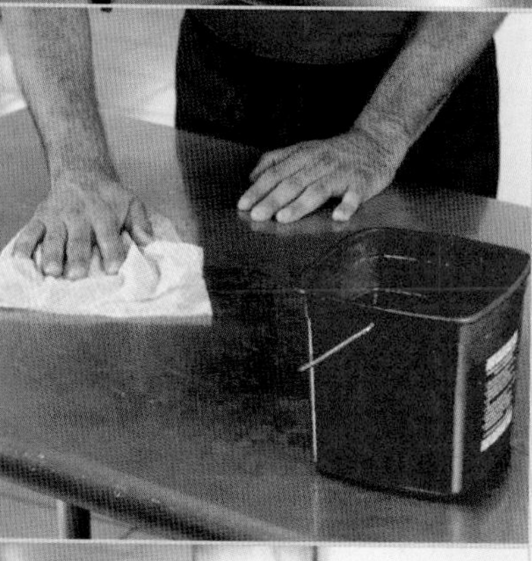

4 Sanitize the surface.
- Use the correct sanitizing solution.
- Prepare the concentration per manufacturer requirements.
- Use the correct tool, such as a cloth towel, to sanitize the surface.
- Make sure the entire surface has come in contact with the sanitizing solution.

5 Allow the surface to air-dry.

When to Clean and Sanitize

All food-contact surfaces need to be cleaned and sanitized at these times:

- After they are used
- Before working with a different type of food, for example between prepping raw chicken and cutting lettuce
- After handling different raw TCS fruits and vegetables, for example between cutting melons and leafy greens
- Any time there is an interruption during a task and the items being used may have been contaminated
- After four hours if items are in constant use

Cleaning and Sanitizing Stationary Equipment

Equipment manufacturers will usually provide instructions for cleaning and sanitizing stationary equipment, such as a slicer. In general, follow these steps:

- Unplug the equipment.
- Take the removable parts off the equipment. Wash, rinse, and sanitize them by hand. You can also run the parts through a dishwasher if allowed.
- Scrape or remove food from the equipment surfaces.
- Wash the equipment surfaces. Use a cleaning solution prepared with an approved detergent. Wash the equipment with the correct cleaning tool, such as a nylon brush or pad or a cloth towel.

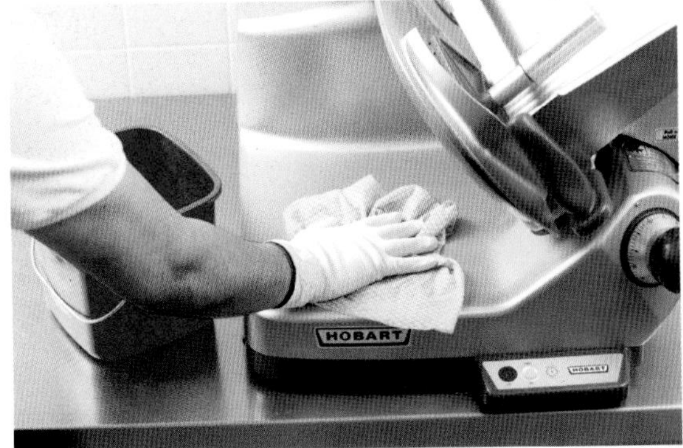

- Rinse the equipment surfaces with clean water. Use a cloth towel or other correct tool.
- Sanitize the equipment surfaces, as the food handler in the photo at left is doing. Make sure the sanitizer comes in contact with each surface. The concentration of the sanitizing solution must meet requirements.
- Allow all surfaces to air-dry. Put the unit back together.

Clean-in-Place Equipment

Some pieces of equipment, such as soft-serve yogurt machines, are designed to have cleaning and sanitizing solutions pumped through them. Because many of them hold and dispense TCS food, they must be cleaned and sanitized every day unless otherwise indicated by the manufacturer.

Dishwashing

There are two methods used by operations to wash dishes: machine dishwashing and manual dishwashing.

Machine Dishwashing

Tableware and utensils are often cleaned and sanitized in a dishwashing machine. The effectiveness of your dishwashing program will depend on the following factors:

- Well-planned layout in the dishwashing area, including a scraping and soaking area and enough space for both dirty and clean items
- Sufficient water supply, especially hot water
- Separate area for cleaning pots and pans
- Devices that indicate water pressure and temperature of the wash and rinse cycles
- Protected storage areas for clean tableware and utensils
- Staff trained to operate and maintain the equipment and use the correct chemicals

High-Temperature Machines

High-temperature machines use hot water to clean and sanitize. If the water is not hot enough, items will not be sanitized. Extremely hot water can also bake food onto the items.

The temperature of the final sanitizing rinse must be at least 180°F (82°C), as shown in the photo at right. For stationary-rack, single-temperature machines, it must be at least 165°F (74°C). The dishwasher must have a built-in thermometer that checks water temperature at the manifold. This is where the water sprays into the tank.

Chemical-Sanitizing Machines

Chemical-sanitizing machines can clean and sanitize at much lower temperatures. Different sanitizers require different temperatures, so follow the manufacturer's dishwashing guidelines.

Dishwashing Machine Operation

Operate your dishwasher according to the manufacturer's recommendations, and keep it in good repair. However, no matter what type of machine you use, you should follow these guidelines.

Cleanliness **Clean the machine as often as needed, checking it at least once a day. Clear spray nozzles of food and foreign objects. Remove mineral deposits when needed. Fill tanks with clean water, and make sure detergent and sanitizer dispensers are filled.**

Preparation Scrape items before washing them. If necessary, items can be rinsed or presoaked. This may be necessary when handling items with dried-on food.

Loading Use the correct dish racks. Load them so the water spray will reach all surfaces, as shown in the photo at left. **NEVER** overload dish racks.

Air-drying Air-dry all items. **NEVER** use a towel to dry items. Doing this could contaminate the items. Make sure items are completely dry before stacking or storing them.

Monitoring Check water temperature, pressure, and sanitizing levels. Take appropriate corrective action if necessary.

Operations using high-temperature dishwashing machines must provide staff with an easy and quick way to measure the surface temperatures of items being sanitized. The method used must provide an irreversible record of the highest temperature reached during the sanitizing rinse. This ensures that the dishwasher can reach correct sanitizing temperatures during operation. Maximum registering thermometers, as shown in the picture at left, and heat-sensitive tape are good tools for checking temperatures.

Manual Dishwashing

Operations often use a three-compartment sink to clean and sanitize large items.

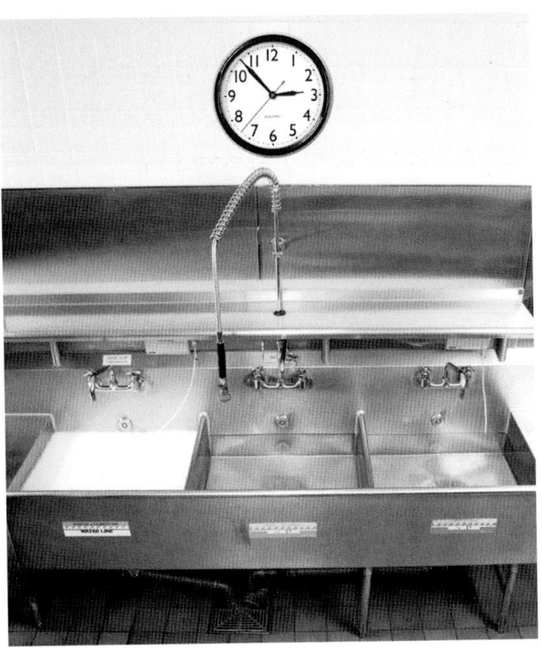

Preparing a Three-Compartment Sink

The sink needs to be set up correctly before use, as shown in the photo at left.

- Clean and sanitize each sink and drainboard.
- Fill the first sink with detergent and water. The water temperature must be at least 110°F (43°C). Follow the manufacturer's recommendations.
- Fill the second sink with clean water. This is not necessary if items will be spray-rinsed instead of being dipped.
- Fill the third sink with water and sanitizer to the correct concentration. Hot water can be used as an alternative. Follow the guidelines on pages 12.4 through 12.6 and the manufacturer's recommendations.
- Provide a clock with a second hand. This will let food handlers time how long items have been in the sanitizing solution.

Cleaning and Sanitizing in a Three-Compartment Sink

Follow these steps to clean and sanitize items in a three-compartment sink.

1 Scrape items before washing them.
If necessary, items can be rinsed or soaked.

2 Wash items in the first sink.

Use a brush, cloth towel, or nylon scrub pad to loosen dirt. Change the water and detergent when the suds are gone or the water is dirty.

3 Rinse items in the second sink.

Spray the items with water or dip them in it. Make sure to remove all traces of food and detergent from the items being rinsed. If dipping the items, change the rinse water when it becomes dirty or full of suds.

4 Sanitize items in the third sink.

Change the sanitizing solution when the temperature of the water or the sanitizer concentration falls below requirements.

NEVER rinse items after sanitizing them. This could contaminate their surfaces.

5 Air-dry items on a clean and sanitized surface. Place the items upside down so they will drain. **NEVER** use a towel to dry items, as it could contaminate them.

Storing Tableware and Equipment

Once utensils, tableware, and equipment have been cleaned and sanitized, they must be stored in a way that will protect them from contamination. Follow these guidelines.

Storage Store tableware and utensils at least six inches (15 centimeters) off the floor. Protect them from dirt and moisture.

Storage surfaces Clean and sanitize drawers and shelves before storing clean items.

Glasses and flatware Store glasses and cups upside down on a clean and sanitized shelf or rack. Store flatware and utensils with handles up, as shown in the photo at left. Staff can then pick them up without touching food-contact surfaces.

Trays and carts Clean and sanitize trays and carts used to carry clean tableware and utensils. Check them daily, and clean as often as needed.

Stationary equipment Keep the food-contact surfaces of stationary equipment covered until ready for use.

Cleaning the Premises

Keeping your operation clean means using the correct tools, supplies, and storage to prevent contamination. Many of the chemicals you will use are hazardous, so you also have to know how to handle them to prevent injury.

For all of your cleaning efforts to come together, you need a master cleaning schedule. Making this schedule work also means training and monitoring your staff to be sure they can follow it.

Using Wiping Cloths

Wiping cloths are often used in operations to wipe up food spills and to wipe down equipment surfaces. There are two types of wiping cloths used in operations—wet cloths and dry cloths. Each has its own requirements. **NEVER** use cloths that are meant for wiping food spills for any other purpose.

Wet cloths Store wet wiping cloths used for wiping counters and other equipment surfaces in a sanitizing solution between uses, as shown in the photo at left. Change the solution when it no longer meets requirements for the sanitizer being used. Always keep cloths that come in contact with raw meat, fish, and poultry separate from other cleaning cloths.

Dry cloths Wiping cloths that will be used to wipe food spills from tableware, such as from a plate during service, must be kept dry while in use. The photo at right shows a dry wiping cloth being used for this purpose. These cloths must **NOT** contain food debris or be visibly dirty during use.

Cleaning Nonfood-Contact Surfaces

Many surfaces in the operation do not normally come in contact with food. These are called **nonfood-contact surfaces**. Examples include floors, walls, ceilings, and equipment exteriors. Because they are not food-contact surfaces, they do not need to be sanitized. However, they do need to be cleaned regularly. This prevents dust, dirt, and food residue from building up. Not only will this prevent the growth of pathogens, but it will also prevent pests.

Cleaning Up after People Who Get Sick

If vomit or diarrhea contacts surfaces in the operation, it must be cleaned up correctly. These substances can carry Norovirus, which is very contagious. Cleaning these surfaces correctly can prevent food from becoming contaminated. It will also keep others from becoming sick.

To be effective, operations must have procedures for cleaning up vomit and diarrhea. These procedures must address specific actions that employees must take to minimize contamination and exposure to food, surfaces, and people. It is critical that employees be trained on these procedures.

Using and Storing Cleaning Tools and Supplies

Cleaning tools can contaminate surfaces if not handled carefully. You can help prevent this by cleaning the tools before storing them and by designating tools for tasks. For example, some operations assign one set of tools for cleaning food-contact surfaces and another for nonfood-contact surfaces. Likewise, one set of tools can be used for cleaning and another for sanitizing. Color-coding each set of tools helps reinforce their different uses. Always use a separate set of tools for cleaning the restroom.

Storing Cleaning Tools and Supplies

Cleaning tools must be stored so that they do not contaminate food and equipment. It is a best practice to store these items in a designated area away from food. Cleaning tools should also be stored in a way that makes it easy to clean the area in which they are stored. The storage area should have the following:

- Good lighting so staff can see chemicals easily
- Hooks for hanging mops, brooms, and other cleaning tools
- Utility sink for filling buckets and washing cleaning tools
- Floor drain for dumping dirty water, as shown in the photo at left

To prevent contamination, **NEVER** clean mops, brushes, or other tools in sinks used for handwashing, food prep, or dishwashing. Additionally, **NEVER** dump mop water or other liquid waste into toilets or urinals.

When storing cleaning tools, consider the following:

- Place mops in a position to air-dry without soiling walls, equipment, or supplies.
- Clean and rinse buckets. Let them air-dry, and then store them with other tools.

Using Foodservice Chemicals

Many of the chemicals used in an operation can be hazardous, especially if they are used or stored the wrong way. One of the biggest dangers is cross-contamination. To reduce your risk, follow these guidelines.

Use Only chemicals approved for use in a foodservice operation should be used. **NEVER** keep chemicals that are not required to operate or maintain the establishment. To prevent contamination, always cover or remove items that could become contaminated before using chemicals. After using chemicals, make sure to clean and sanitize equipment and utensils. Always follow the law and manufacturers' directions when using chemicals.

Storage Chemicals must be stored in their original containers. Some operations also designate specific areas for storing chemicals. Whether or not this is done, chemicals must be kept separate from food, equipment, utensils, and linens. This separation can be done either of these ways:

- By spacing chemicals apart from other items
- By partitioning off chemicals from other items stored in the same area

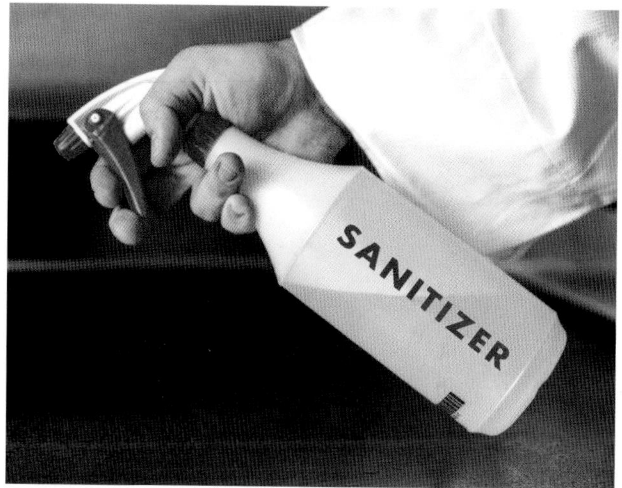

Regardless of the method used, chemicals must always be stored below food, equipment, utensils, and linens.

Labels Chemicals stored in their original container should have a manufacturer's label. That label must include the directions for use and be clear enough to read. If chemicals are transferred to a new working container, the label on that container must list the common name of the chemical. The photo at right shows a working container labeled with the common name of the chemical.

Developing a Cleaning Program

A clean and sanitary operation is a foundation for a successful food safety management system. You can keep your operation in this condition with an effective cleaning program.

To develop your program, first identify what the operation needs. Then create a master cleaning schedule. Also train staff to clean equipment and surfaces correctly. Finally, monitor the program to ensure that it is effective.

Identifying Cleaning Needs

Identify cleaning needs using the following guidelines:

- Review the facility to identify all surfaces, tools, and equipment that need cleaning.
- Look at how cleaning is currently done. Get input from staff. Ask them how and why they clean a certain way. Find out which procedures can be improved.
- Estimate the time and skills needed for each task. Some jobs may be done more efficiently by two or more people. Other jobs might require an outside contractor. Determine cleaning frequency as well.

Creating a Master Cleaning Schedule

Use the information you gather while identifying your cleaning needs to develop a master cleaning schedule. The schedule should include the following.

What should be cleaned Arrange the schedule so that nothing is left out. List all cleaning jobs in one area, or list jobs in the order in which they should be performed. Include both food- and nonfood-contact surfaces as items that need to be cleaned. Keep the schedule flexible enough so that you can adjust it if needed.

Who should clean it Assign each task to a specific person. In general, staff should clean their own areas. Rotate other cleaning tasks to distribute them fairly.

When it should be cleaned Staff should clean and sanitize as needed. Schedule major cleaning when food will not be contaminated or service interrupted—usually after closing. Schedule work shifts to allow enough time as well. Staff rushing to clean before the end of their shifts may cut corners.

How it should be cleaned Provide clearly written procedures for cleaning. Guide staff through the process. Always follow manufacturers' instructions when cleaning equipment. Specify cleaning tools and chemicals by name. Post cleaning instructions near the item to be cleaned.

Choosing Cleaning Materials

Consider the following when selecting cleaning tools and supplies for your operation.

Correct tools and cleaners Select tools and cleaners according to what is identified in the master cleaning schedule. Ask suppliers to suggest which tools and supplies are correct for your operation.

Worn tools Replace worn tools. Dirty or worn tools or equipment may not clean or sanitize surfaces correctly.

Protective gear Provide staff with the correct protective gear, such as aprons, goggles, and rubber gloves.

Implementing the Cleaning Program

Training is critical to the success of a cleaning program. Staff need to understand the tasks you want them to perform and the quality that you expect. Follow these guidelines for a successful cleaning program.

Kickoff meeting Schedule a kickoff meeting to introduce your program to staff. Explain the reason behind it. Stress how important cleanliness is to food safety. If staff understand why they are supposed to do something, they will be more likely to do it.

Training Schedule enough time for training. Work with small groups, as shown in the photo at right, or conduct training by area. Show staff how to clean equipment and surfaces in each area.

Motivation Provide lots of motivation. Reward staff for any job well done. Create small incentives for staff members or teams, such as an award for Clean Team of the Month. Tie performance to specific goals or measurements, such as achieving high marks during regulatory inspections.

Monitoring Once you have implemented the cleaning program, monitor it to make sure it is working. This includes the following:

- Supervise daily cleaning routines.
- Check all cleaning tasks against the master cleaning schedule every day.
- Change the master schedule as needed for any changes in menu, procedures, or equipment.
- Ask for staff input on the program.

Chapter Summary

- Cleaning removes food and other dirt from a surface. Sanitizing reduces the number of pathogens on a surface to safe levels. You must clean and rinse a surface before it can be sanitized. Surfaces can be sanitized with hot water or a chemical sanitizing solution. Then the surface must be allowed to air-dry. Each sanitizing method and sanitizer chemical has specific requirements for use.
- Use the appropriate cleaner for the job. Cleaners are divided into four categories, each with a different purpose. These categories are detergents, degreasers, delimers, and abrasive cleaners. Some categories may overlap.
- All surfaces should be cleaned and rinsed. Food-contact surfaces must be cleaned and sanitized after every use. You should also clean and sanitize each time you begin working with a different type of food or after handling raw TCS fruits and vegetables. Also clean and sanitize surfaces when a task is interrupted. If items are in constant use, they must be cleaned and sanitized every four hours.
- To clean and sanitize a surface, first remove any food from the surface. Then wash and rinse the surface. Finally, sanitize the surface, and let it air-dry.
- Tableware and utensils can be washed in dishwashers or by hand in a three-compartment sink. Always follow manufacturers' instructions when using dishwashers. Make sure your machine is clean and in good working condition. Check the temperature and pressure of wash and rinse cycles daily.
- Before washing items in a three-compartment sink, clean and sanitize the sinks and drainboards. Scrape, rinse, or presoak items before washing them. Then wash them in a detergent solution, and rinse them in clean water. Next, sanitize them for a specific amount of time in either hot water or a chemical sanitizing solution. Finally, they should be air-dried. Once cleaned and sanitized, tableware and equipment should be protected from contamination.
- Wet and dry wiping cloths may be used to wipe up food spills and wipe down equipment surfaces. Wet cloths may be used for wiping equipment surfaces. They should be stored in a sanitizing solution between uses. Clean, dry wiping cloths may be used to wipe food spills from tableware.
- Operations must have procedures for cleaning up vomit and diarrhea. Make sure employees are trained on these procedures and know what to do.
- Chemicals can contaminate food and equipment if the chemicals are not used or stored correctly. Use only chemicals approved for use in a foodservice operation. Before using chemicals, cover or remove items to prevent them from being contaminated. Clean and sanitize equipment and utensils after using chemicals. Store cleaning supplies and tools away from food and equipment.
- Create a master cleaning schedule listing all cleaning tasks. Train staff to follow it. Monitor the cleaning program to keep it effective and supervise cleaning procedures. Make adjustments as needed.

Apply Your Knowledge

Use these questions to review the concepts presented in this chapter.

Discussion Questions

1 When should food-contact surfaces be cleaned and sanitized?

2 How should a three-compartment sink be prepared for dishwashing?

3 What are the steps that should be taken (in order) when cleaning and sanitizing items in a three-compartment sink?

4 How should clean and sanitized tableware, utensils, and equipment be stored?

5 What factors affect the effectiveness of a sanitizing solution?

For answers, please turn to the Answer Key.

Apply Your Knowledge

Something to Think About

Sarah's Dilemma

Sarah noticed that the dirty dishes had started to pile up. She quickly unloaded the dishwashing machine and got a dish cart for the clean dishes. Sarah saw a few crumbs on the cart. To clean it, she dipped a cloth towel in the dishwater in her three-compartment sink and wiped off the crumbs.

In the meantime, the carts of dirty dishes had grown. Sarah quickly loaded a dish rack with as many dishes as she could fit into it. She glanced into the dishwasher before pushing in the rack. She noticed a heavy buildup of mineral deposits on the spray arm and inside the compartment. She closed the door and started the load.

1 What did Sarah do wrong?

____

____

____

____

____

____

____

____

____

____

____

For answers, please turn to the Answer Key.

Apply Your Knowledge

Something to Think About

The New Manager

Andy was just hired as the new general manager at the Twin Trees Family Restaurant. One of his first projects was to create a new cleaning program. He started by taking a walk through the operation. His first stop was the storage area for cleaning tools and supplies. It had a utility sink and a floor drain, but the hot water in the sink was not working. He also noticed two sets of mops and brooms stored on the floor. The storage area was small, but it was well organized and well lit. All the containers were clearly labeled.

Next, Andy watched Clara, a new prep cook, to see how she cleaned and sanitized her areas. Clara cut some melons on a cutting board. Then she wiped it down with a cloth towel. Clara put the cloth towel in a bucket of sanitizing solution to soak while she chopped some fresh spinach. Using the same cloth towel, she wiped down the board after she finished the spinach. Then, she butterflied some pork chops on the same board. Afterward, Clara wiped the board a third time with the same cloth towel.

Andy also watched many other staff members perform cleaning and sanitizing tasks that week. With the help of some senior staff, Andy created a master cleaning schedule.

1 Should Andy suggest any changes to the storage room, tools, or chemicals? If yes, what changes should he suggest?

____

____

2 Did Clara do anything wrong? If yes, what should she have done instead?

____

____

3 What steps should Andy take to make sure everyone follows the master cleaning schedule?

____

____

____

For answers, please turn to the Answer Key.

Study Questions

Circle the best answer to each question.

1 **What is required for measuring the sanitizing rinse temperature in a high-temperature dishwashing machine?**

A Infrared thermometer
B Time-temperature indicator
C Maximum registering thermometer
D Thermocouple with immersion probe

2 **What is an acceptable sanitizing method and contact time for a food-contact surface?**

A Soak the item in very hot water for 7 seconds.
B Soak the item in an iodine solution for 7 seconds.
C Soak the item in a chlorine solution for 7 seconds.
D Soak the item in an ammonia solution for 7 seconds.

3 **If food-contact surfaces are in constant use, how often must they be cleaned and sanitized?**

A Every 4 hours
B Every 5 hours
C Every 6 hours
D Every 7 hours

4 **What must food handlers do to make sure sanitizing solution for use on food-contact surfaces has been made correctly?**

A Test the solution with a sanitizer kit.
B Use very hot water when making the solution.
C Try out the solution on a food-contact surface.
D Mix the solution with equal parts of water.

5 **George is getting ready to wash dishes in a three-compartment sink. What should be his first task?**

A Remove leftover food from the dishes.
B Fill the first sink with detergent and water.
C Clean and sanitize the sinks and drainboards.
D Make sure there is a working clock with a second hand.

Study Questions

6 **Which feature is most important for a chemical storage area?**

A Good lighting
B Single-use towels
C Nonskid floor mats
D Emergency shower system

7 **How should flatware and utensils that have been cleaned and sanitized be stored?**

A With handles facing up
B Below cleaning supplies
C Four inches (10 centimeters) from the floor
D In drawers that have been washed and rinsed

8 **What is the correct way to clean and sanitize a prep table?**

A Remove food from the surface, sanitize, rinse, wash, and air-dry.
B Remove food from the surface, wash, rinse, sanitize, and air-dry.
C Remove food from the surface, wash, sanitize, air-dry, and rinse.
D Remove food from the surface, air-dry, wash, rinse, and sanitize.

9 **Pete the buser poured some cleaner from its original container into a smaller, working container. What else does he need to do?**

A Label the working container with its contents.
B Read the safety data sheet (SDS) for the cleaner.
C Use a new wiping cloth when first using the working container.
D Note on the original container that some cleaner was put into a working container.

10 **What information should a master cleaning schedule contain?**

A What should be cleaned, and when
B What should be cleaned, when, and by whom
C What should be cleaned, when, by whom, and how
D What should be cleaned, when, by whom, how, and why

For answers, please turn to the Answer Key.

Notes

Notes

Rats!

Construction of new subway tunnels had several nearby restaurateurs up in arms. They blamed the construction project for a significant increase in rat activity outside of their operations.

The restaurateurs contacted the engineers for the project and the regulatory authority. They wanted assurances that the rats would be kept out of their operations.

1. **What are some methods that might be used to keep the rats out?**

For answers, please turn to the Answer Key.

13 Integrated Pest Management

Inside This Chapter

- Integrated Pest Management (IPM) Programs
- Identifying Pests
- Working with a Pest Control Operator (PCO)
- Treatment
- Using and Storing Pesticides

Objectives

After completing this chapter, you should be able to identify the following:

- Methods for denying pests access to an operation
- Methods for denying pests food and shelter
- Signs of pest infestation and activity
- How to correctly store pesticides
- How to select a pest control operator (PCO)

Key Terms

Infestation

Integrated pest management (IPM)

Pest control operator (PCO)

Air curtains

Pesticides

Integrated Pest Management (IPM) Programs

Pests, such as insects and rodents, can pose serious problems for restaurants and foodservice operations. Beyond being unsightly to customers, they damage food, supplies, and facilities. The greatest danger from pests is that they can spread diseases, including foodborne illnesses.

Once pests have entered the operation in large numbers—an **infestation**—they can be difficult to eliminate. Developing and implementing an **integrated pest management (IPM)** program is the key. An IPM program uses prevention measures to keep pests from entering the operation and control measures to eliminate those that do get inside.

The best way to ensure your IPM program succeeds is to work closely with a licensed **pest control operator (PCO)**, as shown in the photo at left. These professionals use safe, current ways of preventing and controlling pests.

Prevention is critical in pest control. If you wait until there is evidence of pests in your operation, they may already be there in large numbers.

An IPM program has three basic rules to keep your operation pest-free:

1 Deny pests access to the operation.

2 Deny pests food, water, and shelter.

3 Work with a licensed pest control operator.

Deny Pests Access to the Operation

Pests can enter an operation by traveling inside with deliveries or by entering through openings in the building itself.

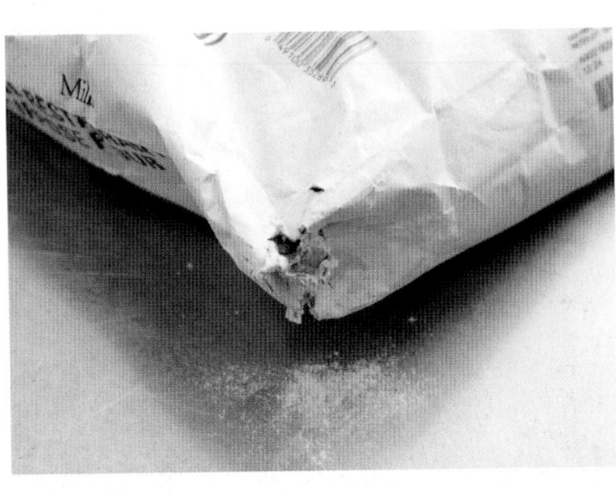

Deliveries

Here is how to prevent pests from entering with deliveries:

- Use approved, reputable suppliers.
- Check all deliveries before they enter your operation.
- Refuse shipments that have pests or signs of pests, as shown in the photo at left. This includes egg cases and body parts (legs, wings, etc.).

Doors, Windows, and Vents

Address the following to prevent pests from entering through doors, windows, and vents.

Screens Screen all windows and vents with screening of at least 16 mesh per square inch. Anything larger might let in mosquitoes or flies. Check screens often. Clean, patch, or replace them as needed.

Self-closing devices and door sweeps Install self-closing devices and door sweeps on all doors. Repair gaps and cracks in door frames and thresholds, such as the one in the photo at right. Use weather stripping on the bottoms of doors with no threshold.

Air curtains Install **air curtains** (also called air doors or fly fans) above or alongside doors. These devices blow a steady stream of air across the entryway. This creates an air shield around doors left open.

Exterior openings Keep all exterior openings tightly closed. Close drive-through windows when not in use.

Pipes

Rodents and insects use pipes as highways through an operation. Consider the following methods of prevention.

Concrete Use concrete to fill holes or sheet metal to cover openings around pipes. The pipes in the photo at right have been sealed with concrete to keep out pests.

Screens Install screens over ventilation pipes and ducts on the roof.

Grates Cover floor drains with hinged grates to keep rodents out. Rats are good swimmers. They can enter buildings through drainpipes.

Floors and Walls

Rodents often burrow into buildings through decaying masonry or cracks in foundations. They move through floors and walls the same way. Seal all cracks in floors and walls, as shown in the photo at right. Use a permanent sealant recommended by your PCO or regulatory authority. Seal spaces or cracks where stationary equipment is fitted to the floor. Use an approved sealant or concrete, depending on the size of the spaces.

Deny Food and Shelter

Pests are attracted to damp, dark, dirty places. A clean operation offers them no food or shelter. The stray pest that might get in cannot thrive or multiply in a clean kitchen. Stick to your master cleaning schedule and follow these additional guidelines.

Garbage Throw out garbage quickly and correctly. Garbage attracts pests and provides them with a breeding ground. Keep garbage containers clean and in good condition. Make sure outdoor containers are tightly covered. Clean spills around garbage containers right away. Wash and rinse containers regularly.

Recyclables Store recyclables in clean, pestproof containers. Keep them as far from your building as regulatory requirements allow. Bottles, cans, paper, and packaging material provide shelter and food for pests.

Storage Store all food and supplies correctly and as quickly as possible. Keep food and supplies away from walls and at least six inches (15 centimeters) off the floor. Use the FIFO (first-in, first-out) method to rotate products, so that pests do not have time to settle into them and breed.

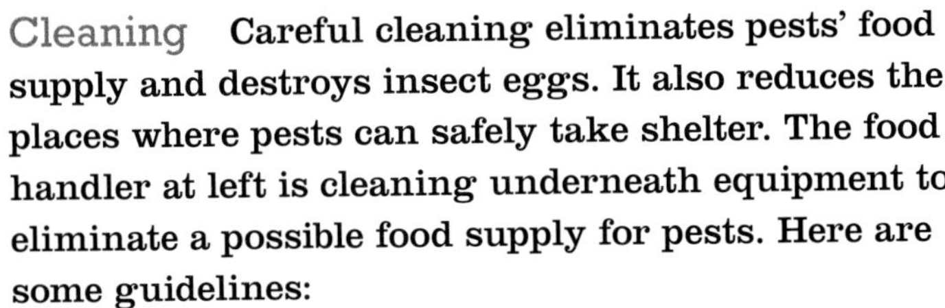

Cleaning Careful cleaning eliminates pests' food supply and destroys insect eggs. It also reduces the places where pests can safely take shelter. The food handler at left is cleaning underneath equipment to eliminate a possible food supply for pests. Here are some guidelines:

- Clean food and beverage spills right away, including crumbs and scraps.
- Clean toilets and restrooms as often as needed.
- Train staff to keep lockers and break areas clean.
- Keep cleaning tools and supplies clean and dry. Store wet mops on hooks rather than on the floor; otherwise roaches can hide in them.
- Empty water from buckets to keep from attracting rodents.

Grounds and Outdoor Dining Areas

Birds, flies, bees, and wasps can be both annoying and dangerous to your customers. As with indoor pests, the key to controlling them is to deny them food and shelter. Here are some guidelines:

- Mow the grass, pull weeds, get rid of standing water, and pick up litter.

- Cover all outdoor garbage containers.
- Remove uneaten food and dirty dishes from tables. Clean dishes as quickly as possible.
- Clean spills as quickly as possible.
- Do not allow staff or customers to feed birds or wildlife on the grounds.
- Install electronic insect eliminators, or zappers, away from food, customers, staff, and serving areas.
- Call your PCO to remove hives and nests.

Identifying Pests

Pests may still get into your operation even if you try to prevent them. They hide in delivery boxes and even ride in on staff's clothing or personal belongings.

It is important to spot signs of pests and determine which type you are dealing with. When you detect pests, record the date, time, and location. Then inform your PCO. Early detection allows the PCO to start treatment as soon as possible.

Flies

Flies are a threat to human health because they feed on garbage and animal waste. For this reason, flies can spread pathogens such as *Shigella* spp.

Cockroaches

Roaches often carry disease-causing pathogens such as *Salmonella* Typhi, fungi, parasite eggs, and viruses. They reproduce quickly and can adapt to certain pesticides. This makes them difficult to control. Many people are also allergic to residue that roaches leave on food and surfaces. There are several types of roaches. Most live and breed in dark, warm, moist, hard-to-clean places. You will often find them in the following areas:

- Behind coolers, freezers, and stoves.
- In sink and floor drains.
- In spaces around hot-water pipes.
- Inside equipment, often near motors and other electrical devices.
- Under shelf liners and wallpaper.
- Underneath rubber mats.
- In delivery bags and boxes.
- Behind unsealed coving (especially rubber-based).

Roaches generally feed in the dark. If you see a cockroach in daylight, you may have a major infestation, because only the weakest roaches come out during the day. If you suspect you have a roach problem, check for the following signs:

- Strong oily odor
- Droppings (feces) that look like grains of black pepper
- Capsule-shaped egg cases that are brown, dark red, or black and possibly leathery, smooth, or shiny in appearance

Rodents

Rodents are a serious health hazard. They eat and ruin food, damage property, and can spread disease. Most rodents have a simple digestive system. They urinate and defecate as they move around a facility. Their waste can both fall into food and contaminate surfaces. Rats and mice are the most common types of rodent. Rodents hide during the day and search for food at night. Like other pests, they reproduce often.

Typically, they do not move far from their nests. Rats travel only 100 to 150 feet away. Mice travel only 10 to 30 feet. Mice can squeeze through a nickel-sized hole to enter a facility. Rats can slip through holes the size of a half dollar. Rats can also stretch to reach an item as high as 18 inches (46 centimeters), jump three feet (one meter) in the air, and even climb straight up brick walls.

Rats and mice have keen senses of hearing, touch, and smell. Plus, they are smart enough to avoid poison bait and poorly laid traps. Effective control of these rodents requires professional knowledge and experience.

A building can be infested with both rats and mice at the same time. Look for the following signs.

Gnawing Rats and mice gnaw to reach food and to wear down their teeth, which are always growing. Rats' teeth can gnaw through pipes, concrete, and wood.

Droppings and urine stains Fresh droppings are shiny and black, as shown in the photo at left. Older droppings are gray. Rodent urine will glow under black (ultraviolet) light.

Tracks Rodents tend to use the same pathways through your operation. If rodents are a problem, you may see dirt tracks along light-colored walls.

Nesting materials Rats and mice build their nests with soft materials such as cloth, hair, feathers, grass, and scraps of paper, as shown in the photo at left.

Holes Rats usually nest in holes in quiet places, often near food and water. Their nests may also be found next to buildings.

Working with a Pest Control Operator (PCO)

Few pest problems are solved simply by spraying **pesticides**—chemical agents used to destroy pests. While you can help reduce the risk of infestation, most pest control should be carried out by professionals. Employ a licensed PCO. Together, you and the PCO can prevent or eliminate pests and keep them from coming back.

You can rely on your PCO to do the following:

- Develop an integrated approach to pest management. This may include a combination of chemical and nonchemical treatments to solve and prevent problems.
- Stay current on new equipment and products.
- Provide prompt service to address problems as they occur. Contracts should include regular visits as well as immediate service when pests are spotted.
- Keep records of all steps taken to prevent and control pests.

How to Choose a PCO

Check references when hiring a PCO and make sure the PCO is licensed (if required by your state). Always require a written service contract that outlines the work to be performed. It clarifies what is expected from both you and the PCO. Here are some things included in a service contract:

- Description of services to be provided, including an initial inspection, regular monitoring visits, follow-up visits, and emergency service.
- Period of service.
- Your duties, including preventive measures and facility preparation before and after treatment.
- Records to be kept by the PCO, including:
  - Pests sighted and trapped; species, location, and actions taken
  - Building and maintenance problems noted and fixed
  - Facility maps or photos showing locations of traps, bait, and problem spots
  - Schedule for checking and cleaning traps, replacing bait, and reapplying chemicals
  - Regular written summary reports from the PCO

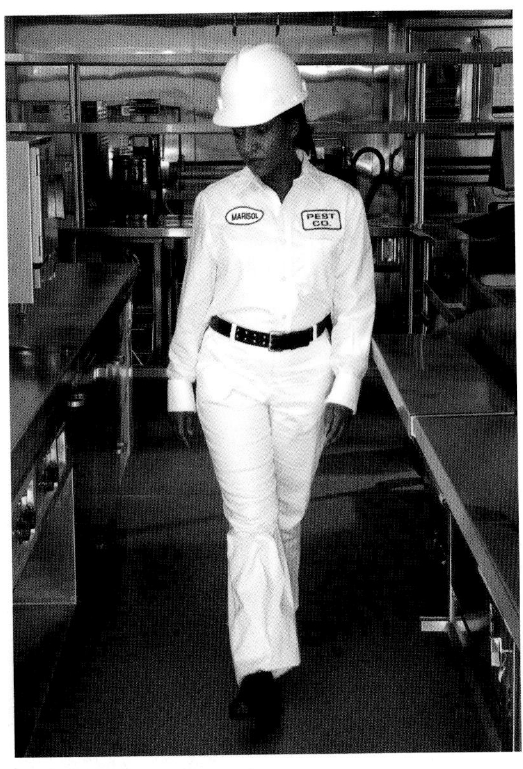

Treatment

Effective treatment starts with a thorough inspection of your facility and grounds, as shown in the photo at left. Give the PCO complete access to the building. The PCO will get a clearer picture of the situation if you help in the following ways:

- Prepare staff to answer the PCO's questions.
- Provide building plans and equipment layouts.
- Point out possible trouble spots.

After the initial inspection, your PCO should provide a treatment plan in writing. In addition to price, the plan should address the following:

- Exactly what treatment(s) will be used for each area or problem and the potential risks involved.
- Dates and times of each treatment (the federal government requires a PCO to provide enough notice to prepare the facility correctly; staff should not be on-site during the treatment).
- Steps you can take to control pests.
- Any building defects that may be a barrier to prevention and control measures.
- Timing of follow-up visits, including plans for the PCO to assess the treatment and suggest alternate treatments if pests reappear.

Control Measures

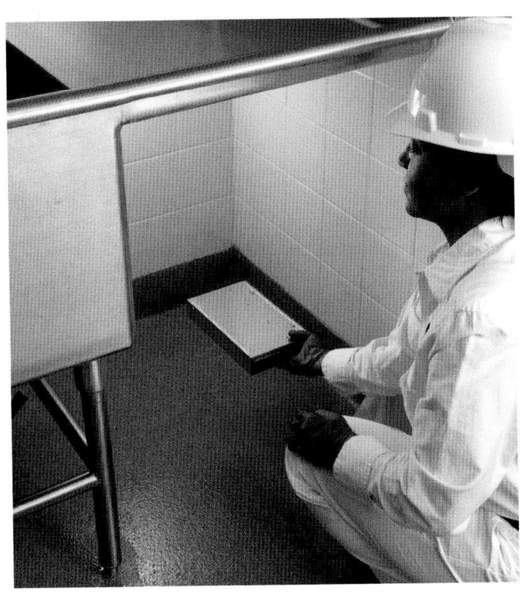

PCOs use pest-control methods that are environmentally sound and safe for operations. They also know which techniques will work best to control the types of pests in your area. New technologies are always being developed. Work with your PCO to determine which pest-control methods are best for your operation. In the photo at left, a PCO has determined that a trap is good for controlling mice in an operation.

Using and Storing Pesticides

Sometimes purchasing and applying pesticides on your own might seem more cost-effective. However, there are many reasons not to do so:

- Applied incorrectly, they may be ineffective or harmful.
- Pests can develop resistance and immunity to pesticides.
- Each region has its own pest-control problems. Control measures may vary.
- Pesticides are regulated by federal, state, and local laws. Some are not approved for use in restaurants or foodservice operations.

Poisonous or toxic pest-control materials should only be applied by a certified applicator. Rely on your PCO to decide whether pesticides should be used in your operation. They are trained to determine the best pesticide for each pest as well as how and where to apply it, as shown in the photo at right.

Here are some other considerations when pesticides will be used.

Timing To minimize the hazard to people, have your PCO use pesticides only when you are closed for business and staff are not on-site.

Preparation When pesticides will be applied, prepare the area to be sprayed by removing all food and movable food-contact surfaces. Cover equipment and food-contact surfaces that cannot be moved, as shown in the photo at right.

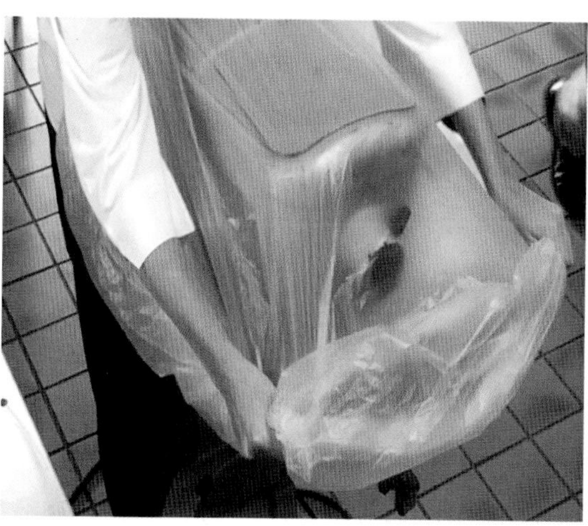

After application Wash, rinse, and sanitize food-contact surfaces after the area has been sprayed.

Safety Data Sheet (SDS) Pesticides are hazardous materials. You should have a corresponding SDS any time one will be used or stored on the premises.

Storage All pesticides used in your facility should also be stored by your PCO. If they are stored on the premises, follow these guidelines:

- Keep pesticides in their original containers.
- Store pesticides in a secure location away from where food, utensils, and food equipment are stored.

Disposal Pesticides should be disposed of by the PCO. Check regulatory requirements before disposing of pesticides yourself. Many are considered hazardous waste. Dispose of empty containers according to manufacturers' directions and your regulatory requirements.

Chapter Summary

- Pests can carry and spread many diseases. Once they have infested a facility, eliminating them can be difficult. Developing and implementing an integrated pest management program is the key.
- An IPM program uses prevention measures to keep pests from entering the operation and control measures to eliminate any pests that do get inside. To be successful, deny pests access to the operation, as well as food and shelter. Also work with a licensed PCO to eliminate pests that do enter.
- Pests can be brought into the operation with deliveries. They can also enter through openings in the building itself. To prevent them from getting inside, check deliveries before they enter your facility. Refuse any shipment in which you find pests or signs of infestation. Screen all windows and vents. Install self-closing doors and air curtains. Keep exterior openings closed when not in use. Fill or cover holes around pipes, and seal cracks in floors and walls.
- A clean and safe operation offers pests little food and shelter. Stick to your master cleaning schedule. Dispose of garbage quickly, and keep all containers clean and tightly covered. Store recyclables as far from your building as allowed. Keep food and supplies away from walls and at least six inches (15 centimeters) off the floor. Rotate food items so pests do not have time to settle into them and breed.
- Roaches live and breed in dark, warm, and moist places. Check for a strong oily odor, droppings that look like grains of black pepper, and egg cases.
- Rodents are a serious health hazard as well. Look for droppings, tracks, holes, nesting materials, and signs of gnawing.
- Rely on your PCO to decide whether pesticides should be used in your operation. PCOs are trained to determine the best pesticide for each pest and how and where to apply it.
- Your PCO should store and dispose of all pesticides used in your facility. If they are stored on the premises, they should be kept in a secure location away from where food, utensils, and equipment are stored.

Apply Your Knowledge

Use these questions to review the concepts presented in this chapter.

Discussion Questions

1 What is the purpose of an integrated pest management program?

2 How can you prevent pests from entering your operation?

3 How can you tell if your operation has been infested with cockroaches or rodents?

4 What are the storage requirements for pesticides?

5 What precautions must be taken both before and after pesticides are applied in your operation?

For answers, please turn to the Answer Key.

Apply Your Knowledge

Something to Think About

The Best Intentions

Now We're Cooking is an operation located in a 90-year-old building. The building is in a shopping area that includes several other restaurants. Fred, the manager, recently remodeled the operation. He chose materials that were easy to clean. All of the new foodservice equipment was designed for ease of cleaning as well. The cleaning procedures listed on Fred's master cleaning schedule were written out in detail and completed by the staff as scheduled with frequent self-inspections. FIFO was followed, and food was stored on metal racks away from walls and six inches (15 centimeters) off the floor.

During a self-inspection two weeks after he finished remodeling, Fred found live cockroaches behind the sinks, in the vegetable-storage area, in the public restrooms, and near the garbage-storage area.

1 What prevention measures might Fred have overlooked in his recent remodeling that could have led to this infestation?

____

____

____

____

____

2 What should Fred do to eliminate the roaches?

____

____

____

____

____

For answers, please turn to the Answer Key.

Study Questions

Circle the best answer to each question.

1 **Who should apply pesticides?**

A Shift manager
B Person in charge
C Pest control operator
D Designated pest staff member

2 **In what type of places are cockroaches typically found?**

A Cold, dry, and light
B Warm, dry, and light
C Cold, moist, and dark
D Warm, moist, and dark

3 **What type of smell may be a sign that cockroaches are present?**

A Strong, oily
B Warm, spicy
C Sharp, musty
D Mild, seaweed

4 **The three basic rules of an integrated pest management program are: work with a PCO; deny pests access; and**

A deny pests food, water, and a nesting or hiding place.
B document all infestations with the local regulatory authority.
C prepare a chemical application schedule and post it publicly.
D notify the EPA that pesticides are being used in the operation.

Study Questions

5 **After pesticides have been applied, food-contact surfaces should be**

A used only after a 20-minute wait.
B checked with a sanitizer test kit.
C washed, rinsed, and sanitized.
D replaced with new equipment.

6 **If pesticides are stored in the operation, where should they be kept?**

A In a secure location, away from food and equipment
B In a glass container, in a walk-in cooler
C In dry storage, on a shelf below the food
D In a plastic container, in any location

7 **To deny pests food and shelter in outside dining areas and around your operation, it is important to**

A mow the grass.
B place extra garbage containers outside.
C spray pesticides around the outside of the facility.
D plant flowers.

8 **Pesticides should be disposed of by**

A the manager.
B the PCO.
C pouring them out and recycling the containers.
D throwing them in an outdoor garbage container.

For answers, please turn to the Answer Key.

Notes

Off on the Wrong Foot

Brian, a new assistant manager, was covering the shift for his boss. Brian had spent most of the morning running around, trying to solve one problem after another.

The operation was just about to open for lunch when there was a knock at the front door. The unfamiliar face asked for the person in charge and said she was there to conduct a health inspection. Brian was in no mood to deal with an inspection. He refused her entry to the operation and told her that the manager was not there and she would have to come back at another time. The inspector told Brian that she could close the operation if he did not let her in. After a few minutes, Brian let her in, but he told her, "You are on your own. I'm by myself and we're getting ready to open. I don't have time for this."

The inspector asked Brian for several documents related to food safety. Brian could not locate the documents and reminded the inspector that he was pressed for time.

The inspector completed the inspection by herself and prepared the results and a final score. She asked to meet with Brian to review the score, discuss the violations, and set up a time frame for things to be corrected. Once again Brian was too busy to meet with her, and he refused to sign the completed inspection.

1 **What did Brian do wrong?**

For answers, please turn to the Answer Key.

14

Food Safety Regulation and Standards

Inside This Chapter

- Government Agencies Responsible for Preventing Foodborne Illness
- The Inspection Process
- Self-Inspections
- Voluntary Controls within the Industry

Objectives

After completing this chapter, you should be able to identify the following:

- Government agencies that regulate food operations
- The importance of regulatory inspections and self-inspections
- The key components of an inspection
- Corrective actions to take when found to be in violation of a regulation

Key Terms

Food and Drug Administration (FDA)

U.S. Department of Agriculture (USDA)

FDA *Food Code*

Centers for Disease Control and Prevention (CDC)

Public Health Service (PHS)

Food codes

Health inspectors

Government Agencies Responsible for Preventing Foodborne Illness

Several government agencies take leading roles in the prevention of foodborne illness in the United States. The **Food and Drug Administration (FDA)** and the **U.S. Department of Agriculture (USDA)** inspect food and perform other critical duties. State and local regulatory authorities create regulations and inspect operations.

Agencies such as the Centers for Disease Control and Prevention (CDC) and the U.S. Public Health Service (PHS) help with food safety as well.

The Role of the FDA

The FDA inspects all food except meat, poultry, and eggs. The agency also regulates food transported across state lines. In addition, the agency issues the **FDA *Food Code*.** This science-based code provides recommendations for food safety regulations. The *Food Code* was created for city, county, state, and tribal agencies. These agencies regulate foodservice for the following groups:

- Restaurants and retail food stores
- Vending operations
- Schools and day-care centers
- Hospitals and nursing homes

Although the FDA recommends that states adopt its published *Food Code*, it cannot require it. The FDA also provides technical support and training. This is available for industry and regulatory agencies.

Other Agencies

Several other agencies have an important role in food safety and the prevention of foodborne illness.

USDA The U.S. Department of Agriculture regulates and inspects meat, poultry, and eggs. The USDA also regulates food that crosses state boundaries or involves more than one state.

CDC The **Centers for Disease Control and Prevention (CDC)** are agencies of the U.S. Department of Health and Human Services. They assist the FDA, USDA, and state and local regulatory authorities by providing the following services:

- Investigating outbreaks of foodborne illness
- Studying the causes and control of disease

- Publishing statistical data and case studies in the *Morbidity and Mortality Weekly Report (MMWR)*
- Providing educational services in the field of sanitation
- Conducting the Vessel Sanitation Program—an inspection program for cruise ships

PHS Like the CDC, the **Public Health Service (PHS)** also assists the FDA, USDA, and state and local regulatory authorities. The PHS conducts research into the causes of foodborne-illness outbreaks. The PHS also assists in investigating outbreaks.

State and local regulatory authorities Regulatory authorities have many responsibilities. Here are some of the responsibilities related to food safety:

- Inspecting operations
- Enforcing regulations
- Investigating complaints and illnesses
- Issuing licenses and permits
- Approving construction
- Reviewing and approving HACCP plans

Regulatory authorities write or adopt **food codes** that regulate retail and foodservice operations. Food codes may differ from the FDA *Food Code*, because these agencies are not required to adopt it. In fact, food codes differ widely from one state or locality to another. For example, some regulatory authorities require hot-holding food temperatures to be 140°F (60°C) or higher, while others require 135°F (57°C) or higher. This can frustrate efforts by the industry to establish uniform food safety standards. Foodservice managers therefore need to consult with their regulatory authorities to find out which regulations apply to their operations.

In a large city, the local regulatory authority will probably be responsible for enforcing regulatory requirements. In smaller cities or in rural areas, a county or state regulatory authority may be responsible for enforcement. In any case, the manager needs to be familiar with the authorities and their enforcement system. State and local **health inspectors** (also called sanitarians, health officials, or environmental health specialists) conduct restaurant and foodservice inspections in most states, as shown in the photo at right. Most are trained in food safety, sanitation, and public-health principles.

The Inspection Process

Having a foodservice inspection program is important for several reasons. The most important reasons, however, are that failing to ensure food safety can risk your guests' health and cost you your business.

All operations that serve food to the public are subject to inspection. An inspection measures whether an operation is meeting minimum food safety standards. It also produces a written report that notes deficiencies. This report helps an operation comply with safe food practices. Keep in mind that you are ultimately responsible for food safety in your operation.

Regulatory requirements guide the inspection. So keep a current copy of your local or state regulations. Be familiar with them. Compare them often to your operation's procedures.

Regulatory authorities have begun using a more risk-based approach when conducting inspections. They often use the five risk factors for foodborne illness and the FDA's public health interventions as guides.

The FDA recommends that regulatory authorities use the following three risk designations when evaluating operations:

- Priority items
- Priority foundation items
- Core items

Priority items are the most critical. These are actions and procedures that prevent, eliminate, or reduce hazards associated with foodborne illness to an acceptable level. Correct handwashing would be considered a priority item.

Priority foundation items are those that support a priority item. Having soap at a handwashing sink is an example.

Core items relate to general sanitation, the facility, equipment design, and general maintenance. Keeping equipment in good repair is an example.

Inspection Frequency

State and local regulatory authorities differ in the frequency of their inspections. Some require inspections for operations at least every six months. Others schedule inspections more or less often.

The frequency will vary depending on the area, type of operation, or food served. Many authorities use a risk-based approach to decide how often they will inspect. Determining factors can include the following.

Size and complexity Larger operations offering many TCS food items might be inspected more frequently.

Inspection history Operations with a history of low sanitation scores or consecutive violations might be inspected more often.

At-risk populations Nursing homes, schools, day-care centers, and hospitals might receive more inspections.

Resources The regulatory authority's workload and number of available inspectors may determine how often it inspects operations.

Steps in the Inspection Process

In most cases, inspectors will arrive without warning. They will usually ask for the person in charge. Make sure your staff know who is in charge of food safety in your absence. Also be aware of your company's policies for handling an inspection.

The following guidelines can help you get the most out of food safety inspections.

Identification Always ask for it, as the manager in the photo at right has done. Also prohibit entry through the back of the operation without the correct ID. Inspectors will volunteer their credentials. Make sure you know the reason for the inspection as well. It could be a routine visit or the result of a guest complaint.

Do not refuse entry to an inspector. Inspectors have the authority to gain access to the operation. They also have the authority to revoke the operation's permit for refusing entry.

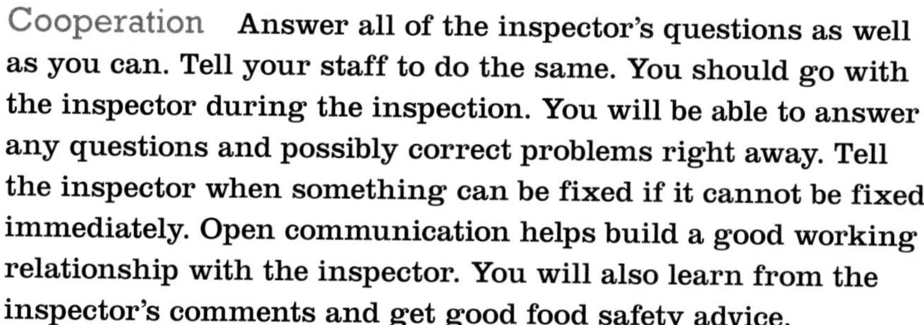

Cooperation Answer all of the inspector's questions as well as you can. Tell your staff to do the same. You should go with the inspector during the inspection. You will be able to answer any questions and possibly correct problems right away. Tell the inspector when something can be fixed if it cannot be fixed immediately. Open communication helps build a good working relationship with the inspector. You will also learn from the inspector's comments and get good food safety advice.

Notes As you walk with the inspector, make note of any problems pointed out. This will help you remember exactly what was said. Make it clear that you are willing to fix any problems. If you believe the inspector is incorrect about something, ask for clarification and note what was mentioned. Then contact the regulatory authority if you are still unsure about something.

Professionalism Be polite and friendly, and treat inspectors with respect. Be careful about offering food, drink, or anything else that could be perceived as trying to influence the report.

Records Be prepared to provide the following records an inspector might request:

- Purchasing records to make sure that food has been received from an approved source
- Pest control operator (PCO) treatment plan
- Proof of food safety knowledge, such as a food protection manager certificate, as shown in the photo at left
- HACCP records (if applicable)
- Temperature logs

You can ask the inspector why these records are needed. If a request seems inappropriate, check with the inspector's supervisor. You can also check with your lawyer about limits on confidential information. Remember that any records you provide will become part of the public record.

Correction After the inspection, the inspector will explain the results and the score, if one is given. Study the inspection report. Discuss any violations and time frames for correction with the inspector. You need to understand the exact nature of a violation. You should also know how a violation affects food safety, how to correct it, and whether or not the inspector will follow up.

You will be asked to sign the inspection report. Signing it acknowledges you have received it. Follow your company's policy regarding this issue.

A copy of the report will then be given to you or the person in charge at the time of the inspection. Keep copies of all reports on file in the operation. You can refer to them when planning improvements and assessing operation goals. Copies of reports are also kept on file at the regulatory authority. They are public documents that may be available to anyone upon request.

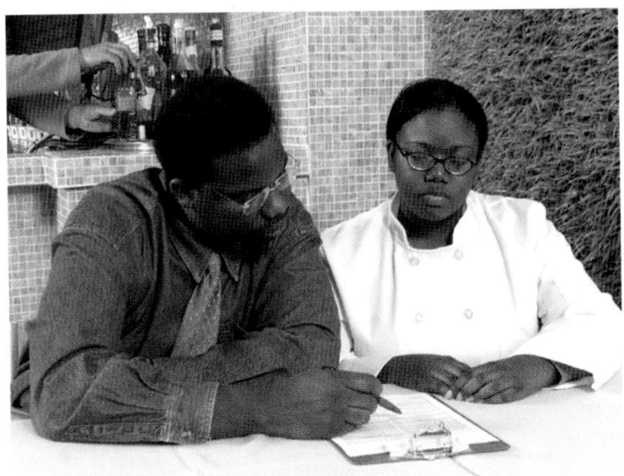

Action Act on any deficiencies noted in the inspection report. The manager and chef in the photo at left are discussing deficiencies in an inspection report. You will need to act on deficiencies within the time given by the inspector. Violations of priority items usually must be corrected within 72 hours. Violations of priority foundation items typically must be corrected within 10 calendar days.

Determine the cause of any deficiencies by reviewing standard operating procedures. Also review the master cleaning schedule, staff training, and food handling practices. Revise current procedures or set up new ones to resolve any problems. Inform staff of the deficiencies and retrain them if needed.

Closure

After careful review, an inspector might determine an operation poses an imminent health hazard to the public. In some states, he or she may ask for a voluntary closure or issue an immediate suspension of the permit to operate. Examples of hazards calling for closure include the following:

- Significant lack of refrigeration
- Backup of sewage into the operation or its water supply
- Emergency, such as a building fire or flood
- Significant infestation of insects or rodents
- Long interruption of electrical or water service
- Clear evidence of a foodborne-illness outbreak related to the operation

If an operation receives a suspension, it must cease operations right away. However, the owner can request a hearing if he or she believes the suspension was unjustified. Such a request often has a time limit (usually within five to ten days of the inspection). Check your regulations for these limits.

The suspension order may be posted at a public entrance to the operation, as shown in the photo at right. This is not required if the operation closes voluntarily. Regulations vary among different authorities. To reinstate a permit to operate, the operation must eliminate the hazards causing the suspension. Then it needs to pass a reinspection and receive written approval to reopen.

Self-Inspections

Well-managed operations perform frequent self-inspections to keep food safe. These are done in addition to—and more often than—regulatory inspections. They can be conducted in-house or by a third-party organization.

A good self-inspection program provides the following benefits:

- Safer food.
- Improved food quality.
- Cleaner environment for staff and guests.
- Higher inspection scores.

Strive to exceed the standards of your regulatory authority. This will help you do well on inspections. Your guests will also recognize your commitment to food safety.

Consider these guidelines when conducting a self-inspection:

- Use the same type of checklist that the regulatory authority uses.
- Identify all risks to food safety.
- After the inspection, meet with staff to review any problems.

Voluntary Controls within the Industry

Few professions have devoted as much effort to self-regulation as the restaurant and foodservice and food-processing industries. Scientific and trade associations, manufacturing firms, and foodservice corporations have made voluntary efforts to raise industry standards through research, education, and cooperation with government.

These organizations have recommended legislative policy, sponsored uniform enforcement procedures, and provided educational opportunities. The results for food safety have included the following:

- Increased understanding of foodborne illness and its prevention.
- Improvements in the safe design of equipment and facilities.
- Industry-wide initiatives to maintain safe food during processing, shipment, storage, and service.
- Efforts to make foodservice laws more practical, uniform, and science-based.

Chapter Summary

- Government control regarding food safety in the United States is exercised at three levels: federal, state, and local.
- Recommendations for restaurant and foodservice regulations are issued at the federal level by the FDA in the form of the FDA *Food Code*. Regulations are written and enforced at the state and local level.
- All operations need to follow practices critical to the safety of the food they serve. The inspection process lets the operation know that it is meeting the minimum standards.
- During the inspection, cooperate with the health inspector and keep the relationship professional. Accompany him or her during the inspection. If the inspector points out a problem, take notes. If a deficiency can be corrected right away, do so. Be prepared to provide records that are requested. Discuss any violations and time frames for correction, and then follow up.
- Well-managed operations will inspect themselves often to keep food safe. These inspections are in addition to those by the regulatory authority. Operations with high food safety standards consider regulatory inspections only a supplement to their own self-inspection programs.

Apply Your Knowledge

Use these questions to review the concepts presented in this chapter.

Discussion Questions

1 What are some hazards that require the closure of an operation?

2 What are the roles of federal, state, and local agencies regarding the regulation of food safety in operations?

3 What should a manager do during and after an inspection?

4 What are some factors that determine the frequency of health inspections in an operation?

For answers, please turn to the Answer Key.

Apply Your Knowledge

Something to Think About

Inspect Thy Self

Brianna was a veteran manager and had been with the company for several years when she was promoted to the company's flagship operation. That operation was where they worked on all new menu concepts and developed all the new recipes that would be used throughout the 42-unit company. Brianna was very proud to have been given a chance to manage this particular operation.

One of the reasons Brianna was promoted was that she had the reputation of always running the cleanest operations in the company, and she always seemed to receive the highest scores on her health inspections.

Brianna had a secret weapon and was determined to use it at her new place. It was a self-inspection system that she had created. It had always kept her one step ahead on inspections and ensured that her staff was keeping food safe.

1 What are the benefits that a self-inspection program provides?

____

____

____

____

____

2 What are some guidelines for conducting a self-inspection?

____

____

____

____

____

For answers, please turn to the Answer Key.

Study Questions

Circle the best answer to each question.

1 **A backup of raw sewage and significant lack of refrigeration can result in**

A a delay of an inspection until the situation is corrected.
B closure of the operation by the regulatory authority.
C improved inspection scores.
D being issued a permit to operate.

2 **A person arrives at a restaurant claiming to be a health inspector. What should the manager ask for?**

A An inspection warrant
B The inspector's identification
C A hearing to determine if the inspection is necessary
D A one-day postponement to prepare for the inspection

3 **Which agency enforces food safety in a restaurant?**

A Centers for Disease Control and Prevention
B Food and Drug Administration
C State or local regulatory authority
D U.S. Department of Agriculture

4 **Who is responsible for keeping food safe in an operation?**

A Food and Drug Administration
B Health inspectors
C Manager/operator
D State health department

For answers, please turn to the Answer Key.

Notes

15

Staff Food Safety Training

What Do You Know?

Katherine was selected by her company to replace a general manager who had been recently promoted. The operation that Katherine was taking over had only been open for a few months. The crew included a lot of young people from the local area who had little experience. Katherine's regional manager advised her that her top priority should be to assess her crew and decide what the food safety training needs were. The operation seemed to be running very well. But, a recent health department inspection revealed that the staff lacked general food safety knowledge. This greatly concerned the company.

This problem had to be immediately addressed. Katherine set out to assess the training needs to determine the gap between what her staff needed to know to perform their jobs versus what they actually knew.

1. **How do you think Katherine should identify her staff's food safety training needs?**

For answers, please turn to the Answer Key.

Inside This Chapter

- Training Staff
- Ways of Training

Objectives

After completing this chapter, you should be able to identify the following:

- Staff duties and specific training needs for each duty
- Ways of training specific to staff and their duties
- How to maintain food safety training records
- How to ensure all staff are trained upon and after being hired

Key Terms

Training need

Training Staff

You do not know how long staff members will be working at your operation. Whether they have been on the job for one day or five years, they need to understand that food safety is important. To make sure you are serving safe food, train your staff when they are first hired and then continue training them.

To ensure staff can handle food correctly, first identify each training need within your operation. A **training need** is a gap between what staff should know to do their jobs and what they actually know.

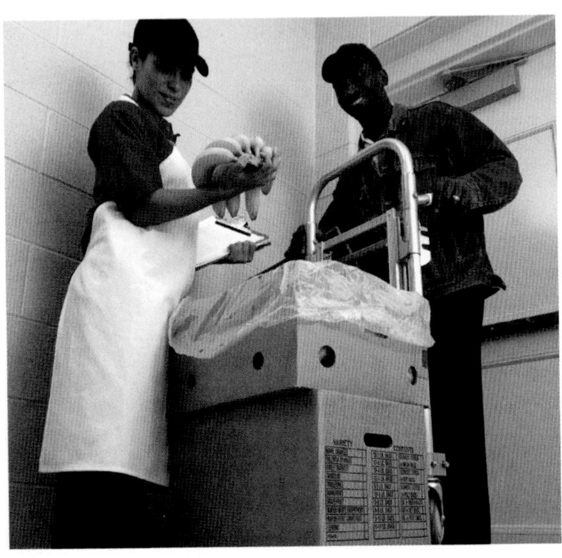

For new hires, the need might be obvious. For experienced staff, the need is not always as clear.

Identifying food safety training needs will require some effort. You can achieve this in several ways:

- Observe performance on the job
- Test food safety knowledge
- Identify areas of weakness

All staff need general food safety knowledge. Other knowledge will be specific to tasks. For example, everyone should know how to wash their hands correctly. However, only receiving staff need to know how to inspect produce during receiving, as shown in the photo at left.

Critical Food Safety Knowledge

You cannot assume new hires will understand your operation's food safety procedures without training. They should begin learning about the importance of food safety on their first day. They should also receive training in the critical areas listed in Table 15.1. Once staff are trained, monitor them to make sure they are following procedures.

Retraining

Staff need to be periodically retrained in food safety. You can do this by scheduling short training sessions, planning meetings to update them on new procedures, or holding motivational sessions that reinforce food safety practices.

Record Keeping

Keep records of all food safety training at your operation. For legal reasons, be sure to document this training when a staff member completes it.

Table 15.1: **Critical Food Safety Knowledge for Staff**

Good Personal Hygiene

- How and when to wash hands
- Where to wash hands
- Other hand-care guidelines including fingernail length, nail polish, covering wounds
- Proper work attire
- Reporting illness

Controlling Time and Temperature

- TCS food
- How to measure the temperature of food
- Holding and storing TCS food
- How to label food for storage
- Temperature requirements when thawing, cooking, cooling, and reheating food

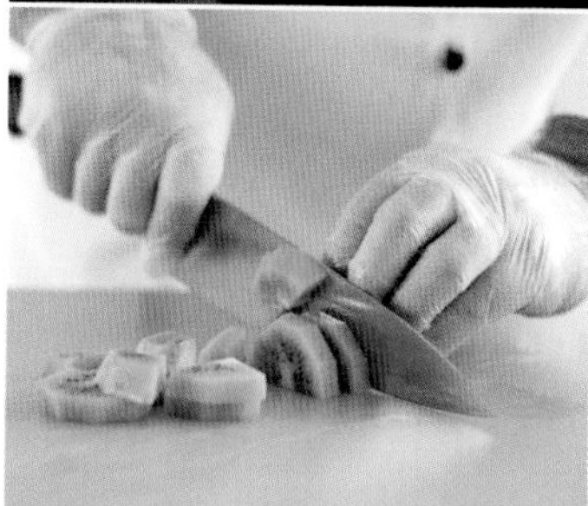

Preventing Cross-Contamination

- Preventing cross-contamination of food during storage, preparation, and service
- Preventing cross-contamination when storing utensils and equipment
- What to do if cross-contamination happens
- What to do for people who have food allergies

Cleaning and Sanitizing

- How and when to clean and sanitize
- The correct way to wash dishes in a three-compartment sink and in a dishwasher
- How to handle cleaning tools and supplies
- Handling garbage
- Spotting pests

Ways of Training

You have several ways to teach staff how to keep food safe. When choosing training, think about what would work best in your operation. Some operations use a traditional approach such as on-the-job training. Others may use a technology-based approach. No one type of training works best, as not everyone learns the same way. Use different methods to achieve the best results.

On-the-Job Training (OJT)

Many operations assign experienced staff to train learners while on the job. Learners perform tasks while the trainers tell them how they are doing.

OJT teaches skills that require thinking and doing. It is good for training staff members one at a time. It can also work for small groups. It is equally effective for teaching skills that require watching someone perform the task correctly.

Success depends on the skill of the person doing the training. Choose the trainer carefully. Before using OJT, also recognize that it takes experienced staff away from their jobs. Plus, it is not as useful for training large groups.

Classroom Training

Today's workforce expects training that will both entertain and teach them. This can be challenging, but it is not impossible. Using an activity-based approach to training can be very effective. People learn by doing rather than by just being told what to do. Your training should include activities that require staff to do something.

Staff should also take part in learning activities. Encourage them to ask questions and allow them to make mistakes. Make them responsible for their own learning as well.

You can use a range of activity-based training to teach food safety to your staff:

- Information search
- Guided discussion
- Role-playing
- Games
- Demonstrations
- Jigsaw design
- Training videos and DVDs

Information Search

Some people are curious and like to explore things on their own. Make use of their interest by having them discover food safety information for themselves. Here is how:

1 Put staff in small groups.

2 Give them questions to answer within a set time.

3 Give them the following types of tools to answer the questions:

- Operations manuals
- Job aids
- Posters, as shown in the image at right
- Staff guides

4 Bring the groups together and have them share what they learned.

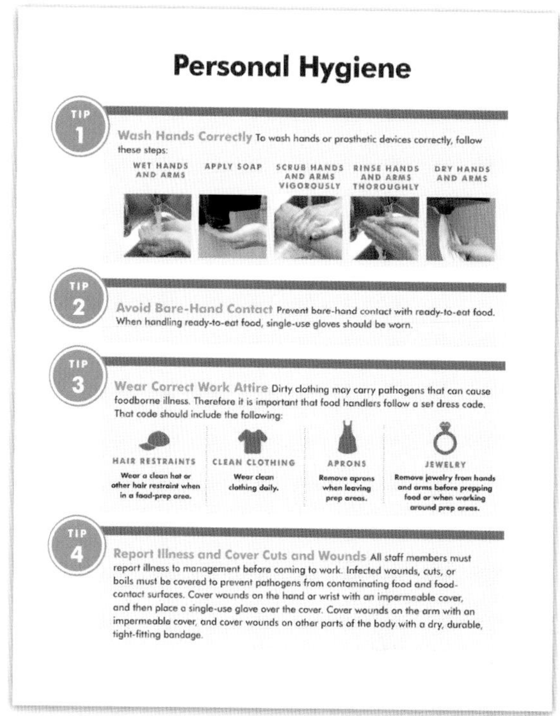

Guided Discussion

Ask staff questions that draw on their knowledge and experience. Encourage them to think and then discuss their thoughts. Each time learners answer a question, follow with another question.

Through this approach, a training session on calibrating thermometers might go something like this:

Instructor: "How can you find out if a cooked chicken breast has reached the correct temperature?"

Learner: "Use a thermometer."

Instructor: "How can you make sure a thermometer's reading is correct?"

Learner: "Calibrate it."

Instructor: "How do you calibrate a thermometer?"

Learner: "By using the ice-point method or the boiling-point method."

Games

A game can help make difficult or boring information seem more exciting. You can also use games to practice information that has already been taught. To be effective, games should be the following:

- Easy to play.
- Fun.
- Suitable for all time frames.
- Easy to bring to the training site.
- Easy to change for the audience and content.

Role-Play

Many trainers use role-playing to teach concepts. However, some learners do not like to role-play because it puts them on the spot. Role-playing can work if you handle it the correct way. Here is how:

1 Prepare a script in advance that shows the correct or incorrect way to perform a skill.

2 Find two volunteers and give them time to rehearse the script. Do this early in the training session. As an alternative, you can play one of the parts in the role-playing exercise.

3 Have the volunteers act out the script.

4 Ask the rest of the group to decide what the role-players did correctly and incorrectly.

Demonstrations

You will often teach specific food safety tasks by showing them to a person or group. Demonstrations are most effective when you follow the Tell/Show/Practice model, as shown in Table 15.2.

Table 15.2: **Demonstrating a Task Using the Tell/Show/Practice Model**

	**Tell** Tell the learner how to do the task. Explain what you are doing and why.
	**Show** Show the learner how to do the task.
	**Practice** Let the learner do the task. As extra practice, have the learner explain how to do the task before showing how to do it. Tell the learner how he or she is doing throughout the practice.

Jigsaw Design

There is an old saying that goes, "You have learned something when you can teach someone else how to do it." The jigsaw method follows this principle. Here is how to use it:

1. Put learners in small groups.
2. Assign a specific food safety topic to each group.
3. Tell each group to read about their topic, discuss it, and decide how to teach it to the other groups.
4. Take one person from each group and form new groups.
5. Have each member in the new group teach his or her topic to the other group members.
6. Bring the groups back together for review and questions.

Training Videos and DVDs

Trainers generally believe that learners retain information from their training sessions in the following ways:

- 10 percent of what they read.
- 20 percent of what they hear.
- 30 percent of what they see.
- 50 percent of what they see and hear.

Videos and DVDs will help your staff see and hear food safety information. This will make them more likely to remember it. Video is also useful for teaching skills that involve motion, such as calibrating a thermometer.

If your staff are learning food safety on their own by video instruction, supplement their training with print materials.

Technology-Based Training

Many operations use technology-based training, such as online learning, to teach food safety. Technology-based training lets you deliver training when and where your staff needs it. It is most appropriate in the following situations:

- Staff work in different locations and/or need the same training at different times.
- When it is too costly to bring staff to the same place.
- Staff need retraining.
- Staff have different levels of knowledge about a topic.
- Staff have different learning skills.
- Staff need to learn at their own pace.
- You want to collect specific information, such as test scores, time spent on different topics, and/or problem areas.

Chapter Summary

- Ensure that staff have the knowledge and skills to handle food safely in your operation.
- First assess your operation's training needs. A training need is a gap between what staff should know to perform their jobs and what they actually know.
- To identify food safety training needs, test your staff's knowledge, observe their performance, or note their areas of weakness.
- All staff need general food safety knowledge. Other knowledge will be specific to tasks. All staff should be retrained periodically.
- Keep records of all food safety training at your operation. For legal reasons, be sure to document this training when a staff member completes it.
- Training can be delivered in various ways. No one type of training works best, as not everyone learns the same way.
- Use different training methods to achieve the best results.

Apply Your Knowledge

Use these questions to review the concepts presented in this chapter.

Discussion Questions

1 How can an operation determine its food safety training needs?

2 What are some methods that can be used to deliver training?

For answers, please turn to the Answer Key.

Apply Your Knowledge

Something to Think About

Technology Saves the Day

Ryan was a genuine success story. He started with the company when he was 17 years old and worked summers and holidays as he moved up from job to job. He had started washing pots and pans and had been promoted into almost every job there was in the back of the house.

He found himself, at age 24, as the director of training for this rapidly growing chain of casual-dining restaurants. Ryan was in charge of coordinating food safety training for all company staff. He worked directly with the company's director of food safety to determine the best way to approach the company's goals for food safety training.

One of the problems Ryan faced was that the company employed over 3,000 people in 18 different states. Ryan did not have a clue about how he could ensure that every staff member in the company would be correctly trained in food safety.

Ryan's background had been in the back of the house and his technology skills were extremely limited. Even though Ryan was not comfortable with technology, he realized that it was the answer to making sure all 3,000 staff members were correctly and uniformly trained.

1 Why do you think Ryan was considering a company-wide technology-based training program?

____

____

____

2 List some of the situations where technology-based training is most appropriate?

____

____

____

For answers, please turn to the Answer Key.

Study Questions

Circle the best answer to each question.

1 **When should staff receive food safety training?**

A When hired, and then periodically after that

B When they do not have foodservice experience

C When a new FDA *Food Code* comes out

D Only when they request it

2 **New staff must be trained in the critical areas of personal hygiene, cleaning and sanitizing, controlling time and temperature, and**

A crisis management.

B equipment handling.

C HACCP plan creation.

D preventing cross-contamination.

3 **The manager's responsibility for staff food safety training is to**

A test staff's food safety knowledge.

B provide all staff with videos and DVDs for training.

C make sure that staff have the knowledge and skills to keep food safe.

D let staff learn on their own.

4 **All new staff should receive training on**

A HACCP.

B crisis management.

C general food safety.

D active managerial control.

5 **What is the first task in training a large group of servers to prevent contamination of food?**

A Assess the training needs of the servers on this topic.

B Make a list of possible information to cover.

C Provide servers with operation manuals on the topic.

D Put the servers into small groups based on service experience.

6 **In which training method does a trainer ask a series of questions to draw on the knowledge and experience of the learners?**

A Information search

B Guided discussion

C Jigsaw design

D Games

For answers, please turn to the Answer Key.

Notes

Notes

Glossary

Note: The number in bold at the end of each entry refers to the chapter in which the term is discussed in detail.

A

Abrasive cleaners. Cleaners containing a scouring agent for scrubbing off hard-to-remove dirt. **12**

Active managerial control. Food safety management system designed to prevent foodborne illness by addressing the five most common risk factors identified by the Centers for Disease Control and Prevention (CDC). **10**

Air curtains. Devices installed above or alongside doors that blow a steady stream of air across an entryway, creating an air shield around open doors. Also called air doors or fly fans. **13**

Air gap. Air space used to separate a water supply outlet from any potentially contaminated source; for example, the air space between a floor drain and the drainpipe of a sink. **11**

A.L.E.R.T. Acronym developed by the FDA to help operations develop a food defense program. A.L.E.R.T. stands for assure, look, employees, reports, and threat. **3**

Anaphylaxis. A severe allergic reaction that can lead to death. **3**

Approved suppliers. Suppliers who have been inspected, are able to provide an inspection report, and who meet applicable local, state, and federal laws. **6**

B

Backflow. Unwanted reverse flow of contaminants through a cross-connection into a drinkable-water system. **11**

Backsiphonage. A backflow that occurs when high water use in one area of an operation creates a vacuum that sucks contaminants into the drinkable water supply. **11**

Bacteria. Single-celled, living microorganisms that can spoil food and cause foodborne illness. **2**

Best-by date. Date by which a product should be eaten for best flavor or quality. **6**

Glossary

Bimetallic stemmed thermometer. The most common and versatile type of thermometer, which measures temperature through a metal stem with a sensor in the end. **5**

Boiling-point method. Method of calibrating a thermometer based on the boiling point of water. **5**

Booster heater. Water heater attached to hot-water lines leading to dishwashing machines or sinks. Raises water to the temperature required for the heat sanitizing of tableware and utensils. **11**

C

Calibration. Process of adjusting a thermometer to a known standard, such as the freezing point or boiling point of water, to ensure that the thermometer gives accurate readings. **5**

Carriers. People who carry pathogens and infect others, yet never get sick themselves. **4**

Centers for Disease Control and Prevention (CDC). Agencies of the U.S. Department of Health and Human Services that investigate foodborne-illness outbreaks, study the causes and control of disease, publish statistical data, provide educational services in the field of sanitation, and conduct the Vessel Sanitation Program. **14**

Cleaning. Removing food and other types of dirt from a surface, such as a countertop or plate. **12**

Concentration. The amount of sanitizer for a given amount of water measured in parts per million (ppm). **12**

Contamination. Presence of harmful substances in food. Some food safety hazards occur naturally, while others are introduced by humans or the environment. **1**

Coving. Curved, sealed edge placed between the floor and wall to eliminate sharp corners or gaps that would be impossible to clean. Coving also eliminates hiding places for pests and prevents moisture from deteriorating walls. **11**

Critical control points (CCPs). In a HACCP system, the points in the process where you can intervene to prevent, eliminate, or reduce identified hazards to safe levels. **10**

Glossary

Cross-connection. Physical link through which contaminants from drains, sewers, or other wastewater sources can enter a drinkable water supply. A hose connected to a faucet and submerged in a mop bucket is an example. **11**

Cross-contact. The transfer of an allergen from a food or food-contact surface containing an allergen to a food that does not contain the allergen. **3**

Cross-contamination. The transfer of pathogens from one surface or food to another. **1**

D

Date marking. A date placed on ready-to-eat TCS food held for more than 24 hours indicating the date by when the food must be sold, eaten, or thrown out. **7**

Degreasers. Detergents that contain a grease-dissolving agent. **12**

Delimers. Cleaning agents used on mineral deposits and other soils that other cleaners cannot remove, such as scale, rust, and tarnish. **12**

Detergents. Cleaners designed to penetrate and soften dirt to help remove it from a surface. **12**

E

Expiration date. Last date recommended for a product to be at peak quality. **6**

F

FAT TOM. Acronym for the conditions needed by foodborne bacteria to grow: food, acidity, temperature, time, oxygen, and moisture. **2**

FDA *Food Code*. Science-based recommendations on food safety regulations for city, county, state, and tribal agencies that regulate foodservice for retail food operations, vending operations, schools and day-care centers, and hospitals and nursing homes. **14**

Fecal–oral route. The transfer of pathogens from a person's feces to his or her hands, and then from that person's unwashed or improperly washed hands to food that is eaten by someone else. A foodborne illness may result. **2**

Glossary

First-in, first-out (FIFO) method. Method of stock rotation in which products are shelved based on their use-by or expiration dates, so oldest products are used first. **7**

Flow of food. Path that food takes through an operation, from purchasing and receiving through storing, preparing, cooking, holding, cooling, reheating, and serving. **5**

Food allergen. A naturally-occurring protein in food or in an ingredient that some people are sensitive to. When enough of an allergen is eaten, the immune system mistakenly considers it harmful and attacks the food protein. This can result in an allergic reaction. **3**

Food and Drug Administration (FDA). Federal agency that inspects all food except meat, poultry, and eggs; regulates food transported across state lines; and issues the FDA *Food Code*. **14**

Food codes. State or local food safety regulations for retail and foodservice operations. **14**

Food defense program. Program developed and implemented by an operation to prevent deliberate contamination of its food. **3**

Food safety management system. Group of programs, procedures, and measures designed to prevent foodborne illness by actively controlling risks and hazards throughout the flow of food. **10**

Foodborne illness. Illness carried or transmitted to people by food. **1**

Foodborne-illness outbreak. An incident in which two or more people experience the same illness symptoms after eating the same food. An investigation is conducted by the state and local regulatory authorities, and the outbreak is confirmed by a laboratory analysis. **1**

Fungi. Pathogens that can spoil food and sometimes make people sick. Molds and yeasts are examples. **2**

H

HACCP. Food safety management system based on the idea that if significant biological, chemical, or physical hazards are identified at specific points within a product's flow through the operation, they can be prevented, eliminated, or reduced to safe levels. **10**

HACCP plan. Written document based on HACCP principles describing procedures a particular operation will follow to ensure the safety of food served. *See HACCP.* **10**

Glossary

Hair restraint. Device used to keep a food handler's hair away from food and to keep the individual from touching his or her hair. **4**

Hand antiseptics. Liquids or gels used to lower the number of pathogens on the skin's surface. Hand antiseptics should only be used after correct handwashing, not in place of it. **4**

Health inspectors. City, county, or state staff members who conduct foodservice inspections. Health inspectors are also known as sanitarians, health officials, and environmental health specialists. **14**

High-risk populations. People susceptible to foodborne illness due to the effects of age or health on their immune systems, including preschool-age children, elderly people, and people with compromised immune systems. **1**

I

Ice-point method. Method of calibrating thermometers based on the freezing point of water. **5**

Imminent health hazard. A significant threat or danger to health that requires immediate correction or closure to prevent injury. **10**

Immune system. The body's defense system against illness. People with compromised immune systems are more susceptible to foodborne illness. **1**

Impermeable. A material that does not allow liquid to pass through it; for example, a bandage or finger cot. **4**

Infestation. Situation that exists when pests overrun or inhabit an operation in large numbers. **13**

Inspection stamp. A stamp indicating that a carcass or package of meat has been inspected by the USDA or a state department of agriculture. **6**

Integrated pest management (IPM). Program using prevention measures to keep pests from entering an operation and control measures to eliminate any pests that do get inside. **13**

J

Jaundice. A yellowing of the skin and eyes, which can be a symptom of a foodborne illness. **2**

Glossary

K

Key drop delivery. The receipt of food by a foodservice operation while it is closed for business. **6**

M

Microorganisms. Small, living organisms that can be seen only through a microscope. There are four types of microorganisms that can contaminate food and cause foodborne illness: bacteria, viruses, parasites, and fungi. **2**

Minimum internal temperature. The required minimum temperature the internal portion of food must reach to sufficiently reduce the number of pathogens that might be present. This temperature is specific to the type of food being cooked. Food must reach and hold its required internal temperature for a specified amount of time. **8**

Mobile units. Portable foodservice operations, ranging from concession vans to full field kitchens. **9**

Mold. Type of fungus that causes food spoilage. Some molds produce toxins that can cause foodborne illness. **2**

N

Nonfood-contact surfaces. Surfaces in an operation that do not normally come in contact with food, such as floors, walls, ceilings, and equipment exteriors. **12**

NSF. Organization that develops and publishes standards for the design of sanitary equipment. It also assesses and certifies that equipment has met these standards. **11**

O

Off-site service. Service of food to someplace other than where it is prepared or cooked, including catering and vending. **9**

Onset time. Time it takes for the symptoms of a foodborne illness to appear after exposure to the pathogen, toxin, or parasite that caused the illness. This time varies depending on the type of foodborne illness and other factors. **2**

Glossary

P

Parasite. Organism that needs to live in a host organism to survive. Parasites can be found in water and inside many animals, such as cows, chickens, pigs, and fish. **2**

Partial cooking (par cooking). Intentionally stopping the cooking process to cool a food item, so cooking can be finished just before service or sale. **8**

Pathogens. Illness-causing microorganisms. **2**

Pest control operator (PCO). Licensed professional who uses safe, current methods to prevent and control pests. **13**

Pesticides. Chemicals used to destroy pests, usually insects. **13**

pH. A measure of acidity on a scale of 0 to 14.0, with 0 being highly acidic, 7.0 being neutral, and 14.0 being highly alkaline. **2**

Pooled eggs. Eggs that are cracked open and combined in a common container. **8**

Porosity. Extent to which liquids are absorbed by a material. The term is usually used in relation to flooring material. **11**

Potable. Drinkable; for example, potable water is water that is safe to drink. **11**

Public Health Service (PHS). A federal agency that conducts research into the causes of foodborne illness outbreaks and assists with the investigation of outbreaks. **14**

R

Ready-to-eat food. Any food that can be eaten without further preparation, washing, or cooking; for example, cooked food, washed fruits and vegetables (whole and cut), and deli meats. Bakery items, sugars, spices, and seasonings are also considered ready to eat. **1**

Reduced-oxygen packaged (ROP) food. Food packaged in a way that reduces the amount of oxygen available in order to slow microbial growth. ROP methods include sous vide, modified atmosphere packaged (MAP), and vacuum packaging. **7**

Resiliency. Ability of a surface to react to a shock without breaking or cracking; usually used in relation to a flooring material. **11**

Glossary

S

Sanitizing. Reducing the number of pathogens on a surface to safe levels. **12**

Sell-by date. Date that tells a store how long to display a product for sale. **6**

Shellstock identification tag. A tag that identifies when and where shellfish were harvested and the supplier. **6**

Slacking. Process of gradually thawing frozen food in preparation for deep-frying. **8**

Spore. Form that some bacteria can take to protect themselves when nutrients are not available. Spores can revert back to a form capable of growth. **2**

T

TCS food. Food that requires time and temperature control to limit the growth of pathogens. TCS stands for time and temperature control for safety. **1**

Temperature danger zone. The temperature range between 41°F and 135°F (5°C and 57°C), within which most foodborne microorganisms rapidly grow. **2**

Temporary units. Operations that function in a location for typically no more than 14 days; for example, foodservice tents or kiosks set up for food fairs, special celebrations, or sporting events. **9**

Thermistors. Thermometers that check food temperature through a sensor on the tip of a metal probe. **5**

Thermocouples. Thermometers that check food temperature through a sensor on the tip of a metal probe. **5**

Time-temperature abuse. When food has stayed too long at temperatures that are good for the growth of pathogens; for example, when food is not held or stored correctly, not cooked or reheated correctly, or not cooled correctly. **1**

Time-temperature indicator (TTI). Time and temperature monitoring device attached to a food shipment to determine if the product's temperature has exceeded safe limits during shipment or storage. **5**

Glossary

Toxins. Poisons produced by pathogens, plants, or animals. Some toxins occur in animals as a result of their diet. **2**

Training need. Gap between what staff should know to do their jobs and what they actually know. **15**

U

U.S. Department of Agriculture (USDA). Federal agency responsible for regulating and inspecting meat, poultry, and eggs, and food that crosses state boundaries or involves more than one state. **14**

Use-by date. Last date recommended for a product to be at peak quality. **6**

V

Variance. Document issued by a regulatory agency that allows a regulatory requirement to be waived or changed. **8**

Virus. Smallest of the microbial food contaminants. Viruses rely on a living host to reproduce. **2**

Vacuum breaker. A mechanical device that prevents backsiphonage by closing a check valve and sealing the water supply line shut when water flow is stopped. **11**

W

Water activity (a_w). Amount of moisture available in food for bacteria to grow. It is measured on a scale from 0.0 to 1.0, with 1.0 having the most moisture available. **2**

Water hardness. The amount of minerals in water. **12**

Y

Yeast. Type of fungus that can cause food spoilage. **2**

Answer Key

1 Keeping Food Safe

Page Activity

1.0 Baked Potato Outbreak

1 Baked potatoes are a TCS food, and pathogens can grow well in them. They need time and temperature control to limit this growth. The baked potatoes at the café were time-temperature abused. They were not cooled correctly after baking, and they were stored at room temperature for a long period of time. This provided the perfect conditions for pathogens on the potatoes to grow, which caused the outbreak. To prevent this, the potatoes should have been removed from the foil after baking, and then correctly cooled. Then they should have been stored in a cooler.

1.13 Discussion Questions

1 The potential costs associated with foodborne-illness outbreaks include the following:

- Loss of guests and sales
- Loss of reputation
- Negative media exposure
- Lawsuits and legal fees
- Increased insurance premiums
- Lowered staff morale
- Staff absenteeism
- Staff retraining
- Closure of the operation
- Human costs, such as lost work, medical costs, long-term disability, and death

Answer Key

2 As people age, there are changes in their organs. For example, stomach-acid production decreases as people get older. This allows more pathogens to enter the intestines. A change in the stomach and intestinal tract also allows the body to store food for longer periods. This gives toxins more time to form.

3 The three major types of contaminants are biological, chemical, and physical. Biological contaminants include bacteria, viruses, parasites, and fungi. Chemical contaminants include foodservice chemicals such as cleaners, sanitizers, and polishes. Physical hazards include foreign objects such as metal shavings, staples, bandages, glass, and dirt. Naturally occurring objects, such as fish bones in fillets, are another example.

1.14 Something to Think About: Undercooked Chicken Sends Children to the Hospital

1 The chicken that the children ate was time-temperature abused. It was not cooked enough to kill pathogens, which resulted in the outbreak. The manager of the operation should have been monitoring food handlers to ensure that all food was being cooked to required internal temperatures. The manager and food handlers must also make sure that food is being checked with calibrated thermometers.

2 The reason so many children got sick was because preschool-age children have a higher risk of getting a foodborne illness. That is because they have not had enough time to build up a strong immune system.

1.15 Something to Think About: With Power Comes Responsibility

1 As the person in charge in his operation, Russell will be held accountable by the regulatory authority to make sure the following standards are met:

- Food is not prepared in a private home or in a room where people are living or sleeping.
- People other than food handlers are restricted from prep, storage, and dishwashing areas. If other people are allowed in these areas, steps are taken to protect food, utensils, and equipment from contamination.

Answer Key

- Maintenance and delivery workers follow food safety practices while in the operation.
- Staff handwashing is monitored in the operation.
- The inspection of deliveries is monitored to ensure that food is received from an approved source, is received at the correct temperature, and has not been contaminated.
- Food delivered after-hours is monitored to make sure it is received from an approved source, stored in the correct location, protected from contamination, and accurately presented.
- Food handlers are monitored to make sure TCS food is cooked to required temperatures. Temperatures are checked using calibrated thermometers.
- Food handlers are monitored to make sure TCS food is cooled rapidly.
- Consumer advisories are posted notifying guests of the risk of ordering raw or partially cooked food.
- Cleaning and sanitizing procedures are monitored to make sure that sanitizer solutions are at the correct temperature and concentration and remain in contact with items for the correct amount of time.
- Guests are notified that they must use clean tableware when returning to a self-service area.
- Staff are handling ready-to-eat food with utensils or single-use gloves.
- Staff are trained in food safety, including allergy awareness.
- Staff, including conditional staff, are reporting illnesses and symptoms of illness that can be transmitted through food.
- Food safety procedures are written down, implemented, and maintained where required by the regulatory authority.

1.16 Study Questions

1 C

2 D

3 B

4 C

5 D

6 C

7 C

8 D

Answer Key

2 Understanding the Microworld

Page Activity

2.0 *Shigella* Outbreak

1 The outbreak could have been prevented if the cook had reported his illness to management. Most likely the cook suffered from diarrhea. If he had told management, they would have been required to exclude the cook from the operation. This most certainly would have prevented the outbreak. Another thing that may have prevented it was correct handwashing. The cook failed to wash his hands several times throughout the day. This was a critical mistake, especially if he failed to wash his hands after using the restroom.

2 To prevent an outbreak like this in the future, owners and management should do the following:

- Reinforce the importance of reporting illness with food handlers.
- Exclude from the operation food handlers who have diarrhea or have been diagnosed with an illness from *Shigella* spp.
- Remind food handlers of the importance of handwashing. If necessary, retrain them on how, when, and where to wash hands.
- Control flies inside and outside the operation.

2.30 Discussion Questions

1 The six conditions that support the growth of bacteria are:

- Food: Carbohydrates or proteins.
- Acidity: Food that contains little or no acid.
- Temperature: Temperatures between 41°F and 135°F (5°C and 57°C).
- Time: The longer food spends at temperatures between 41°F and 135°F (5°C and 57°C), the more opportunity bacteria in the food have to grow to unsafe levels.
- Oxygen: Some bacteria grow with oxygen, others grow without it.
- Moisture: Food with high levels of available moisture.

2 The two FAT TOM conditions that are easiest to control are time and temperature. To control time, limit how long TCS food spends in the temperature danger zone. To control temperature, keep TCS food out of the temperature danger zone.

Answer Key

3 An outbreak of Norovirus can be prevented by practicing good personal hygiene. This is the most important prevention measure and includes the following:

- Excluding staff with diarrhea and vomiting from the operation
- Excluding staff who have been diagnosed with Norovirus from the operation
- Washing hands
- Avoiding bare-hand contact with ready-to-eat food

4 Food must be purchased from an approved, reputable supplier. This is the single most important prevention measure.

5 The "Big Six" pathogens include the bacteria *Shigella* spp., *Salmonella* Typhi, nontyphoidal *Salmonella*, and Shiga toxin-producing *E. coli*, and the viruses Hepatitis A and Norovirus. These pathogens have been singled out by the FDA because they are highly infectious.

2.31 Something to Think About: Rice Makes Children Sick

1 The illness was caused by the bacteria *Bacillus cereus*. It is commonly linked with cooked rice, including fried rice. The outbreak occurred because the pathogen was allowed to grow when the rice was cooled incorrectly and held at the wrong temperature. Once this occurred, the bacteria formed a toxin, which, when eaten, made the children sick.

2.32 Study Questions

1 C

2 A

3 D

4 C

5 A

6 C

7 A

8 B

9 B

10 B

Answer Key

3 Contamination, Food Allergens, and Foodborne Illness

Page Activity

3.0 Man Hospitalized after Allergic Reaction

1 The allergic reaction could have been prevented if there had been good communication in the restaurant between the server and the kitchen staff. Kitchen staff should also have taken the necessary steps to prevent cross-contact between the guest's steak and any shellfish prepped in the kitchen. Putting the steak on a grill used to cook shellfish led to cross-contact. In the future, separate grills should be used for shellfish and other grilled products. If that is not possible, then this should be communicated to guests with shellfish allergies.

3.11 Discussion Questions

1 There are several ways to keep food safe from physical contaminants:

- Purchase food from approved, reputable suppliers.
- Closely inspect the food you receive.
- Take steps to make sure no physical contaminants can get into food in your operation. This includes making sure that food handlers practice good personal hygiene.

2 There are several ways to keep chemicals from contaminating food:

- Make sure chemicals are approved for use in a foodservice operation.
- Purchase chemicals from approved, reputable suppliers.
- Store chemicals away from prep areas, food-storage areas, and service areas.
- Separate chemicals from food and food-contact surfaces by spacing and partitioning.
- Do not store chemicals above food or food-contact surfaces.
- Use chemicals for their intended use and follow manufacturers' directions.
- Only handle food with equipment and utensils approved for foodservice use.

Answer Key

- Make sure the manufacturers' labels on original chemical containers are readable.
- Follow the manufacturers' directions and local regulatory requirements when throwing out chemicals.

3 There are several ways to prevent the deliberate contamination of food:
- Make sure that the products you receive are from safe sources.
- Monitor the security of products in the operation.
- Know who is in the operation.
- Keep information related to food defense accessible.
- Identify what you will do and who you will contact if there is suspicious activity or a threat at your operation.

4 There are several measures that can be taken by both service staff and kitchen staff to ensure the safety of guests with food allergies.

Service staff:

- Describe dishes so guests know how they are prepared.
- Tell guests if the food they are allergic to is in the menu item.
- Identify any secret ingredients.
- Suggest menu items that do not contain the food that the guest is allergic to.
- Clearly mark the order for the guest with the identified food allergy.
- Deliver food to the guest with the allergy separately from other food delivered to the table.

Kitchen staff:

- Check recipes and ingredient labels to confirm that the allergen is not present.
- Wash, rinse, and sanitize cookware, utensils, and equipment before prepping food. If possible, use a separate set of cooking utensils just for allergen special orders.
- Make sure the allergen does not touch anything for guests with food allergies, including food, beverages, utensils, equipment, and gloves.
- Wash your hands and change gloves before prepping food.
- Use separate fryers and cooking oils when frying food for guests with food allergies.
- Label food packaged on-site.

Answer Key

3.13 Something to Think About: The 1984 Rajneeshee Bioterror Attack

1 Guests should have been monitored as they used the salad bars. A staff member should have been assigned to monitor guests. Not only would this have helped prevent the accidental contamination of food by guests, but it may have stopped the terrorists from deliberately contaminating it.

3.14 Study Questions

1 A

2 B

3 D

4 C

5 A

6 D

4 The Safe Food Handler

Page Activity

4.0 Hepatitis A Scare

1 If the food handler had symptoms, the situation could have been prevented if he or she had immediately reported them to management and management had excluded the food handler from the operation. The outbreak might also have been avoided if the food handler practiced correct and frequent handwashing while working, especially after using the restroom. Management must always remind staff of the importance of reporting illnesses.

Answer Key

4.18 Discussion Questions

1 Staff must meet the following work attire requirements:

- Wear a clean hat or other hair restraint.
- Wear clean clothing daily.
- Remove aprons when leaving food-preparation areas.
- Remove jewelry from hands and arms before preparing food or when working around prep areas.

2 The following personal behaviors can contaminate food:

- Wiping or touching the nose
- Rubbing an ear
- Scratching the scalp
- Touching a pimple or an infected wound or boil
- Running fingers through the hair

3 How an infected wound is covered depends on where it is located:

- Cover wounds on the hand or wrist with an impermeable cover, such as a bandage or finger cot. Next, place a single-use glove over the cover.
- Cover wounds on the arm with an impermeable cover, such as a bandage. The wound must be completely covered.
- Cover wounds on other parts of the body with a dry, durable, tight-fitting bandage.

4 Food handlers must follow these procedures when wearing gloves to handle food:

- Wash hands before putting on gloves when starting a new task.
- Choose the correct glove size.
- Hold gloves by the edge when putting them on. Avoid touching the glove as much as possible.
- Check gloves for rips and tears after they have been put on.
- Never blow into gloves.
- Never roll gloves to make them easier to put on.
- Never wash and reuse gloves.

Answer Key

5 These staff health problems pose a possible threat to food safety:

- Infected wound or boil that is not properly covered. Restrict the food handler from working with exposed food, utensils, and equipment.
- Sore throat with fever. Restrict the food handler from working with exposed food, utensils, and equipment. Exclude the food handler from the operation if you primarily serve a high-risk population.
- Persistent sneezing, coughing, or a runny nose that causes discharges from the eyes, nose, or mouth. Restrict the food handler from working with exposed food, utensils, and equipment.
- Vomiting, diarrhea, or jaundice from an infectious condition. Exclude the food handler from the operation. Food handlers who vomit or have diarrhea cannot return to work unless they have had no symptoms for at least 24 hours, or have a written release from a medical practitioner. Food handlers with jaundice must be reported to the regulatory authority. Food handlers who have had jaundice for seven days or less must be excluded from the operation. They cannot return to work unless they have a written release from a medical practitioner and approval from the regulatory authority.
- A foodborne illness caused by one of these pathogens and symptoms of diarrhea or vomiting: Norovirus; *Shigella* spp.; nontyphoidal *Salmonella*; or Shiga toxin-producing *E. coli*. Exclude the food handler from the operation. Report the situation to the regulatory authority. Work with the medical practitioner and the local regulatory authority to determine when the employee can safely return to the operation and/or carry out regular food-handling duties.
- A foodborne illness caused by one of these pathogens: Hepatitis A or *Salmonella* Typhi. Exclude the food handler from the operation. Report the situation to the regulatory authority. Some food handlers diagnosed with an illness may not experience symptoms, or their symptoms may have ended. Work with the medical practitioner and the local regulatory authority to determine whether the food handlers must be excluded from the operation or restricted from working with exposed food, utensils, and equipment. The medical practitioner and regulatory authority will also determine when the employees can safely return to the operation and/or carry out their regular food-handling duties.

Answer Key

4.20 Something to Think About: Robert's Day

1 Robert and his manager made the following errors:

- Robert did not report his illness to the manager before coming to work.
- Robert did not take a bath or shower before work.
- Robert wore a dirty uniform to work.
- Robert should have removed his watch and rings (with the exception of a plain band) before prepping and serving food.
- Robert did not wear a hair restraint.
- Robert did not wash his hands before handling the raw chicken.
- Robert did not wash his hands after handling the raw chicken.
- The manager did not ask about Robert's symptoms. If Robert were to report that he had diarrhea, the manager should have sent him home.
- Robert did not wash his hands correctly after taking out the garbage.
- Robert did not wash his hands correctly after using the restroom.
- Robert did not dry his hands correctly after washing them. He got them dirty again when he wiped them on his apron.
- Robert wore his apron into the restroom.
- The manager did not make sure the restroom was stocked with paper towels.
- Robert touched the ready-to-eat chicken with his contaminated hands.
- Robert was eating chicken while prepping food.

4.21 Something to Think About: Kurt's Dilemma

1 Jackie should not have asked Kurt to come to work. By doing so she was inviting a potential foodborne-illness outbreak. Kurt was vomiting and had diarrhea. These are two symptoms that require a manager to exclude a food handler from an operation.

2 Not only should Jackie have told Kurt to stay home, but she should have told him to stay there until he was symptom-free for at least 24 hours. As an alternative, Kurt could have been asked to get a doctor's release to return to work.

Answer Key

4.22 Study Questions

1 C
2 D
3 C
4 A
5 B
6 B
7 B
8 C
9 D
10 A

5 The Flow of Food: An Introduction

Page Activity

5.0 University Outbreak

1 Here is what could have been done to prevent this situation from occurring:

- The operation should have supplied food handlers with color-coded cutting boards to keep things separate when prepping different types of food. For example, it could have supplied yellow cutting boards for prepping raw chicken, and green cutting boards for prepping produce—like the lettuce. Of course it would be critical to train food handlers on the correct use of each color.
- The food handler should have cleaned and sanitized all work surfaces, equipment, and utensils after each task, including the knife and cutting board.
- The operation could have chosen to purchase prepared lettuce to eliminate the necessity of chopping it for their chicken Caesar salads.

Answer Key

5.11 Discussion Questions

1 Food is being time-temperature abused whenever it is handled in the following ways:

- It is cooked to the wrong minimum internal temperature.
- It is held at the wrong temperature.
- It is cooled or reheated incorrectly.

2 Cross-contamination can be prevented in the operation by:

- Using separate equipment when preparing each type of food
- Cleaning and sanitizing all work surfaces, equipment, and utensils after each task
- Preparing raw meat, fish, and poultry and ready-to-eat food at different times (when using the same prep table)
- Purchasing ingredients that require minimal preparation

3 These are the steps for calibrating a thermometer using the ice-point method:

1 Fill a large container with ice. Use crushed ice if you have it. Add tap water until the container is full. Stir the mixture well.

2 Put the thermometer stem or probe into the ice water. Make sure the sensing area is completely submerged. Wait 30 seconds or until the indicator stops moving. Do not let the stem or probe touch the sides or bottom of the container.

3 Adjust the thermometer so it reads 32°F (0°C). To calibrate a bimetallic stemmed thermometer, adjust it by holding the calibration nut with a wrench or other tool. To calibrate a thermocouple or thermistor, follow the manufacturer's directions.

Answer Key

5.12 Something to Think About: Cross-Contamination Stops Truck in Its Tracks

1 The food truck operator should have used separate equipment for preparing different kinds of food. Also, he could have prevented cross-contamination by prepping raw and ready-to-eat food at different times. Finally, the food truck operator should have washed, rinsed, and sanitized his utensils and equipment after each task.

5.13 Something to Think About: Tour Cancelled by Outbreak

1 The food in the box lunches was time-temperature abused. Because the box lunches were stored in the warm luggage compartment of the bus, pathogens on the food grew and made the food unsafe.

2 The box lunches should have been stored in a way that would have kept the food out of the temperature danger zone. The food needed to be held at 41°F (5°C) or lower.

5.14 Study Questions

1 C

2 C

3 D

4 C

5 C

6 C

7 A

8 B

Answer Key

6 The Flow of Food: Purchasing and Receiving

Page Activity

6.0 More Than They Bargained For

1 The chef purchased the fish from an unapproved source. This put her customers at risk for a foodborne illness.

2 The chef should have purchased her fish from approved, reputable suppliers. These suppliers have been inspected and can show you an inspection report. They also meet applicable local, state, and federal laws. Barracuda are a predatory tropical reef fish and should be used with caution because they are commonly linked with ciguatera fish poisoning.

6.14 Discussion Questions

1 Here are some general guidelines for receiving food safely:

- Have suppliers deliver food when there is time to inspect it.
- Make specific staff responsible for receiving. Train them to follow food safety procedures, and provide them with the tools they need to receive and inspect deliveries.
- Make sure there is enough trained staff to receive and inspect food promptly.
- Plan ahead for deliveries. Make sure that equipment is clean and there is enough storage space to hold deliveries.
- Inspect deliveries immediately upon receipt. Start by inspecting the overall condition of the delivery trucks. Then inspect the food. Count quantities, check for damage, and look for items that might have been repacked or mishandled. Spot-check weights. Take sample temperatures of all TCS food.
- Inspect and store each delivery before accepting another one.

Answer Key

2 Here are some general guidelines for inspecting food:

- Make sure TCS food is received at safe temperatures. Take sample temperatures of all TCS food. Receive cold TCS food at 41°F (5°C) or lower unless otherwise specified. Receive hot TCS food at 135°F (57°C) or higher.
- Make sure packaging is intact and clean and protects food and food-contact surfaces from contamination. Reject items with damaged packaging, including leaks, dampness, or water stains.
- Make sure items have the correct documentation and stamps.
- Make sure food quality is acceptable and meets your operation's standards.

3 Here is how to check the temperature of each product:

- Fresh poultry: Insert the thermometer stem or probe into the thickest part of the poultry. The center is usually the thickest part. The temperature should be 41°F (5°C) or lower.
- Carton of milk: Open the carton and insert the thermometer stem or probe into the milk. Fully immerse the sensing area. The stem or probe must not touch the carton. The temperature should be 45°F (7°C) or lower when receiving the milk. However, it must be cooled to 41°F (5°C) or lower in four hours.

4 A shipment of fresh poultry should be rejected for any of the following conditions:

- Purple or green discoloration around the neck
- Dark wing tips (red tips are acceptable)
- Stickiness under wings or around joints
- Abnormal or unpleasant odor
- Temperature above 41°F (5°C)

5 Cans must be rejected for the following reasons:

- Holes and visible signs of leaking
- Severe dents in the can seams
- Deep dents in the can body
- Missing labels
- Swollen or bulging ends
- Rust

Answer Key

6.16 Something to Think About: A Decision to Make

1 All food must be purchased from approved, reputable suppliers. Because an approved supplier is one that is inspected, the partners should ask the supplier for a copy of a recent inspection report to see if the supplier meets applicable laws.

6.17 Something to Think About: Delivery Decision Could Cost Them

1 Betty should have asked the delivery driver to come back later. Deliveries must be made when staff have enough time to inspect them promptly. By putting the food away without inspecting it, Sunnydale missed an important opportunity to identify problems with the food. Problems may include food that:

- Was not delivered at the correct temperature
- Was damaged or mishandled
- Had been thawed and refrozen
- Had expired code dates
- Showed signs of a pest infestation

6.18 Study Questions

1 D
2 B
3 B
4 A
5 C
6 D
7 B
8 D
9 D
10 D

7 The Flow of Food: Storage

Page Activity

7.0 Fatal Outbreak Linked to Incorrect Storage Practices

1 The packages of raw ground beef should have been stored separately from the ready-to-eat rolls and cartons of chocolate milk. If that was not possible, then the ground beef should have been stored below these items. This would have prevented the juices from the raw ground beef from dripping onto ready-to-eat food and causing the outbreak.

7.14 Discussion Questions

1 The recommended top-to-bottom order for storing the items in the same cooler is:

- Pecan pie
- Raw trout
- Uncooked beef roast
- Raw ground beef
- Raw chicken

2 Live shellfish must be stored in its original container at an air temperature of 41°F (5°C) or lower. Shellstock identification tags must be kept on file for 90 days from the date the last shellfish was sold or served from the container.

3 The label must include the following information:

- Common name of the food or a statement that clearly identifies it.
- Quantity of the food.
- Ingredients and subingredients in descending order by weight if the item contains two or more ingredients.
- Artificial colors and flavors.
- Chemical preservatives.
- Name and place of business of the manufacturer, packer, or distributor.
- Source of each major food allergen contained in the food. This is not necessary if the source is already part of the common name of the ingredient.

4 Many operations use the first-in, first-out (FIFO) method to rotate their refrigerated, frozen, and dry food during storage. Here is one way to use the FIFO method:

1 Identify the food item's use-by or expiration date.

2 Store items with the earliest use-by or expiration dates in front of items with later dates.

3 Once shelved, use those items stored in front first.

4 Throw out food that has passed its manufacturer's use-by or expiration date.

7.15 Something to Think About: Storage Problems at Enrico's

1 Here are the storage errors that occurred:

- A food handler at the restaurant failed to shut the door to the walk-in freezer. This could have warmed the interior of the freezer and allowed products to thaw.
- Alyce placed the case of sour cream into an already overloaded refrigerator. This could prevent good airflow and make the unit work harder to stay cold.
- The stockpot of soup should not have been stored on the floor of the cooler. Food must be stored at least six inches (15 centimeters) off the floor.
- Alyce should not have stored the fresh salmon above the ready-to-eat soup. The salmon could drip fluids into the soup, cross-contaminating it. Ready-to-eat food must always be stored above raw meat, poultry, and seafood.
- Alyce should not have stored the ground beef near the door, which is the warmest part of the unit. Raw meat, poultry, and seafood should be stored in the coldest part of the unit.
- Mary was lining the shelving with aluminum foil. This can restrict airflow in the unit.

Answer Key

7.16 Something to Think About: A Second Chance

1 Here are some things that Chase and his staff should consider:

- Determine where meat, poultry, and seafood will be stored. Ideally they will want to store it in the coldest part of the unit, away from the door.
- Ensure that there is at least one air-temperature measuring device in each storage unit. For coolers and freezers, the device must be located in the warmest part of the unit.
- Install cold curtains in walk-in coolers and freezers to help maintain temperatures in the units.
- Purchase open shelving for walk-in coolers and freezers. This will help ensure good airflow in the units. The shelving should also ensure that food is stored at least six inches (15 centimeters) from the floor.
- Identify the designated storage location for each stored product. This includes both food and nonfood items, such as paper napkins and single-use cups.
- Purchase storage containers intended for food.
- Identify the storage location for dirty linen.
- Establish a procedure for the correct storage order for raw and ready-to-eat food.
- Determine how to rotate food using the FIFO method.

7.17 Study Questions

1 C

2 C

3 C

4 D

5 A

6 C

7 C

8 A

9 B

10 D

Answer Key

8 The Flow of Food: Preparation

Page Activity

8.0 Undercooked Meatballs Lead to Fatal Outbreak

1 Simply browning the outside of the meatballs was not enough to reduce the *Salmonella* on them to a safe level. The only way to do that is to cook them to a minimum internal temperature of 165°F (74°C) for 15 seconds. To be sure that the meatballs had reached this internal temperature, the chef should have checked them with a thermometer.

8.19 Discussion Questions

1 The minimum internal cooking temperatures are:

- Poultry: 165°F (74°C) for 15 seconds
- Fish: 145°F (63°C) for 15 seconds
- Pork: 145°F (63°C) for 15 seconds (roasts for four minutes)
- Ground beef: 155°F (68°C) for 15 seconds

2 The four correct methods for thawing food are:

- Thaw it in a refrigerator at a product temperature of 41°F (5°C) or lower.
- Submerge it under running, drinkable water at a temperature of 70°F (21°C) or lower.
- Thaw it in a microwave oven if it will be cooked immediately afterward.
- Thaw it as part of the cooking process as long as the product reaches the required minimum internal cooking temperature.

3 There are a number of methods that can be used to cool food, including:

- Using ice-water baths
- Stirring food with an ice paddle
- Using a blast chiller or tumble chiller
- Adding ice or cold water as an ingredient

Answer Key

4 The rules for correctly cooking food in a microwave include:

- Cover food to prevent the surface from drying out.
- Rotate or stir food halfway through the cooking process to allow heat to reach the food more evenly.
- Let food stand for at least two minutes after cooking to let the food temperature even out.
- Check the temperature in at least two places to make sure the food is cooked through.
- Heat seafood, poultry, and eggs to 165°F (74°C).

8.20 Something to Think About: Something's Fishy

1 Here is what John did wrong:

- He failed to wash his hands before starting work and between the different prep tasks.
- He failed to thaw the shrimp correctly. When food is thawed under running water, the temperature of the water should be 70°F (21°C) or lower. Also, he should have cleaned and sanitized the food prep sink first.
- He took out more whole salmon from the walk-in cooler than he could prepare in a short period of time. He also left the salmon out while he prepped the shrimp. These mistakes subjected the salmon to time-temperature abuse.
- He failed to clean and sanitize the knife, cutting board, and worktable correctly and at the right times. He should have cleaned and sanitized them before prepping the salmon, before prepping the shrimp, before returning to work on the salmon, and after finishing the salmon. These mistakes could allow pathogens to spread.

Answer Key

8.21 Something to Think About: Chicken on the Fly

1 Here is what Aiden did wrong:

- He prepared a large batch of batter.
- He added new batter to old batter.
- He overloaded the fryer baskets.
- He did not allow the fryer oil temperature to recover before lowering the next basket of chicken into the fryer.
- He failed to use a thermometer to check the oil and food temperatures.

2 Here is what Aiden should have done differently:

- Aiden should have prepped the batter in smaller amounts. This would help prevent time-temperature abuse of both the batter and food being coated during preparation.
- He should have thrown out the unused batter at the end of the shift.
- He should have placed an amount of chicken in the fryer basket that would maximize cooking efficiency while still allowing the fryer oil to maintain the correct temperature.
- He should have allowed the fryer oil temperature to recover between batches.
- He should have used a thermometer to check the fryer oil and food temperatures.

8.22 Study Questions

1 A

2 B

3 B

4 D

5 C

6 D

7 A

8 C

9 C

10 D

Answer Key

9 The Flow of Food: Service

Page Activity

9.0 One Hundred Sickened by Norovirus Outbreak

1 The food handler should have reported the vomiting and diarrhea to management the week before the outbreak. He also should have been washing his hands correctly, especially after using the restroom. Food handlers carrying pathogens, such as Norovirus, can easily transfer them to food if they do not wash their hands correctly after using the restroom.

9.13 Discussion Questions

1 To minimize contamination in self-service areas:

- Protect food on display using sneeze guards, display cases, or packaging.
- Label food located in self-service areas.
- Do not let guests refill dirty plates or use dirty utensils at self-service areas.
- Stock food displays with the correct utensils for dispensing food.

2 The longer the time between preparation and consumption, the greater the risk that food will be exposed to contamination or time-temperature abuse. To prevent these hazards do the following:

- Pack food in insulated food-grade containers. They should be designed so food cannot mix, leak, or spill.
- Clean the inside of delivery vehicles regularly.
- Practice good personal hygiene when distributing food.
- Check internal food temperatures. If containers or delivery vehicles are not maintaining the correct temperature, reevaluate the length of the delivery route or the efficiency of the equipment being used.
- Label food with a use-by date and time and with reheating and service instructions for staff at off-site locations.
- Store raw meat, poultry, and seafood and ready-to-eat items separately.

Answer Key

3 TCS food can be displayed or held without temperature control under the following conditions:

It is not for a primarily high-risk population.

Cold Food

- It was held at 41°F (5°C) or lower before removing it from refrigeration.
- It does not exceed 70°F (21°C) while it is being served.
- It has a label that specifies both the time it was removed from refrigeration and the time it must be thrown out.
- It is sold, served, or thrown out within six hours.

Hot Food

- It was held at 135°F (57°C) or higher before removing it from temperature control.
- It has a label that specifies when the item must be thrown out.
- It is sold, served, or thrown out within four hours.

4 When serving catered food off-site:

- Ensure there is safe water for cooking, dishwashing, and handwashing.
- Make sure garbage is stored away from food-prep, storage, and serving areas.
- Store food properly. Use insulated containers to hold TCS food. Wrap raw meat and store it on ice. Deliver dairy products in a refrigerated vehicle or on ice. Store ready-to-eat food separately from raw meat, poultry, and seafood.
- Serve cold food in containers on ice or in chilled, gel-filled containers. Or hold the food without temperature control according to guidelines.
- Label any leftovers given to guests. Provide instructions on storage and reheating and a discard date.

Answer Key

9.15 Something to Think About: In the Weeds

1 Here is what Jill did wrong:

- She packed the deliveries in cardboard boxes.
- She failed to make sure that the internal temperature of the food on the serving line was checked at least every four hours. This would have alerted her to the fact that the steam table was not maintaining the correct temperature and that the casserole was in the temperature danger zone.

2 Here is what Jill should have done:

- She should have packed the food in food-grade, insulated containers.
- She should have checked the temperature of the food on the service line at least every four hours. Doing it this way means that any food not at the correct temperature would need to be thrown out. Because the casserole was only 130°F (54°C), she should have thrown it out. As an alternative, Jill could have checked the temperature of items on the serving line every two hours. This would have left time for corrective action.

9.16 Something to Think About: Megan's Day

1 Megan made the following errors:

- She tasted the food on the guest's plate.
- She failed to wash her hands after clearing the dirty dishes from the table.
- She failed to clean the table correctly after busing it. Megan should not have wiped the table with the cloth she kept in her apron.
- She incorrectly scooped ice into glassware. Megan should not have used the glass itself to retrieve ice from the bin. Using a glass this way could cause it to chip or break in the ice.
- She re-served bread and butter that had been previously served to a guest. Uneaten bread or rolls should never be re-served to other guests.
- She failed to wash her hands after scratching a sore. By scratching it and not washing her hands afterward, she could easily have contaminated everything else she touched.

Answer Key

2 Here is what Megan should have done:

- She should not have tasted food from the guest's plate.
- She should have washed her hands after clearing the table and before she touched the water glasses.
- When cleaning tables between guest seatings, if food bits or spills are present, Megan should use the correct cleaning tool, such as a cloth towel, to remove the debris. Megan should have then cleaned the table with a clean cloth that was stored in a sanitizer solution (see Chapter 11).
- She should have used tongs or an ice scoop to get ice.
- She should have served a fresh basket of bread and butter.
- She should have washed her hands immediately after scratching the sore.

9.17 Study Questions

1 D

2 D

3 C

4 A

5 C

6 B

7 B

8 A

9 B

10 B

Answer Key

10 Food Safety Management Systems

Page Activity

10.0 Blue Skies Handles It Correctly

1 Here is what the owner of the café did correctly:

- She took each complaint seriously and expressed concern to the guests.
- She filled out an incident report after each call.
- She contacted the regulatory authority when she realized that she had received similar complaints.
- She cooperated with the regulatory authority to determine the cause of the outbreak.

10.21 Discussion Questions

1 The following programs are a foundation for a food safety management system:

- Personal hygiene program
- Food safety training program
- Supplier selection and specification program
- Quality control and assurance program
- Cleaning and sanitation program
- Standard operating procedures (SOPs)
- Facility design and equipment maintenance program
- Pest control program

2 There are many ways to achieve active managerial control in the operation. According to the Food and Drug Administration (FDA), you can use simple tools such as training programs, manager supervision, and the incorporation of SOPs. Active managerial control can also be achieved through more complex solutions, such as a HACCP program. Monitoring is critical to the success of active managerial control. Food will be safe if managers monitor critical activities in the operation. Managers must take the necessary corrective action when required. They must also verify that the actions taken to control the risk factors for foodborne illness are actually working.

Answer Key

3 The seven HACCP principles are:

- Principle 1: Conduct a hazard analysis.
- Principle 2: Determine critical control points (CCPs).
- Principle 3: Establish critical limits.
- Principle 4: Establish monitoring procedures.
- Principle 5: Identify corrective actions.
- Principle 6: Verify that the system works.
- Principle 7: Establish procedures for record keeping and documentation.

4 Certain specialized food-prep processes require a variance from the regulatory authority. They include the following:

- Smoking food as a method to preserve it (but not to enhance flavor).
- Using food additives or adding components, such as vinegar, to preserve or alter it so it no longer requires time and temperature control for safety.
- Curing food.
- Custom-processing animals. For example, this may include dressing deer in the operation for personal use.
- Packaging food using reduced-oxygen packaging (ROP) methods. This includes MAP, vacuum-packed, and sous vide food. *Clostridium botulinum* and *Listeria monocytogenes* are risks to food packaged in these ways.
- Packaging fresh juice on-site for sale at a later time, unless the juice has a warning label that complies with local regulations.
- Sprouting seeds or beans.
- Offering live shellfish from a display tank.

Answer Key

10.22 Something to Think About: Trouble at Nathan's

1 Here is what was wrong with the way Nathan handled the crisis:

Nathan forgot that, despite his best efforts, a foodborne illness or other crisis could still occur. He was not prepared for it. One of his most obvious problems was that he had no communication with the media. He also failed to communicate with his key audiences, which included both his staff and his customers.

2 Here is what should have been done differently:

In addition to his HACCP program, Nathan needed a crisis management program. He should have started by developing a crisis management team, which would have certainly included his chef and general manager. Nathan definitely could have benefitted from having a crisis communication plan. This would have included a trained spokesperson, as well as a list of media responses that could have been used in the event of an outbreak. He also needed a plan for communicating with his staff and customers. He should not have relied on the media alone to get the word out. The press should not have access to staff. They should be directed by staff to the designated spokesperson.

10.23 Something to Think About: Maria's Challenge

1 Here is what Maria did wrong:

- She started by identifying CCPs.
- She determined that the critical limit for grilled hamburgers was cooking them to 150°F (66°C) for 15 seconds.
- She determined that critical limits would be monitored by checking for doneness using feel and color.
- She failed to determine how to verify whether the HACCP plan was working as intended.
- She failed to include record keeping in her HACCP plan.

Answer Key

2 Here is what Maria should have done differently:

- She should have started creating her HACCP program by conducting a hazard analysis.
- She should have established the correct critical limit for grilled hamburgers. This would include cooking them to 155°F (68°C) for 15 seconds.
- She should have identified a method for determining if her HAACP program was working as intended. This might have included checking records to determine if critical limits were being met and CCPs were actually being controlled.
- She should have identified records that should be kept. These would be important when verifying whether the HACCP program was working as intended.

10.24 Study Questions

1 B

2 D

3 A

4 A

5 C

6 B

7 B

8 D

Answer Key

11 Safe Facilities and Equipment

Page Activity

11.0 Café Owners Stopped from Opening

1 Here is what the owners need to fix in order to open for business:

- The floor tiles that are cracked must be replaced. Once installed, flooring must be kept in good condition and be replaced if damaged or worn.
- New adhesive should be applied to the loose coving so it can be adhered to the wall. Coving tile or strip must adhere tightly to the wall. This will help eliminate hiding places for insects.
- A service call should be placed to make sure the ventilation system is working correctly. It will probably also need to be cleaned.
- Any household equipment in the restaurant needs to be replaced with a commercial equivalent. Only commercial foodservice equipment should be used in operations. Household equipment is not built to withstand heavy use.
- The cutting boards need to be replaced because they have several large cracks.
- The hot water supply to the handwashing sinks in the restroom will need to be fixed. Restroom handwashing sinks must have hot and cold water available for handwashing.
- The Dumpster lid must be replaced. Outdoor garbage containers must have tight-fitting lids and their drain plugs must be in place except during cleaning.

Answer Key

11.21 Discussion Questions

1 One of the most important considerations when selecting flooring for food-preparation areas is the material's porosity, or the extent to which it will absorb liquids. Avoid high porosity flooring. Its absorbency often makes it ideal for pathogen growth. Flooring should also be smooth, durable, and easy to clean. It should resist wear and help prevent slips.

2 A backup of raw sewage in an operation is cause for immediate closure of the area, correction of the problem, and thorough cleaning. If the backup is a significant risk to the safety of food, service must be stopped. Then the local regulatory authority must be notified.

3 To prevent backflow in an operation:

- Avoid creating a cross-connection. Do not attach a hose to a faucet unless a backflow prevention device, such as a vacuum breaker, is attached.
- Install air gaps where necessary. This is the only sure way to prevent backflow. An air gap is an air space that separates a water supply outlet from a potentially contaminated source.

4 Sources of approved water include:

- Approved public water mains
- Private water sources regularly maintained and tested
- Closed portable water containers
- Water transport vehicles

If an operation uses a private water supply, such as a well, rather than an approved public source, it should check with the local regulatory authority for information on inspections, testing, and other requirements. Nonpublic water systems should be tested at least annually, and the report kept on file in the operation.

Answer Key

5 The requirements of a handwashing station include:

- Hot and cold running water that is drinkable, and meets temperature and pressure requirements.
- Soap in liquid, bar, or powder form.
- A way to dry hands. Disposable paper towels or a continuous towel system that supplies the user with a clean towel can be used. Hands can also be dried with a hand dryer using either warm air or room-temperature air delivered at high velocity.
- A garbage container. This is required if disposable paper towels are used.
- A clearly visible sign or poster that tells staff to wash hands before returning to work. The message should be in all languages used by staff in the operation.

Handwashing stations are required in restrooms or directly next to them. Handwashing stations are also required in areas used for food prep, service, and dishwashing. Handwashing sinks must be used only for handwashing and not for any other purpose. Make sure adequate barriers are present on handwashing sinks or that there is an adequate distance between handwashing sinks and food and food-contact surfaces. Make sure these stations work correctly and are well stocked and maintained. They must also be available at all times. Handwashing stations cannot be blocked by portable equipment or stacked full of dirty kitchenware.

6 When installing stationary equipment:

- Put floor-mounted equipment on legs at least six inches (15 centimeters) high. Another option is to seal it to a masonry base.
- Put tabletop equipment on legs at least four inches (10 centimeters) high. Or, seal it to the countertop.

Answer Key

11.22 Something to Think About: Go or No-Go

1 The manager appeared to handle the sewage backup correctly. First, she evaluated the situation and determined there was no significant risk to food or food-contact surfaces. This allowed her to remain open. When there is a backup of sewage, the affected area should be closed right away. Then the problem must be corrected and the area thoroughly cleaned. Again, the manager followed the correct procedures. She closed the prep area and contacted building management to get a plumber. She also assigned a staff member to clean up the backup.

11.23 Something to Think About: Where There's Smoke

1 The ventilation system is not working correctly. When this happens, grease and condensation will build up on walls and ceilings.

2 The regional manager should ask the store manager to schedule maintenance on the ventilation system. It is also likely that the ventilation and ductwork needs to be cleaned. This should be performed periodically by a professional.

11.24 Study Questions

1 D
2 D
3 B
4 C
5 A
6 A
7 A
8 B
9 A
10 C
11 B

12 Cleaning and Sanitizing

Page Activity

12.0 Slicer Tied to Outbreak

1 The outbreak could have been prevented if the slicer had been cleaned and sanitized correctly. In general, stationary equipment, such as slicers, should be cleaned and sanitized following these steps:

- Unplug the equipment.
- Take the removable parts off the equipment. Wash, rinse, and sanitize them by hand. You can also run the parts through a dishwasher if allowed.
- Scrape or remove food from the equipment surfaces.
- Wash the equipment surfaces. Use a cleaning solution prepared with an approved detergent. Wash the equipment with the correct cleaning tool such as a nylon brush or pad, or a cloth towel.
- Rinse the equipment surfaces with clean water. Use a cloth towel or other correct tool.
- Sanitize the equipment surfaces. Make sure the sanitizer comes in contact with each surface. The concentration of the sanitizer must meet requirements.
- Allow all surfaces to air-dry. Put the unit back together.

12.19 Discussion Questions

1 Food-contact surfaces must be cleaned and sanitized at the following times:

- After they are used
- Before working with a different type of food
- After handling different raw TCS fruits and vegetables
- Any time there is an interruption during a task and the items being used may have been contaminated
- After four hours if items are in constant use

Answer Key

2 Set up a three-compartment sink before use as follows:

- Clean and sanitize each sink and drain board.
- Fill the first sink with detergent and water. The water temperature must be at least 110°F (43°C). Follow the manufacturer's recommendations.
- Fill the second sink with clean water. This is not necessary if items will be spray-rinsed instead of being dipped.
- Fill the third sink with water and sanitizer to the correct concentration. Hot water can be used as an alternative. Follow guidelines for using sanitizers and the manufacturer's recommendations.
- Provide a clock with a second hand.

3 These are the steps that must be taken when cleaning and sanitizing items in a three-compartment sink:

1. Scrape items before washing them. If necessary, rinse or soak items.
2. Wash items in the first sink. Use a brush, cloth towel, or nylon scrub pad to loosen dirt. Change the water and detergent when the suds are gone or the water is dirty.
3. Rinse items in the second sink. Spray the items with water or dip them in it. Make sure to remove all traces of food and detergent from the items being rinsed. If dipping the items, change the rinse water when it becomes dirty or full of suds.
4. Sanitize items in the third sink. Change the sanitizing solution when the temperature of the water or the sanitizer concentration falls below requirements. Never rinse items after sanitizing them. This could contaminate their surfaces. The only exception to this rule applies to dishwashing machines that can safely rinse items after they have been sanitized.
5. Air-dry items on a clean and sanitized surface. Place items upside down so they will drain. Never use a towel to dry items, as it could contaminate them.

Answer Key

4 Clean and sanitized tableware, utensils, and equipment should be stored in the following way:

- Store tableware and utensils at least six inches (15 centimeters) off the floor. Protect them from dirt and moisture.
- Clean and sanitize drawers and shelves before storing clean items.
- Store glasses and cups upside down on a clean and sanitized shelf or rack. Store flatware and utensils with handles up so staff can then pick them up without touching food-contact surfaces.
- Clean and sanitize trays and carts used to carry clean tableware and utensils. Check them daily, and clean as often as needed.
- Keep the food-contact surfaces of stationary equipment covered until ready for use.

5 Several factors affect the effectiveness of a sanitizer. The most critical include concentration, water temperature, contact time, water hardness, and pH.

12.20 Something to Think About: Sarah's Dilemma

1 Sarah made these mistakes:

- She did not clean and sanitize the cart for clean tableware.
- She did not rinse, scrape, or soak the dirty dishes before putting them into the dish rack.
- She overloaded the dish rack.
- She did not clean the heavy mineral deposits from the machine before starting the day.

Answer Key

12.21 Something to Think About: The New Manager

1 Yes. Andy should suggest these changes for the storage area:

- Fix the hot water.
- Install hooks for hanging up the mops and brooms.

2 Yes. Clara should have washed, rinsed, and sanitized the cutting board at these times:

- Before cutting the melons
- After cutting the melons and before chopping the spinach
- After chopping the spinach and before butterflying the pork chops
- After butterflying the pork chops

3 Andy should take these steps to make sure everyone follows the master cleaning schedule:

- Train the staff on the cleaning and sanitizing tasks.
- Supervise daily cleaning routines.
- Check all cleaning tasks against the master cleaning schedule daily.
- Change the master schedule as needed for any changes in the menu, procedures, or equipment.
- Ask staff during meetings for input on the program.

12.22 Study Questions

1 C
2 C
3 A
4 A
5 C
6 A
7 A
8 B
9 A
10 C

Answer Key

13 Integrated Pest Management

Page Activity

13.0 Rats!

1 Methods that can be used to keep the rats out include:

- Installing self-closing doors and door sweeps
- Repairing gaps and cracks in door frames and thresholds
- Keeping all exterior openings tightly closed
- Filling holes around pipes
- Covering floor drains with hinged grates
- Sealing cracks in floors and walls

Most importantly the restaurateurs need to work with their PCO to keep the rats out.

13.11 Discussion Questions

1 The purpose of an integrated pest management program is to prevent pests from entering the operation and eliminate any pests that do get inside.

2 To prevent pests from entering your operation:

- Use approved, reputable suppliers. Check all deliveries before they enter your operation. Refuse shipments that have pests or signs of pests, such as egg cases and body parts.
- Screen all windows and vents with at least 16 mesh per square inch screening.
- Install self-closing devices and door sweeps on all doors.
- Repair gaps and cracks in door frames and thresholds. Use weather stripping on doors with no thresholds.
- Install air curtains above or alongside doors.
- Keep all exterior openings closed tightly.

Answer Key

- Use concrete to fill holes or sheet metal to cover openings around pipes.
- Install screens over ventilation pipes and ducts on the roof.
- Cover floor drains with hinged grates.
- Seal all cracks in floors and walls.

3 Signs of a cockroach infestation include:

- Strong oily odor
- Droppings (feces) that look like grains of black pepper
- Capsule-shaped egg cases that are brown, dark red, or black and possibly leathery, smooth, or shiny in appearance

Signs of a rodent infestation include:

- Signs of gnawing
- Urine stains revealed by black (ultraviolet) light
- Droppings that are shiny and black (fresh) or gray (older)
- Tracks
- Nesting materials, such as scraps of paper, cloth, hair, and other soft materials
- Holes in quiet places, near food and water, and next to buildings

4 All pesticides used in your operation should also be stored by your PCO. If they are stored on the premises, follow these guidelines:

- Keep pesticides in their original containers.
- Store pesticides in a secure location away from where food, utensils, and food equipment are stored.

5 To minimize the hazard to people, have your PCO use pesticides only when you are closed for business, and staff are not on-site. When pesticides will be applied, prepare the area to be sprayed by removing all food and movable food-contact surfaces. Cover equipment and food-contact surfaces that cannot be moved. Wash, rinse, and sanitize food-contact surfaces after the area has been sprayed. Anytime pesticides are used or stored on the premises, you should have corresponding Safety Data Sheets (SDS), because pesticides are hazardous materials.

Answer Key

13.12 Something to Think About: The Best Intentions

1 Fred may have overlooked several measures for preventing pests. First, he may not be inspecting deliveries before they enter his operation. This is important since pests can enter an operation with deliveries. Perhaps Fred is not keeping exterior openings tightly closed when not in use. He may also have failed to seal openings around pipes, or sealed cracks in floors and walls. Maybe Fred did not think about installing door sweeps on his doors, or there are cracks in his door frames or thresholds.

2 Fred needs to contact a pest control operator to help him eliminate the roaches. The PCO will also be able to help him determine how the roaches are getting into the operation and decide the best way to fix the problem.

13.13 Study Questions

1 C

2 D

3 A

4 A

5 C

6 A

7 A

8 B

Answer Key

14 Food Safety Regulation and Standards

Page Activity

14.0 Off on the Wrong Foot

1 Here is what Brian did wrong:

- He failed to ask the inspector for identification.
- He refused the inspector entry to the operation.
- He was not cooperative.
- He failed to walk with the inspector during the inspection or take notes.
- He failed to provide the records asked for by the inspector.
- He was not polite or friendly, nor did he treat the inspector with respect.
- He failed to discuss any violations or time frames for correction with the inspector.

14.10 Discussion Questions

1 The following hazards require the closure of an operation:

- Significant lack of refrigeration
- Backup of sewage into the operation or its water supply
- Emergency, such as a building fire or flood
- Significant infestation of insects or rodents
- Long interruption of electrical or water service
- Clear evidence of a foodborne-illness outbreak related to the operation

Answer Key

2 The FDA and USDA inspect food and regulate food transported across state lines. The FDA also issues the FDA *Food Code*, which is the government's recommendations for food safety regulations. The CDC and the PHS assist the FDA and the USDA by conducting research into the causes of foodborne-illness outbreaks. State and local regulatory authorities write or adopt food codes that regulate retail and foodservice operations. These codes differ widely from one state or locality to another. State and local regulatory authorities enforce these food codes. In addition, they investigate complaints and illnesses, issue licenses and permits, and approve construction.

3 During an inspection, a manager should do the following:

- Ask for identification.
- Cooperate.
- Take notes.
- Keep the relationship professional.
- Be prepared to provide records requested by the inspector.

After the inspection, the manager should do the following:

- Discuss violations and time frames for correction with the inspector.
- Act on all deficiencies noted in the report by determining why each problem occurred, and then establish new procedures or revise existing ones. It may also be necessary to retrain staff.

4 Factors that determine the frequency of a health inspection include:

- Size and complexity of the operation. Larger operations offering a large number of TCS food items might be inspected more frequently.
- Inspection history of the operation. Operations with a history of low sanitation scores or consecutive violations might be inspected more frequently.
- Clientele's susceptibility to foodborne illness. Nursing homes, schools, day-care centers, and hospitals might receive more frequent inspections.
- Workload of the local health department and the number of inspectors available.

Answer Key

14.11 Something to Think About: Inspect Thy Self

1 A self-inspection program provides the following benefits:

- Safer food
- Improved food quality
- Cleaner environment for staff and customers
- Higher inspection scores

2 Consider these guidelines when conducting a self-inspection:

- Use the same type of checklist that the regulatory authority uses.
- Identify all risks to food safety.
- After the inspection, meet with staff to review any problems.

14.12 Study Questions

1 B

2 B

3 C

4 C

Answer Key

15 Staff Food Safety Training

Page Activity

15.0 What Do You Know?

1 A training need is a gap between what staff needs to know to perform their jobs and what they actually know. Katherine most likely identified her staff's food safety training needs by:

- Observing performance on the job.
- Testing their food safety knowledge.
- Identifying areas of weakness.

15.9 Discussion Questions

1 An operation can determine its food safety training needs by doing the following:

- Testing staff members' food safety knowledge
- Observing staff job performance
- Questioning or surveying staff members to identify areas of weakness

2 Methods that can be used to deliver training include:

- On-the-job training
- Classroom training
- Information search
- Guided discussion
- Games
- Role-play
- Demonstrations
- Jigsaw design
- Training videos and DVDs
- Technology-based training

Answer Key

15.10 Something to Think About: Technology Saves the Day

1 Technology-based training would allow Ryan to deliver food safety training when and where staff members needed it. It also could ensure that all staff received the same information.

2 Technology-based training is most appropriate when:

- Staff work in different locations and/or need the same training at different times.
- It is costly to bring staff to the same place.
- Staff need retraining.
- Staff have different levels of knowledge about a topic.
- Staff have different learning skills.
- Staff need to learn at their own pace.
- You want to collect specific information, such as time spent on different topics, test scores, number of tries until the training was finished, and/or problem areas.

15.11 Study Questions

1 A

2 D

3 C

4 C

5 A

6 B

Index

Index

Index

Index

Index

Index

Index

Index

Index

Index

U

V

Index